RACIALLY SEPARATE
OR
TOGETHER?

McGRAW-HILL SERIES IN SOCIOLOGY

Consulting Editor:
OTTO N. LARSEN   University of Washington

McGraw-Hill Book Company

RACIALLY SEPARATE OR TOGETHER ?

THOMAS F. PETTIGREW
professor of social psychology
harvard university

new york   st. louis   san francisco   düsseldorf   johannesburg
kuala lumpur   london   mexico   montreal   new delhi   panama
rio de janeiro   singapore   sydney   toronto

RACIALLY SEPARATE
OR
TOGETHER?

Library of Congress Catalog Card Number 75-137130

07-049717-6
07-049718-8

3 4 5 6 7 8 9 0 VBVB 7 9 8 7 6 5 4 3 2 1

This book was set in Helvetica by Vail-Ballou Press, Inc.,
and printed on permanent paper and bound by Vail-Ballou
Press, Inc. The designer was Paula Tuerk; the drawings were
done by John Cordes, J. & R. Technical Services, Inc. The
editors were Ronald Kissack and Susan Gamer. Annette
Wentz supervised production.

to Ann and Mark

# PREFACE

This book has grown out of my deep conviction that genuine racial integration can and must be achieved in the United States. Both the book and the conviction that underlies it derive from my experience as a social psychologist and a specialist in race relations. I have taught race relations to thousands of college students, spoken to hundreds of audiences, and acted as a consultant for government agencies, school systems, and civil rights groups and lawyers. All these activities have contributed to the content of the book; in fact, most of the content was developed first for lectures.

Because of the nature of the book, I am grateful to an unusually large number of people. The finest part of teaching at a university such as Harvard is the colleagues and students one has, and many of my colleagues and students have given me much help. I am indebted especially to Miss Susan Heidel, whose enthusiasm in helping to assemble this book kept up my own motivation. I am also greatly indebted, of course, to my coauthors of several chapters: Professor Kurt Back of Duke University (Chapter 5), Professor J. Michael Ross of the University of California at San Diego and Professor Thomas Crawford of the University of California at Berkeley (Chapter

9), and Mr. Robert Riley of Harvard University (Chapter 10). I wish to thank, too, Professor James Jones of Harvard University and Professor Albert McQueen of Oberlin College for their invaluable criticism. And I appreciated the considerable help I have received from my publisher, in particular from Miss Susan Gamer and Mr. Ronald D. Kissack.

I am also grateful to the many helpful students in my two courses in race relations at Harvard University (Social Relations 134 and Social Relations 284), and to the many audiences I have had the privilege of addressing through the years. As they will note, their comments, criticisms, and suggestions were heard and remembered. I must also express my gratitude to the late Gordon Willard Allport, my graduate teacher at Harvard, who encouraged me to continue in the field of race relations when few others did.

Finally, outdoing the patience of even my students, audiences, and teachers is that of my wife and son, to whom this book is dedicated.

Earlier versions of many of the chapters or parts of chapters have appeared as published articles. I am grateful to the following editors and publishers for their kind permission to adapt and use these articles:

The M.I.T. Press (Cambridge, Massachusetts), for permission to adapt parts of my chapter "Racial Issues in Urban America" in Bernard J. Frieden and William W. Nash, Jr. (eds.), *Shaping an Urban Future: Essays in Memory of Catherine Bauer Wurster,* 1969. Material from this source appears in Part 1.

Basic Books (New York), for permission to adapt parts of my chapter "The Negro and Education: Problems and Proposals" in Irwin Katz and Patricia Gurin (eds.), *Race and the Social Sciences,* 1969. Material from this source appears in Chapter 4.

Harvard Educational Review, for permission to adapt parts of my article "Race and Equal Educational Opportunity" [Winter, 1968, Volume 38 (1), pp. 66–76]. This material appears in Chapter 4.

Basic Books (New York), for permission to adapt parts of a chapter that I coauthored with Kurt Back: "Sociology in the Desegregation Process: Its Use and Disuse" in Paul F. Lazarsfeld, William H. Sewell, and Harold L. Wilensky (eds.), *The Uses of Sociology,* 1967. Material from this source appears in Chapter 5.

American Psychologist, for the use of parts of my article, "Social Psychology and Desegregation Research" (1961, Volume 16, pp. 105–112), copyright 1961 by the American Psychological Association and reproduced by permission. Material adapted from this source appears in Chapter 6.

University of Nebraska Press (Lincoln, Nebraska), for permission to adapt parts of my chapter "Social Evaluation Theory: Convergences and Applications" in David Levine (ed.), *Nebraska Symposium on Motivation,* 1967. The material appears in Chapter 7.

Basic Books (New York), for permission to adapt parts of my chapter "Parallel and Distinctive Changes in Anti-Semitic and Anti-Negro Attitudes" in Charles Herbert Stember (ed.), *Jews in the Mind of America,* 1966. Material from this source appears in Chapter 8.

Trans-action, for permission to adapt parts of an article I coauthored with J. Michael Ross and Thomas Crawford: "Negro Neighbors—Banned in Boston" [September–October, 1966, Volume 3 (6), pp. 13–18]. This material appears in Chapter 9.

Houghton-Mifflin (Boston), and the American Academy of Arts and Sciences, for permission to adapt parts of my chapter "Complexity and Change in American Racial Patterns: A Social Psychological View" in Talcott Parsons and Kenneth B. Clark (eds.), *The Negro American,* 1966. This material appears in Chapter 11.

The Journal of Social Issues, for permission to adapt parts of my article "Racially Separate or Together?" [January, 1969, Volume 25 (1)]. Material from this source appears in Chapter 12.

Thomas F. Pettigrew

CONTENTS

RACIALLY SEPARATE
OR
TOGETHER?

INTRODUCTION

White racism in the United States is the central concern of this book, which focuses on a straightforward thesis: *Genuine racial integration is a necessary condition for the eradication of white racism at both the individual and institutional levels.* If this thesis is to be correctly understood, three matters must be clarified at the outset: (1) the definition of "genuine racial integration"; (2) the critical distinction between individual prejudice and institutional restrictions; and (3) the type of remedial strategy that is implied by this thesis.

(1) "Racial integration" is used to describe biracial situations characterized by cross-racial acceptance. For genuine integration to exist, the two races must be of equal status and have equal access to resources; ideally, they should be working together cooperatively for common goals. "Racial integration," then, is not to be confused with mere desegregation or with the assimilation of black Americans into so-called "white American standards"—two misinterpretations common in the mass media. There is, of course, precious little racial integration fitting this rigorous definition in the United States today.

(2) "White racism," if it is to have any practical use-

fulness beyond supplying the epithet "white racist," must be thought of as operating at two levels: the individual and the institutional. Anti-Negro attitudes held by individuals—attitudes which under certain circumstances often manifest themselves in anti-Negro behavior—are the most obvious result of white racism and typically receive the most attention. Yet the National Advisory Commission on Civil Disorders, in its forthright report in 1968, correctly emphasized that there is an even more critical manifestation of white racism at the institutional level. Institutional racism is evident—even prevalent—in churches, universities, business firms, governments, professions, unions, and other societal institutions whose normal modes of operation restrict choices for black Americans. The way such an institution operates may not have been established with any reference to race; it may not have been conceived, set up, or maintained by bigoted individuals: nevertheless, the resulting product narrows the opportunities of Negroes just as effectively as if it had been designed specifically to do so. Positive action is required to root out these institutional forms of racism; and it can be expected that such action will be resisted precisely because these institutional forms have generally served their original, nonracial, purposes effectively. We shall be discussing both individual and institutional white racism and how the two levels support one another.

(3) The thesis that genuine integration is necessary for eradicating white racism at both levels is, obviously, integrationist. But it would be a mistake to suppose that the thesis implies simply that we should strive to bring black and white Americans together. Once "racial integration" is adequately defined and the two levels of white racism are clearly understood, it becomes clear that a more complex and differentiated remedial strategy is required. I do not attempt to prescribe a complete cure for our racial problems; but I do present certain specific recommendations and a broad outline of an

overall strategy. These recommendations concentrate upon institutional change, because the analyses given throughout the book indicate that this is the most fruitful approach.

I am fully aware that this book does not offer a complete treatment of race relations in the United States from their historical origins to their present form. Nor is it about the "black experience," which has been a prominent topic recently. Rather, it presents a particular perspective on the racial issue, focusing on individual and institutional racism and contending that true racial integration is a necessary remedy for racism. Each of the five parts contributes to this theme.

Part 1 examines four kinds of institutional racism in the urban context, where the racial crisis is most severe, presenting the issues and recommending remedies. The four areas covered are law enforcement, housing, employment, and education. Needless to say, these areas do not exhaust the many critical aspects of race relations; but they do illustrate the depth and complexity of institutional limitations on the choices open to Negro Americans. Even the most privileged blacks have at some time in their lives faced racial discrimination in one or more of these areas.

Part 2 examines the role of the social sciences in understanding and combatting racism at both the individual and institutional levels. In American race relations, this role has been more potential than actual; Chapters 5 and 6 concentrate on describing this potential as well as some of the actual accomplishments. First we will look at the potential of sociology in understanding the process of racial desegregation; then we will examine a social-psychological analysis of conformity as it influences anti-Negro attitudes of white Southerners.

Part 3 extends this kind of social-psychological analysis to changes since World War II in racial attitudes of both black and white Americans. Chapter 7 addresses itself to a fundamental question: Why did unrest among black

Americans culminate in the 1960s? In earlier years, racism was more intense and hardship more severe; why, then, did widespread public expression of dissatisfaction and demand for change by Negroes not occur earlier? Or why was it not deferred until the 1980s? Why the 1960s? The attempt to answer this question will show us the ways, not particularly obvious, in which institutional alterations affect the mood of black America. Chapter 8 traces the shifts in the racial opinions of whites over these same twenty-five years. By comparing changes in anti-Negro attitudes with changes in anti-Semitic attitudes, we can get a new perspective on what amounts to a fundamental shift in attitudes of majority groups toward minority groups. There are some surprises to be found here; the much publicized "white backlash" turns out upon closer examination to be a myth revealing basic misconceptions about white prejudice.

Part 4 discusses two more recent developments of white racism at the individual level, analyzing in some detail the support of two well-known anti-Negro politicians: Louise Day Hicks of Boston, an ardent advocate of so-called "de facto" school segregation (Chapter 9), and Governor George Wallace of Alabama (Chapter 10). Who are the Boston voters favoring Mrs. Hicks, and who are the Northern voters favoring Governor Wallace? Answers to these questions will help to clarify a number of important aspects of white racism as it expresses itself in ballots. We shall learn that white racism does not operate in a psychological vacuum, as many current discussions of it appear to assume: rather, it is bolstered or countered by other values. The supporters of Wallace and Mrs. Hicks are anti-Negro, to be sure, but they are also characterized by fears and beliefs perhaps equally important to recognize—interestingly, they share some of these feelings with black Americans.

Finally, Part 5 draws together the various threads of the book and considers explicitly the argument that racial integration is a societal imperative. Chapter 11 explores the degree and type of interracial contact occurring in the United States today. This is not easy to describe, for American racial patterns are in considerable flux and present an extremely complex picture. Chapter 12 considers the basic assumptions of racial separatists, white and black, in the light of the data and principles developed throughout the book. Chapter 12 presents a broad outline of an overall strategy within which can be placed the various remedial recommendations described in earlier chapters; this recommended strategy calls for a mixed approach—increased integration combined with programs of productive enrichment of the ghetto.

From this brief description, it should be clear that this book has been shaped by my work in social psychology. But I would be less than candid if I did not point out that it has also been shaped by my feelings as an American living through this difficult period, and as a Southerner with an abiding distrust of racial segregation. Yet, as a social scientist, I have tried to avoid some of the narrowness and sensationalism that has characterized much of the current discussion of race relations in the United States. And I believe that the facts presented in this book, as well as the theories explaining and binding them together, support my distrust of separatism.

My work as a social psychologist specializing in race relations over the past fifteen years has been a fascinating and bewildering experience. During the 1950s, one was considered a bit odd, perhaps monomaniacal on the subject of race; opportunities to apply one's specialization and funds for research were difficult to obtain. The problem was to convince white Americans that serious injustices did exist, and that to correct them would require profound changes in the structure of American society. The 1960s were very different. When the first sit-ins by students began at lunch counters in the South in

1960 and 1961, race relations took hold of the headlines; and since then racial events have never been out of the headlines for long. Suddenly, the demand for specialists in race relations outstripped the supply, and research funds finally became available. Many white Americans became acutely aware of the situation, and a new problem arose: how to provide direction for this new awareness, how to convert unproductive guilt into useful action. As we enter the 1970s, this problem has not been solved. As a result, the decade is beginning in a new atmosphere, a mood of pessimism or even despair. Many fear that perhaps the country can never achieve a harmonious interracial society; indeed, many fear that America as it now exists cannot solve any of its serious problems. Our involvement in Vietnam has contributed to this mood, which must be counted as another of the tragic consequences of this long, costly, and unpopular war. And since 1969, the Nixon administration has also contributed importantly to the mood of despair by its startlingly retrogressive actions in race relations. In its eagerness to renew the Republican Party by means of a "southern strategy," it seems unable to decide between a policy of "benign neglect" and one of "malignant attention."

This book is addressed to this mood of despair. There are things to be done and the means to do them. And the approach presented here is not only aimed at encouraging a more affirmative attitude but is also grounded in the practical realities of the issue as well as in theoretical considerations. The analyses and conclusions presented here were developed partly out of research and study, partly out of numerous race-relations courses I have taught to several thousand college students, partly out of hundreds of speeches I have made to audiences throughout the nation, partly out of direct consulting with government agencies and public school systems, partly out of work with civil rights groups and lawyers.

Both my research and my own experiences convince me that the Kerner Commission on Civil Disorders was correct when it concluded that "our nation is moving toward two societies, one black, one white—separate and unequal." I wrote this book in the belief that this trend is wrong, dangerous, and reversible. My answer to the question posed by the title—racially separate or together?—is that we must be together. This is not a matter of doing something "for" blacks or "for" whites; it is a matter of making American society viable in the future.

Frank Lloyd Wright, when asked to suggest a solution to the physical problems of Pittsburgh, gestured grandly toward its grimy hills and exclaimed, "Abandon it! Abandon it!"

Many current observers of the city scene are also tempted, in moments of despair, to advise abandonment. In addition to problems of clogged traffic, deteriorating schools, slum housing, rising crime rates, an eroding tax base, and water and air pollution, the increasingly serious racial issues in our cities surely encourage pessimism. The cities, however, have become too essential in our complex society to allow the luxury of Wright's solution. We must, instead, continue the long-term struggle to improve urban existence. A substantial portion of our attention must be given to resolving the racial issue.

Proposed solutions to the physical difficulties of the cities often revolve around metropolitan planning and cooperation. Alone, the inner city simply does not have the

PART ONE

THE NEGRO AND THE CITY [1]

resources, financial or other, to mount a sustained attack on such vast problems as traffic, slums, and pollution. This point applies as well to racial issues. Indeed, the future of race relations in America is directly dependent upon the success of metropolitan cooperation.

In this century the black American has become an urbanite. Three out of every four Negro Americans today live in cities; only one in four did so as recently as 1910. This shift represents a massive process of migration involving many millions of uprooted people. The dimensions and character of this historical process provide the larger perspective within which we must view current racial issues in urban America.

Significant Negro migration to the city began during World War I. European hostilities simultaneously provided large war orders for American industry and stemmed the tide of immigrant labor, thereby opening up new employment opportunities for Negroes willing to migrate. Labor recruiters encouraged the process, and young Negroes in vast numbers began what one demographer describes as "the greatest and most significant sociological event of our country's recent history." [2]

Not all of this human surge, however, was stimulated by the attractive pull of new jobs; there were significant "push" factors as well. The high birth rate among rural Southerners, the mechanization of agriculture in the South, the boll weevil, government programs limiting agricultural production, and, finally, the shift of cotton cultivation to the Southwest and West—during the past half-century these factors almost starved the Negro off farms in the South.

The resulting migration increased to enormous proportions in the 1920s. During the depression years, the pace slowed, but it accelerated rapidly again with the entry of the United States into World War II and continued during the 1950s and 1960s. Between 1950 and 1966, over two million Negro Southerners broke their home ties and left the South. During this period total Negro population in

the North and West increased by almost four million.[3]
Negroes in the North and West are now so numerous
that natural increase rather than migration provides the
greater part of black growth there. This wider distribution of Negro Americans throughout the nation has made
absurd the time-honored segregationist claim that race
relations are a Southern problem and should be left exclusively to the South to solve. Now that virtually as
many Negroes live outside the South as in it, race relations are clearly a national concern.

But this national concern has a strongly urban cast.
Today a greater proportion of black Americans than white
Americans are urban dwellers; Negroes, too, are concentrated in our largest metropolitan centers. The twelve
largest central cities now contain over two-thirds of the
Negro population outside the South and one-third of the
total Negro population in the United States. Since 1950
the Negro populations in Chicago, Detroit, Cleveland, St.
Louis, Milwaukee, and San Francisco—and probably
New York and Los Angeles—at least doubled. By 1968,
seven cities were over 30 percent Negro, and Washington, D. C., was two-thirds Negro.[4] Today more Negroes
live in the New York metropolitan area than in any single
Southern state, more Negroes live in metropolitan Chicago than in the entire state of Mississippi, and more Negoes live in metropolitan Philadelphia than in the entire
states of Arkansas and Kentucky combined.

Dramatic as these data are, they understate the mass
movement of black Americans over the past two generations by showing merely the net result of those moving to
cities minus those few who move back to rural areas.
There is, in addition, considerable movement back and
forth between cities; and although this does not appear
in these figures, it accounts for an increasing proportion
of migrants. Consequently, if the old stereotype of the
Negro sharecropper is outdated, so, too, is the stereotype of the urban Negro as a raw migrant fresh from the
hinterland. The typical pattern is for Negroes to come to

a Northern city, not from the farm, but from a Southern city. These Negroes tend to be better-educated Negro Southerners, though their educational level is still below that of the typical Negro Northerner.[5] In addition, many Negroes migrate from one Northern city to another, and these intercity migrants are often skilled and well educated.

The stereotype of the raw migrant particularly leaves out the growing number of Negroes who were born and raised in cities and have never experienced rural living. The urban-born Negro American, especially in the North, is truly the newest "new Negro." He is young, somewhat better educated and skilled, far more militant, and less religious than his parents. He has grown up with great aspirations through a time of promised change and has seen those aspirations largely thwarted. The emergence and growth of this new and unsatisfied Negro segment are the demographic ingredients in the racial dynamite that exists in metropolitan America today.

In the near future, American race relations will be even more closely connected with the city. In 1970, black Americans numbered over twenty-two million and constituted 11 percent of the nation's population; by 1984— to select a fateful year—they will probably number between thirty and thirty-three million and constitute about 12 percent of the nation's population. Most of this growth will be absorbed by our largest metropolitan centers in the North and West, the next largest amount by continued growth of metropolitan centers in the South. The demographer C. Horace Hamilton predicts: "Ultimately, if present migration trends continue, from 75 to 85 percent of the Negro population will live outside of the South." [6] At any rate, this expansion will produce Negro majorities in many central cities. Cleveland, Detroit, Baltimore, and Philadelphia in the North, and Atlanta, New Orleans, and Memphis in the South may soon, like Washington and Newark, have black majorities.

Another important projection is the age profile of the

Negro population. With a median age in the early twenties, Negroes are a young group, and the unusually high Negro birth rates from 1948 on, rates that did not level off until 1957, mean that 12- to 21-year-old Negroes will be especially numerous from 1969 to 1978. Since riots are often sparked by this age group, the potential for urban racial disturbances will remain ominously high for some years to come. The high proportion of young Negroes also makes clear the urgent need for expanded civic services and opportunities, for more public schools, recreational facilities, welfare programs, and housing, and for a larger labor market. The need far exceeds present plans for expansion in most of our major urban areas, largely because of costs. These are the social costs incurred by any rapidly growing and migrating group, costs which the central city cannot and should not be expected to bear alone. Federal funding at an order of magnitude not yet envisioned will be absolutely essential. Equally important, there must be metropolitan involvement in this funding if it is to have any hope of success.

From a national perspective, the migration of blacks to the cities should not be viewed exclusively in terms of costs, for this movement contains many positive features. It has prevented an uneconomic piling up of near-peasant Negroes in the South's depressed agricultural areas. The South, it is true, loses its investment in young migrants who go North, but at the same time the migrants add to the Northern cities' young, productive labor force. In addition, the shift from farm to city has been more responsible for Negroes' gains in income, education, health, and housing during the past twenty-five years than has the concurrent reduction in racial discrimination.[7] Finally, urbanization has created a more sophisticated people capable of effective protest, a people more cognizant of what discrimination over the years has denied them and more eager to benefit from the full rights of American citizenship.

These advantages to the nation as a whole would

*probably outweigh local disadvantages were it not for
the enforced segregation of Negroes into central-city
ghettos. When Negroes are concentrated into blighted
and underserviced areas, all the problems of rapid
growth are multiplied for both the Negroes and the cities.
It is this pattern of racial separation that provides the
backdrop for the four key racial issues confronting urban
America today: law enforcement, housing, employment,
and education. We shall now consider each of these
issues in turn.*

Footnotes

1. Part One is an updated and expanded version of the author's 1967 Catherine Bauer Wurster Lecture. An earlier version is published as: T. F. Pettigrew, "Racial Issues in Urban America," in B. Frieden and W. Nash (eds.), *Shaping an Urban Future: Essays in Memory of Catherine Bauer Wurster* (Cambridge, Mass.: M.I.T. Press, 1969), pp. 47–94.
2. H. C. Hamilton, "The Negro Leaves the South," *Demography,* 1964, Vol. 1, p. 294. Thus, the five states of the Deep South —South Carolina, Georgia, Alabama, Mississippi, and Louisiana—lost 400,000 Negroes through out-migration from 1910 to 1920.
3. National Advisory Commission on Civil Disorders, *Report* (Washington, D. C.: U. S. Government Printing Office, 1968), pp. 241–242.
4. *Ibid.,* p. 243.
5. This process leads to the unusual phenomenon of depressing the median education levels of Negroes for both the place of origin and the place of destination.
6. Hamilton, *op. cit.,* p. 294. Rates of Negro out-migration from the South in the 1960s have declined from those of the 1950s. Nevertheless, percentages of nonwhites in Southern metropolitan areas with populations of less than half a million have started to decline, unlike metropolitan areas of all sizes in the rest of the nation. L. Schnore and H. Sharp, "Racial Changes in Metropolitan Areas, 1950–1960," *Social Forces,* 1963, Vol. 41, pp. 247–253.
7. T. F. Pettigrew, *A Profile of the Negro American* (Princeton: Van Nostrand, 1964), pp. 180–181.

CHAPTER ONE

RACE AND THE POLICE

No one can view urban race relations today without becoming concerned about the administration of justice in
general and relations between the police and blacks in
particular. The administration of justice is marred by racial discrimination even in the courts of some of our leading cities. Consider, for example, the dramatic racial
differences uncovered by Marvin Wolfgang in his examination of criminal homicide in Philadelphia from 1948
through 1952.[1] Among defendants receiving a court trial,
81 percent of the Negoes were found guilty as opposed to
62 percent of the whites; for each level of charge, Negroes
received more severe sentences, despite the facts that
they had more often been provoked by their victims and
that fewer of them possessed a previous police record.
These data are consistent with other studies on arrests,
commitment, parole, and execution conducted throughout
the United States.[2]

Equally disturbing are routine relations between the
police and Negroes. Such interactions, strained to begin
with, are rapidly deteriorating still further in many of our
major cities; in some cities, such as Los Angeles and

Springfield, Massachusetts, relations have broken down completely. Charges of police brutality are made repeatedly, with the term "brutality" referring to use by the police of racially derogatory terms as well as physical abuse. Negroes are also understandably suspicious when all-white police review boards exonerate their fellow officers from all charges lodged against them by Negroes.

It is not surprising, then, that serious race riots can be predicted by studying the "police variable"; considerable research confirms this point. Allen Grimshaw has contrasted the generally poor response of local police forces to the nation's major race riots in this century with the typically efficient response of the military. He believes the key difference is that the police are often seen by blacks as biased representatives of the white world, while Federal forces are seen as racially neutral arbiters.[3] Two major studies of the Detroit race riot of 1943 clearly document harsh treatment of Negroes by the police.[4] The Detroit police, virtually all white, arrested hundreds of Negroes but few whites and killed seventeen Negroes but no whites. In general, cities with relatively large Negro representation on their police forces have had fewer race riots in this century than comparable cities.[5]

Incidents involving the police triggered the 1965–1967 riots in New York City, Los Angeles, Chicago, Cleveland, and Detroit, and the hostilities during these riots were especially directed at the police. The 1965 riot in the Watts section of Los Angeles is particularly instructive in this regard. Two years earlier, a comparative study of relations between the police and Negroes in Los Angeles, San Francisco, and Oakland, conducted by the California Advisory Committee to the United States Commission on Civil Rights, had noted the typical "storm warnings" before the riot in Los Angeles. What the committee discovered in Los Angeles was the same as what observers of the 1943 riot in Detroit has reported: [6] hostile officials, increasing distrust of the police by Negroes, mounting charges of "police brutality," virtually no communication between the force and the Negro community, flagrant use by the police of racially offensive language, and largely segregated assignments for the few Negroes on the force.[7] It did not require a prophet to foresee a clash of major proportions in Los Angeles.

The Kerner Commission reported similar findings in its study of recent race riots. In practically every city that had riots since the summer of 1964, abrasive relationships between the police and Negroes had been a major source of grievances, tension and, ultimately, disorder. In predominantly Negro precincts in one city, the Commission found that over three-fourths of the white policemen expressed prejudiced attitudes toward Negroes; only 1 percent of the policemen expressed sympathetic attitudes toward them. Studies made in 1966 and 1967 showed that over 75 percent of the black men in Watts and Detroit believed there was some form of police brutality.[8]

The position of the police is not enviable. They must carry out unpopular duties in a hostile ghetto as agents of the white world. They are a conspicuous and available symbol of hated white authority. Many urban policemen see themselves as lonely and unappreciated guardians of law and order, increasingly alienated from the larger society, white as well as black.[9] Wilson found in Chicago that a majority of police sergeants who completed a questionnaire in 1960 and again in 1965 felt that civilians generally did not cooperate with the police in their work, that the police department did not have the respect of most citizens of Chicago, that their civilian friends would criticize the department to their faces, and that most people obey the law only from fear of getting caught.[10] The former glamour of policework has tarnished, pay and promotion opportunities remain relatively poor, competing employment opportunities have expanded, and even the Supreme Court of the United States seems to many of the police to have become pro-criminal and anti-police. In short, the urban police sense a serious loss of occupational status, while at the same time they view the status of Negroes as rapidly rising.

The ultimate encroachment upon the status of the police is the pressure to hire black policemen. Much like the medieval guilds (especially as they survive today in the building-trade unions), our Eastern and Midwestern police forces have served as traditional enclaves of employment. Ingroup ethnic ties have bound the force together, and the ethnic *gemeinschaft* has formed the basis for high morale and respect from society. The existence of such kinship and social bonds explains much of the resistance to hiring Negro officers. Even though the efficacy of a racially mixed force is now widely recognized, the police forces of most cities still have extremely poor Negro representation. Only about 5 percent of the policemen of New York and Detroit are Negroes, and the figure is even smaller in such cities as Oakland and Boston. Of twenty-eight police departments that responded to a Kerner Commission survey, the median percentage of Negro policemen was 6 percent, while the median percentage of Negroes in the population was 24 percent. In Philadelphia the two percentages were closest: 29 percent of the population was nonwhite and 20 percent of the police force was nonwhite.[11] For supervisory personnel, the disproportionate representation of Negroes is even worse. The Kerner Commission survey revealed the following ratios: one in every twenty-six Negro policemen is a sergeant; the ratio for whites is one in twelve. One in every 114 Negroes is a lieutenant; the ratio for whites is one in twenty-six. One in every 235 Negroes is a captain or above; the ratio for whites is one in fifty-three.[12]

Difficult as the assignment of the urban police admittedly is, and no matter how much they may deserve sympathy for the squeezed position in which they find themselves, two facts inescapably remain: increasingly tense relations between Negroes and the police are the most accurate storm warnings of impending race riots, and those cities with significant numbers of Negroes on their police forces had fewer such upheavals. We can sympathize, then, but we cannot accept the threatened view many policemen hold of race relations.

Furthermore, the police by their own actions often exacerbate an already tense situation. Research by William Kephart in Philadelphia reveals a direct link between personal bigotry and harsh treatment of Negroes.[13] More than half the city's district patrolmen found it "necessary" to be more strict with black offenders than white offenders. These same men also harbored the most unfavorable attitudes toward Negro policemen: they more often objected to riding with a Negro patrolman, resented taking orders from a "well-qualified" Negro sergeant or captain, felt there were too many Negroes on the force, and preferred that Negro policemen not be assigned to their districts.

The ever-present danger in the area of law enforcement is that a set of self-fulfilling prophecies will spiral among both police and Negroes. The police anticipate resistance when dealing with Negroes, and Negroes anticipate mishandling by the police. Each side expects trouble from the other and acts accordingly. The reciprocal expectations, then, actually elicit the provocative behavior each side predicts and fears.

The contribution of the police to the emotion-charged situation in which they find themselves in the ghetto varies considerably among urban police forces. James Wilson distinguishes three contrasting "styles" of police departments in his *Varieties of Police Behavior: The Management of Law and Order in Eight Communities.*[14] The "service style" is typical of homogeneous middle-class white communities, especially suburbs, and is the least relevant to relations between the police and blacks, except that "outsiders" in the area are principally viewed as "troublemakers." The "legalistic style" takes a *gesellschaft* stance, formalizes law enforcement, breaks the pattern of personal relations, and is usually initiated by reform-minded chiefs. Considered by many a major step forward, this style can become in some ways the most harmful of all to relations between police and Negroes, as the Los Angeles force under the late Chief Parker illustrates. But it is Wilson's third form, the "watchman style," that has traditionally created racial tension. Departments characterized by this style ignore many minor violations and use law more as a means of maintaining minimal order than of regulating conduct. Circumstances of person and condition are taken seriously into account. Thus infractions by upper-status whites are often excused, while infractions by Negroes, particularly lower-status Negroes, either are ignored or lead to arrests, depending on the seriousness of the matter and the race of the victim. The departments in the watchman style typically recruit locally, have extremely poor pay, give only minimal training, and are staffed by people with low levels of education. Legalistic-style forces at their best are clear improvements over these outdated departments.

Remedial Action

The spiral of distrust is easier to prevent than it is to alter, once it has become established, but three short-run remedies are often mentioned: better training, new procedures for handling complaints, and recruitment of Negroes. Training of recruits and in-service training often include "human relations," but the effectiveness of such training will depend on informal communications and attitudes about race sanctioned within the force. If police review boards rarely regard complaints by Negroes seriously, if the force is slow to hire Negro officers, if the chief publicly denounces civil rights protests—then no race relations training ever devised will alter the actual daily practices of the patrolman. Police forces are structured hierarchically; only if those in charge desire changes in this area and direct their subordinates accordingly can special police training in minority relations prove useful.

Citizens' complaints against the police constitute a critical focal point. Police review boards and other internal arrangements for handling such complaints have generally failed to gain public confidence, precipitating demands in many localities for civilian review. Although the police uniformly and heatedly reject such demands, seeing civilian review as yet another blow to their status and authority, the goal of public confidence in procedures for reviewing complaints can and must be met. For example, San Mateo County, California, has evolved a formal procedure that does not include a civilian review board but has nevertheless gained wide favor in the community.[15] A review board combining high-ranking police officials and respected white and black citizens is also a possibility.

The most important remedy is substantial representation of Negroes on urban police forces. Token desegregation and restricted assignments for Negro officers conspicuously communicate to the public that the force is racially biased. In defense, police officials complain that few Negroes apply and many who do cannot meet the eligibility standards. They provide two reasons for this paucity of qualified candidates. First, Negroes who meet police standards can find higher-paid work elsewhere. Second, Negroes are thought to shun police work "because such employment isolates them from the Negro community." [16] Yet sufficient motivation on the part of a police force can overcome these obstacles. As in other occupational realms today, remedial training and extensive on-the-job experience could enable many promising Negro applicants to meet regular standards. This would be especially true once word spread throughout the Negro community that the force was sincerely seeking and preparing Negroes for equal-status employment. The second problem, isolation from the Negro community, is in part a function of the fact that only token numbers of Negro policemen are involved so far. Once a force reaches a significant percentage—20 to 25 percent, for instance, rather than today's typical figure of 6 percent—the black community would have less reason to suspect the Negro officer of being a tool of a white institution.

The 1966 report of the White House Conference "To Fulfill These Rights" and the 1968 U. S. Riot Commission report are in basic agreement in their suggestions for improving relations between the police and the community. The report of the White House Conference called upon the Federal government to establish "assistance programs in the areas of recruitment, testing, selection, training, organization and pay" of the police.[17] It also suggested the establishment of a National Police Cadet Training Corps for high school graduates.[18] States were urged to hire qualified minority-group members for state highway patrols, to set minimum police standards through uniform state examinations and licensing, and to provide in-service training programs and college educations for police officers.

The two reports gave similar recommendations for the upgrading of local police departments. They suggested facilitating the filing of complaints and making such filing possible on a neighborhood level. The drafting and publication of guidelines for action by the police were urged for areas such as investigations, demonstrations and arrests, where the conduct of the police can create tension. The recommendation was also made that local departments hire 17- to 21-year-old men as Community Service Officers to strengthen community relations programs.

It was also suggested that regulations prohibiting police misconduct be enforced. "Police misconduct—whether described as brutality, harassment, verbal abuse or discourtesy—cannot be tolerated even if it is infrequent. It contributes directly to the risk of civil disorder." [19] Police departments were urged to hire more blacks and to offer incentives to attract good officers to work in ghetto areas.

Although these suggestions are important and urgent, the problem reaches far beyond the police. The policeman is a symbol of the entire law-enforcement system; and it is noteworthy that both reports also recommended the reform of criminal court systems to ensure equal treatment and justice for all. The policeman is also a symbol of our entire society; as long as Negroes are discriminated against in education and jobs and are segregated into blighted ghettos, profound resentment among Negroes will be stirred, and problems of law enforcement will persist. These other problems—problems of housing, employment, and education—will be examined in the next three chapters.

Footnotes

1. M. E. Wolfgang, *Patterns in Criminal Homicide* (Philadelphia: University of Pennsylvania Press, 1958), pp. 299–307.

2. T. F. Pettigrew, *A Profile of the Negro American* (Princeton: Van Nostrand, 1964), Chapter 6.

3. Military units are also far more interracial than most police forces. For the general point see: A. D. Grimshaw, "Actions of the Police and the Military in American Race Riots," *Phylon*, 1963, Vol. 24, pp. 271–289. See also A. D. Grimshaw, "Urban Racial Violence in the United States: Changing Ecological Considerations," *American Journal of Sociology*, 1960, Vol. 66, pp. 109–119.

4. A. M. Lee and N. D. Humphrey, *Race Riot* (New York: Dryden Press, 1943), and R. Shogan and T. Craig, *The Detroit Race Riot* (Philadelphia: Chilton, 1964).

5. S. Lieberson and A. R. Silverman, "Precipitants and Conditions of Race Riots," *American Sociological Review*, 1965, Vol. 30, pp. 887–898; M. Bloombaum, "The Conditions Underlying Race Riots as Portrayed by Multidimensional Scalogram Analysis: A Reanalysis of Lieberson and Silverman's Data," *American Sociological Review*, 1968, Vol. 33, pp. 76–91.

6. Lee and Humphrey, *op. cit.*, pp. 114–116.

7. California Advisory Committee to the United States Commission on Civil Rights, *Police–Minority Group Relations in Los Angeles and the San Francisco Bay Area* (Washington, D. C.: U. S. Government Printing Office, August 1963); hereafter this is cited as California Advisory Committee.

8. National Advisory Commission on Civil Disorders, *Report* (Washington, D. C.: U. S. Government Printing Office, 1968), pp. 299–306.

9. J. Q. Wilson, "Police Morale, Reform and Citizen Respect: The Chicago Case" (unpublished paper, Dept. of Government, Harvard University). Wilson notes that thorough police reform and professionalization during recent years in Chicago have not significantly altered the force's poor morale and sense of isolation.

10. J. Q. Wilson, *Varieties of Police Behavior: The Management of Law and Order in Eight Communities* (Cambridge, Mass.: Harvard University Press, 1968), p. 27.

11. National Advisory Commission on Civil Disorders, *op. cit.,* pp. 321–322.

12. *Ibid.,* p. 316.

13. W. M. Kephart, *Racial Factors and Urban Law Enforcement* (Philadelphia: University of Pennsylvania Press, 1957).

14. J. Q. Wilson, *Varieties of Police Behavior: The Management of Law and Order in Eight Communities, op. cit.,* pp. 140–226.

15. California Advisory Committee, *op. cit.,* pp. 29–31. The procedure involves the calling in by the police of interested civil rights organizations to observe the investigation of incidents which could lead to complaints against the police.

16. *Ibid.,* pp. 34–35.

17. White House Conference "To Fulfill These Rights," *Council's Report and Recommendations to the Conference* (Washington, D. C.: U. S. Government Printing Office, 1966), pp. 90–94.

18. One important consideration underlying the idea of such a training corps is that many otherwise qualified high school graduates who now wish to embark upon a police career cannot meet the usual age requirement of twenty-one years. The corps, therefore, would be for graduates of high school during the years of nineteen to twenty-one.

19. National Advisory Commission on Civil Disorders, *op. cit.,* p. 305.

CHAPTER TWO

RACE AND HOUSING

"Since the Supreme Court decision on desegregation of schools," the housing expert Catherine Wurster wrote in 1955, "the frontier for race relations has been shifting more and more to the housing field. . . . Residential segregation vs. nonsegregation is certain to be a lively political issue, nationally and locally, for some time to come." [1]

During the ensuing years, residential segregation has indeed intensified as a "lively political issue." The housing trends of recent years readily explain this heightened concern. In the 212 Standard Metropolitan Statistical Areas as a group, from 1960 to 1969, the central cities experienced an annual decline of 0.5 percent in white population and an annual gain of 2.7 percent in black population. By 1965, four out of five nonwhites in metropolitan areas lived in the central cities, compared with less than two out of every five whites. [2] The concentration of Negroes in the central city is found in every region of the country, though it is strongest in the East and Midwest. Moreover, the trends in every region indicate that still larger percentages of Negroes and smaller percentages of whites will live in the central cities of the future. Apart from the previously discussed in-migration of Negroes, natural increase will cause this: while Negroes of childbearing age live chiefly in the central city, whites of that age are disproportionately found in the newly developed suburbs.[3]

Even these striking comparisons between suburban rings and central-cities grossly understate the concentration of blacks, for within both suburbs and central cities they are still further segregated into particular neighborhoods. For the median city in the United States in 1960, the Taeubers found that 88 percent of all Negro households would have to move from their present Negro block to a predominantly white block before racially random residential patterns would exist. In some cities the separation could hardly become more complete: based on the same test, Miami, Fort Lauderdale, and Orlando, Florida, and Odessa, Texas, all had a 98 percent index of racial segregation. Even the least segregated city, San Jose, California, had an index of 60 percent. Within this narrow range, Northeastern (particularly New England) and Western cities tended to have the lowest indices, Midwestern cities somewhat higher ones, and Southern cities the highest of all.

From 1940 to 1950, segregation in housing increased throughout the nation; from 1950 to 1960, it continued to rise in the South while decreasing slightly in other regions.[4] But data for the mid-1960s suggest that housing segregation has increased since 1960 even in the North. In Buffalo and Rochester, for example, the percentage of Negroes living in census tracts with 75 percent or more Negroes doubled from 1960 to 1965.[5] "It is evident . . . that the general trend is toward polarization rather than dispersion of the nonwhite population." [6]

Survey research by the National Opinion Research Center (N.O.R.C.) in the late 1960s adds another dimension to this bleak picture.[7] Using a broader concept of "neighborhood" than the immediate block, this investigation led to an estimate that one out of five Americans live in interracial neighborhoods with comparable housing for both races. But sociability across the races among neighbors is apparently slight. A number of related factors were isolated by N.O.R.C., but the most important of these was simply opportunity. Northern whites were found to be more neighborly with Negroes than Southern whites; better education led to more neighborliness in the North but not in the South; and pro-integration attitudes in both regions were associated with more biracial neighborliness. Most critical, though, was the straightforward finding that the more closely a neighborhood approaches racial balance, the more widespread cross-racial contact becomes. But as the percentage of blacks increases, the *rate* of interracial contact declines.

In addition, the relatively few Negroes who do maintain suburban homes are also generally segregated. For example, the Negro population in the suburban ring of metropolitan Chicago increased from 44,000 to 78,000 between 1950 and 1960. Yet the Taeubers have demonstrated that 83 percent of this apparent improvement occurred either in heavily "Negro suburbs" or in industrial suburbs with Negro ghettos of their own.[8]

The Causes of Housing Segregation

Indeed, there is an especially devastating aspect to the separation of Negroes. Index comparisons reveal that Negro Americans are far more segregated residentially than white Americans in low-status occupations or minority nationality groups, a fact which cannot be explained by the relative poverty of Negroes. "Economic factors," state the Taeubers flatly, "cannot account for more than a small portion of observed levels of racial residential segregation." [9] Consequently, they conclude, "improving the economic status of Negroes is unlikely by itself to alter prevailing patterns of racial residential segregation." [10] At least five interrelated factors are more important than poverty: Federal housing policies, blatant racial discrimination, the tight supply of low-income housing, suburban zoning barriers, and binding ties within the black community. Let us examine these factors.

Federal policies. Federal housing policy, from the National Housing Act of 1935 until 1950, strove diligently and effectively to establish racial segregation in the more than eleven million units constructed during this critical period. From 1950 to 1962, Federal housing policy was officially neutral but in practice still segregationist. Finally, President Kennedy's limited antidiscrimination executive order in 1962 set an important precedent and ushered in the present Federal housing policy that is best described as ineffectively integrationist. These three decades of Federal mismanagement must now be counteracted. Perhaps, what the law giveth, the law can take away.

Our present plight has come about in a number of ways. The Federal Housing Administration's mortgage insurance program and the Veterans Administration's loan guarantee program both encouraged suburban home ownership with more liberal terms, but they generally discriminated economically and racially against Negroes. "If a neighborhood is to retain stability," the FHA manual asserted for years, "it is necessary that properties shall be continued to be occupied by the same social and racial classes." [11] Indeed, Eunice and George Grier cite two cases in which the FHA actually drove developers who insisted upon racially open policies out of business.[12] As these efforts encouraged whites to leave the central city, public housing developments concurrently helped to seal the Negroes in. Large and often unattractive projects were constructed within the central city and were segregated by design.[13]

The final blow came with the initiation of urban renewal. In city after city, this program has been utilized to clear slums and convert the land to heavier tax-bearing uses, typically removing low-income Negroes in the process to make way for upper-income whites. The caustic slogan "Negro removal" has been well justified.[14] Further erosion of low-income housing has come from Federally financed highways that frequently affect black neighborhoods disproportionately in their search for inexpensive routes.[15]

The racial results of these various Federal efforts have been well described by the Griers: "If the FHA, VA, and public housing programs have helped produce metropolitan areas which increasingly resemble black bullseyes and white outer rings, urban renewal has too often created small white or largely white areas in the center of the bullseyes—simultaneously causing the black ghettos to expand outward even further." [16] This Federally influenced pattern is now widely recognized, with a summary indictment rendered by the 1966 White House Conference "To Fulfill These Rights":

Housing policy—both governmental and private—has traditionally ignored the needs of the nonwhite and the economically disadvantaged. . . . The slums and ghettos have grown larger, overcrowding has been intensified, and the alienation of the ghetto dweller has become a national crisis. Too often, public housing and urban renewal programs have aggravated rather than ameliorated the degree of segregation and congestion.[17]

Nevertheless, few of the model city and urban renewal projects now under way in communities throughout the nation promise positive remedies, in part because they are typically confined within city boundaries and thus are antimetropolitan in their effects.

Racial discrimination. Attention to mistakes at the Federal level should not blind us to an even more important factor in creating residential separatism: blatant racial discrimination. In all American cities today there exist two essentially separate housing markets—one for whites, another for blacks. The prejudicial attitudes which lurk behind this pattern of exclusion are intense, well known, and pervasive. Suffice it here to note that roughly two-to-one majorities favoring residential segregation have characterized the results of referenda in Akron, Detroit, Seattle, and the state of California; and opinion surveys reveal a surprising resistance to housing integration even among many college-educated respondents who at least pay lip service to desegregation in other respects.

This blatant discrimination has set the scene for ghetto race riots by fostering overcrowding, inferior facilities, and inflated rents. Negroes are squeezed into Watts under conditions four times as congested as those in the rest of Los Angeles; [18] in Atlanta, Negroes constitute over a third of the population but claim only one sixth of the city's developed residential land; [19] and for the nation as a whole during the 1950s, the number of overcrowded units among nonwhites increased by a million and a third while it declined among whites by one fifth of a million.[20]

Overcrowding such as this reflects the inferior housing available in the separate black market. Differences in housing quality are especially conspicuous in the South, but they are also marked in Northern metropolitan areas. In 1960, Negro-owned housing units of an average Northern city were three times more likely to be substandard than white-owned units, and units rented by Negroes were over twice as likely to be substandard as units rented by whites.[21] In Boston in 1960, for example, ten of thirteen predominantly Negro census tracts were among the city's worst areas in housing quality, and in eleven more than 95 percent of the units had been built before 1940.[22] To put it briefly, the predominantly Negro areas of the nation's cities are characterized by overcrowded old buildings of sharply inferior quality.

Income differentials, of course, contribute to housing differentials, but discrimination augments economics to create this great disparity. The median monthly rents paid by white and Negro residents in Northern metropolitan areas in 1960 were *not* significantly different ($77 for whites and $73 for Negroes), but the differences in quality were enormous.[23] A rigorous analysis of Chicago in 1956 concluded that nonwhites had to pay roughly $15 per month more than whites to secure comparable housing.[24] Given their considerably smaller incomes, most Negroes must therefore devote a much larger share of their resources to shelter; in 1960, about a third of all metropolitan Negro tenants spent more than 35 percent of their annual income in gross rent; less than a fifth of metropolitan white tenants did so.[25]

Blacks have made definite gains in housing quality in recent years. In the entire nation from 1950 to 1960, the percentage of nonwhites living in adequate, standard housing doubled,[26] and home ownership among Negroes rose from 35 percent to 38 percent.[27] Since 1960, the proportion of nonwhite households living in housing that either is dilapidated or lacks basic plumbing facilities has decreased sharply in all areas, especially in large cities. Yet in 1968 24 percent of nonwhite households still lived in such dwellings, compared with only 6 percent of white households.[28] Gains among Negroes, then, have not kept pace with gains among whites, and these gains have not eradicated the dual housing market. The gains among Negroes are largely a function of farm-to-city migration and the acquisition by middle-class Negroes of older homes left behind in the central city by suburban-bound whites, rather than a function of a genuine relaxation of discrimination.[29]

The trends are even less encouraging for poor Negroes. During the 1950s, the number of nonwhites living in substandard housing increased from 1.4 to 1.8 million, even though the number of substandard units declined. Statistics available for the period since 1960 indicate that this trend may be continuing. There has been little decline in the number of occupied dilapidated units in metropolitan areas, and surveys in New York City and Watts actually show an increase in the number of such units.[30]

Efforts to end housing discrimination have been feeble and ineffective. By mid-1965, sixteen states and the District of Columbia, together covering almost half of the population, had barred discrimination in a major portion of their private housing supply.[31] In addition, over five hundred private fair-housing committees are operating throughout the country, most of them strategically located in metropolitan suburbs. And, belatedly, the Federal government enacted an initial fair housing act in 1968.

Yet neither the laws nor the committees have produced substantial progress. In general, both the laws and citizens' committees apply a case-by-case approach, relying upon individual complaints or contacts; the problem has such deep roots, however, that only direct and patterned confrontation with the housing industry as a whole offers any hope for substantial improvement.[32]

The housing shortage. In addition to fashioning new Federal policies and halting discrimination, there must be vigorous, positive remedial actions to swell the available supply of low- and middle-income housing if the segregationist trend in our metropolitan centers is to be stemmed, let alone reversed. The White House Conference "To Fulfill These Rights" summarized the situation as follows:

> More than one million new houses per year are required to take care of the housing needs of the expanding population. To replace existing stock at the rate of just one percent annually would require another half million houses. In addition, there are more than 10 million substandard houses in stock now and millions of others are too old or in too poor condition to last until they are replaced at the prevailing annual rate of one or two percent. A production rate of two million units annually is a conservative estimate of requirements. The present rate of production is only about 1.4 million, and practically all of this new stock is priced beyond the reach of families below the median income level. At least half, preferably more, of the new stock should be made available to low and moderate income families. . . . As far as the production of housing in the lower cost brackets is concerned the economy has been in paralysis for years. At present it is being strangled to death. . . . Now, when the housing industry needs priming, is a particularly propitious time to offer incentives for builders to supply housing for low and moderate income families.[33]

One indication of this short supply of modest-income shelter is the backed-up demand for public housing.[34] In

Massachusetts in 1965, for example, there were 42,000 units of publicly assisted housing. These limited facilities had an annual turnover of only 6,000 units, while 25,000 families remained on the waiting list, where they are joined by an additional 15,000 eligible applicants each year.[35]

Not only is modest-income housing scarce, but poor blacks are largely restricted to that part of the market which lies within the ghetto. Typically, this ghetto market is located close to the central business district and is characterized by high rates of social disorganization. The fringes of the ghetto farthest from the disorganization are generally inhabited by upper-status Negroes who can afford better housing and have acquired homes in formerly white neighborhoods.[36]

Suburban zoning barriers. Further essentials for the distribution of Negroes throughout the metropolitan area include alterations in suburban zoning and a willingness among Negroes to venture into formerly all-white suburbs. By replacing unenforceable restrictive covenants with more evasive zoning regulations, many suburbs have become, in Charles Abrams' words, the "new Mason-Dixon lines of America." Sometimes these zoning devices are nakedly direct: when a union tried to build houses for its Negro members in Milpitas, California, the area was immediately rezoned for industrial use; when a private developer tried to construct integrated housing in Deerfield, Illinois, the town condemned the land for a park.[37] Sometimes zoning ordinances and building codes are rigorously enforced for Negroes but not for whites. "State governments have clothed these suburban jurisdictions," as the White House Conference "To Fulfill These Rights" concludes, "with the power to zone the use of the land and to control the issuance of building permits in such a manner that only housing for the affluent can be built there." [38] In short, what Federal policies, direct discrimination, and the scarcity of modest-income housing have left undone, the white suburb's zoning methods have completed.

Bernard Frieden places suburban zoning in a broader context by pointing out that restrictive policies, such as required size of lot and minimum dwelling cost, result in part from local tax pressures.[39] Like the central city's efforts to upgrade revenues through urban renewal, the suburb is eager to attract residents who will contribute to local taxes more than they will require in social services. Too many suburban officials reason that the Negro is a problem for "downtown." Clearly, such an attitude cannot be appeased much longer if the racial dynamite in our cities is to be deactivated.

Ties within the black community. Frieden also notes that restrictive zoning practices in the suburbs nourish racial fears and prejudices. Indeed, the public has thoroughly adapted to the long-established practices and patterns of the dual housing markets. White Americans frequently accept the sales promotion of the real estate industry and are easily frightened into thinking that their security is dependent upon separation from Negro Americans. For their part, many middle-class Negroes have so accommodated to exclusion that few challenge the existing patterns even when the law and other circumstances favor change. This was shown in a study of Boston's middle-income Negroes.[40] Despite numerous incentives and favorable circumstances, only nine of 250 families (less than 4 percent) moved to interracial areas during a critical sixteen-month period.[41] For that matter, less than 20 percent of these prosperous Negro Bostonians made any realistic effort to investigate suburban housing. And by the late 1960s black separatist ideology added further impetus to this phenomenon—a factor which we shall treat in detail in Chapter 12.

Remedial Strategies

Detailed remedial strategies for the achievement of residential integration in urban America can only evolve over time, but we must begin now. The goal is not to eliminate the black neighborhood, but to convert it from an isolated racial prison to an ethnic area of choice. This effort, to be successful, must be metropolitan, that is, projected for an entire metropolitan area; it must be systemic, carefully intermeshed with other components of the urban structural system, such as mass transit, education, and employment; and it must be interactive, fostering optimal interracial contact. Admittedly, these are rigorous specifications, but a plethora of concrete ideas which appear promising are now available.

On the metropolitan level, the White House Conference "To Fulfill These Rights" urged that public housing authorities assume responsibility for entire metropolitan areas. It also called for area-wide "land banks," and state-initiated housing development corporations modeled after industrial development groups, which would promote the spread of modest-income housing throughout the metropolis.[42] Frieden suggests a number of ways suburban zoning practices might be countered: court challenges to exclusionary controls; legislation reallocating zoning authority only to large municipalities and counties; and extra state and Federal aid to communities with low-income families, to reverse the present economic incentive to exclude the poor.[43]

The ultimate weapon, of course, would be to cut off state and Federal funds to communities which resist inclusive residential policies. A bolder use of Title VI of the 1964 Civil Rights Act in Northern as well as Southern situations is necessary.[44] Short of this, however, considerable progress could still be made if future Federal urban grants (1) were kept almost exclusively metropolitan in character, so that they required formal cooperation between suburbs and the central city; (2) provided not only housing aid but a coordinated package for the whole urban system; and (3) gave bonus points and incentive funds for previous metropolitan cooperation. Several current HUD programs which require review of a community's proposal by a metropolitan planning commission are forerunners of this new approach to Federal funding.

Packaged metropolitan Federal grants of this type logically encourage a systemic approach. Thus, the "model cities" strategy is a far more systemic attack than the typical bulldozer demolition accomplished by urban renewal. If only the model cities program had actively required metropolitan involvement, it could have served as a model for the new and needed Federal approach to urban grants.

Systemic planning also calls for a careful assessment of the social needs of each metropolitan system. While the White House Conference's recommendation of two million new modest-income housing units a year for the entire nation is sufficient as a gross specification, each particular area has its own unique mix of low-, medium-, and high-income housing requirements based upon its income profile and projected labor-force expansion. Programs must be tailored to suit these individual conditions.

A final aspect of a systemic approach is consideration of available resources and an attempt to put them to productive use. In the housing field, a number of techniques could be used to help develop adequate low-income shelter out of current substandard stock: state involvement in enforcement of local housing codes; strengthened judicial powers, including court-administered withholding of rent to force basic repairs and use of a court housing investigator analogous to the probation officer; state guarantee of rehabilitation-loan funds; and new procedures for the disposition of buildings abandoned because of stricter code enforcement.[45] Related possibilities include the allocation of Federal funds to support long-overdue research in low-cost housing and the establishment of a massive National Housing Corporation that would combine public and private interests in the manner of the Communications Satellite Corporation.[46]

Together with metropolitan and systemic concerns, any remedy for Negro housing must also foster positive interaction between Negroes and whites. A prerequisite is the elimination of racial discrimination and the dual housing markets that now exist. While the 1968 Federal civil rights law marked a vital step toward open-housing legislation, realistic enforcement of the measure is still needed. In the meantime, significant progress could be made by converting state antidiscrimination commissions and private fair-housing groups from case-by-case, complaint-based efforts to patterned action. Nondiscriminatory practices should also be made a requirement in state licensing of real estate agents.

Direct action to achieve interracial contact is also possible. A precedent-setting example is the sparsely supported Federal rent supplement program. Heretofore, American public housing has segregated the poor, Negroes and others, from the rest of society in a latter-day version of the poorhouse. Such segregation virtually guarantees the evolution of deviant norms and values by seriously limiting contact with other Americans. Rent supplements mark an important break with these past mistakes by promoting vitally needed equal-status contact between the advantaged and the disadvantaged. To be effective, however, funding must be substantially increased, and the veto power that local jurisdictions now have over implementation of the program in their communities must be eliminated. The rent supplement concept also suggests similar measures for subsidizing home ownership among the poor. A few observers argue that, in the American tradition of giving land to homesteaders, low-income families should be given housing without cost providing they maintain it. Others stress the need for subsidized incentives and technical assistance in a variety of cooperative efforts.[47]

Whatever course is pursued, it must be kept in mind that mere contact between persons of different races and classes does not necessarily generate tolerance. In fact, contact may actually lead to conflict and intolerance; the conditions of the contact are crucial. Social psychologists have studied this problem in a variety of situations, including public housing, and have generally concluded that prejudice is alleviated when the two groups possess equal status in the situation, seek common goals, depend cooperatively upon each other, and interact with the positive support of authorities, custom, or law.[48] We shall consider these four conditions in detail in later chapters. Here it need only be said that careful planning can nurture the creation of these conditions in the public housing of the future.

The issue of race in housing poses a formidable problem for urban America; the metropolitan-wide programs to counter it must necessarily be varied and complex. The White House Conference stated confidently: "The dimensions of this program are staggering—but they are no larger than America's space ventures, the demands for defense, or the tremendous growth of the nation's economy. Americans are conditioned to thinking big. They can think big enough to cope with this problem as well." [49] The Griers remind us of the stakes: "The choice is not merely between segregation and desegregation, but between wholesale destruction of property and human values and the continued growth and security of American society itself." [50]

Footnotes

1. C. B. Wurster, "The Pattern of Urban and Economic Development: Social Implications," *The Annals*, 1956, Vol. 305, pp. 60–69. Though we will explore the definitions of these terms more fully in Chapters 4, 5, and 12, "segregation" refers here simply to a block, neighborhood, or area which is overwhelmingly white or black in residential composition; "desegregation" to a block, neighborhood, or area with a substantial mixture of both white and black residents; and "integration" to a desegregated block, neighborhood, or area with a considerable amount of cross-racial acceptance and contact.

2. T. Clemence, "Residential Segregation in the Mid-Sixties," *Demography*, 1967, Vol. 4, p. 563; U. S. Depts. of Labor and Commerce, *The Social and Economic Status of Negroes in the United States, 1969* (Washington, D. C.: U. S. Government Printing Office, 1970), pp. 6–7.

3. The meaning of such trends has been calculated for metro-

politan Philadelphia by George Schermer. He notes that a yearly outflow of 8,000 Negro households to white areas would be required just to keep Negro areas from expanding further. To reverse the trend and spread the Negro population evenly throughout metropolitan Philadelphia by the year 2000 would require at a minimum the entry of 9,700 Negro households annually into presently white areas and the reciprocal movement of 3,700 white households into presently Negro areas. The absence of such shifts and the continued growth of central cities means that these minimal estimates will progressively increase. Quoted in E. and G. Grier, "Equality and Beyond: Housing Segregation in the Great Society," in T. Parsons and K. B. Clark (eds.), *The Negro American* (Boston: Houghton Mifflin, 1966), p. 535.

4. K. E. Taeuber and A. F. Taeuber, *Negroes in Cities* (Chicago: Aldine, 1965).

5. National Advisory Commission on Civil Disorders, *Report* (Washington, D. C.: U. S. Government Printing Office, 1968), p. 467.

6. T. Clemence, *op. cit.,* p. 568.

7. N. Bradburn, S. Sudman, G. Gockel, J. Noel, and C. Rottsolk, "Neighboring: Social Integration in Integrated Neighborhoods" (unpublished paper of the National Opinion Research Center, University of Chicago, February, 1969).

8. Taeuber and Taeuber, "The Negro Population in the United States," in J. P. Davis (ed.), *The American Negro Reference Book* (Englewood Cliffs, N. J.: Prentice-Hall, 1966), pp. 132–136. Other analyses indicate that Chicago is typical in the extent of its suburban segregation; see Taeuber and Taeuber, *Negroes in Cities,* pp. 55–62.

9. *Ibid.,* p. 2.

10. *Ibid.,* p. 95.

11. Quoted by C. Abrams, "The Housing Problem and the Negro," in Parsons and Clark, *op. cit.,* p. 523.

12. E. and G. Grier, *Privately Developed Interracial Housing* (Berkeley: University of California Press, 1960), Chapter 8.

13. In those relatively few public housing projects which have achieved full racial integration, striking gains in positive racial attitudes have occurred among both the Negro and white tenants. See M. Deutsch and M. Collins, *Interracial Housing: A Psychological Evaluation of a Social Experiment* (Minneapolis: University of Minnesota Press, 1951); M. Jahoda and P. West, "Race Relations in Public Housing," *Journal of Social Issues,* 1951, Vol. 7, pp. 132–139; D. M. Wilner, R. Walkley, and S. W. Cook, *Human Relations in In-*

terracial Housing: A Study of the Contact Hypothesis (Minneapolis: University of Minnesota Press, 1955); and E. Works, "The Prejudice-Interaction Hypothesis from the Point of View of the Negro Minority Group," *American Journal of Sociology*, 1961, Vol. 67, pp. 47–52.

14. Writes Abrams: "In the United States, from 69 to 72 per cent of those who have been displaced from their homes by urban renewal projects have been Negroes, while only a tiny fraction of the new houses built on the sites have been open to them . . . In Stockton, California, a renewal project not only leveled a whole Negro neighborhood but destroyed 32 Negro churches in the process." Abrams, *op. cit.*, p. 514.

15. Even in St. Paul, Minnesota, which is 97 percent white, freeway displacement struck Negroes hardest by eliminating the housing for 311 Negro households. This number represented 72 percent of all of the displacement and 14 percent of the city's Negro housing. Furthermore, only 35 percent of those displaced Negro householders who sought housing outside of the ghetto obtained it, while all the displaced white householders who sought such housing obtained it. F. J. Davis, "The Effects of a Freeway Displacement on Racial Housing Segregation in a Northern City," *Phylon*, 1965, Vol. 26, pp. 209–215.

16. E. and G. Grier, "Equality and Beyond," *op. cit.*, p. 533.

17. White House Conference "To Fulfill These Rights," *Council's Report and Recommendations to the Conference* (Washington, D. C.: U. S. Government Printing Office, 1966), pp. 57, 69.

18. Abrams, *op. cit.*, p. 513.

19. C. B. Motley, "The Legal Status of the Negro in the United States," in Davis, *op. cit.*, p. 501.

20. J. H. Douglass, "The Urban Negro Family," in Davis, *op. cit.*, p. 345. The shifting base between "Negroes" and "nonwhites" is made necessary by the lack of comparable data on many indices, but the distortion thus generated is minimal and insignificant since Negroes constituted in 1960 over 90 percent of the nation's "nonwhites."

21. Taeuber and Taeuber, "The Negro Population in the United States," *op. cit.*, p. 140.

22. T. F. Pettigrew, "Metropolitan Boston's Race Problem in Perspective," in Joint Center for Urban Studies of M.I.T. and Harvard, *Social Structure and Human Problems in the Boston Metropolitan Area* (Cambridge, Mass.: Joint Center for Urban Studies of M.I.T. and Harvard, 1965), p. 39.

23. Taeuber and Taeuber, "The Negro Population in the United States," *op. cit.*, pp. 139–140.

24. B. Duncan and P. M. Hauser, *Housing a Metropolis—Chicago* (New York: Free Press, 1960).

25. Taeuber and Taeuber, "The Negro Population in the United States," *op. cit.*, p. 140.

26. M. P. Yankauer and M. B. Sunderhauf, "Housing: Equal Opportunity to Choose Where One Shall Live," *Journal of Negro Education, 1963 Yearbook*, 1963, Vol. 32, No. 4, pp. 402–414.

27. Douglass, *op. cit.*, p. 345.

28. U. S. Depts. of Labor and Commerce, *op. cit.*, p. 57.

29. Research on this phenomenon in Toledo leads McKee to predict a growing opposition to urban renewal and highway construction dislocations by these more numerous Negro homeowners. J. B. McKee, "Changing Patterns of Race and Housing: A Toledo Study," *Social Forces*, 1963, Vol. 41, pp. 253–260.

30. National Advisory Commission on Civil Disorders, *op. cit.*, p. 467.

31. E. and G. Grier, "Equality and Beyond," *op. cit.*, p. 544.

32. For documentation of the ineffectiveness of complaint procedures in antidiscrimination legislation, see L. Mayhew, *Law and Equal Opportunity: A Study of the Massachusetts Commission Against Discrimination* (Cambridge, Mass.: Harvard University Press, 1968). For documentation of blatant discrimination even in a small city (Schenectady, New York), which has a tiny Negro population and operates under a relatively well-administered state antidiscrimination statute, see N. A. Mercer, "Discrimination in Rental Housing: A Study of Resistance of Landlords to Non-White Tenants," *Phylon*, 1962, Vol. 23, pp. 47–54.

33. White House Conference "To Fulfill These Rights," *op. cit.*, pp. 62–63.

34. Public housing accounts for about 1 percent of the nation's housing. *Ibid.*, p. 58.

35. Special Commission on Low-Income Housing, *Decent Housing For All* (Boston, March 1965).

36. L. F. Schnore, "Social Class Segregation among Non-Whites in Metropolitan Centers," *Demography*, 1965, Vol. 2, pp. 126–133.

37. Abrams, *op. cit.*, p. 516.

38. White House Conference "To Fulfill These Rights," p. 58.

39. B. J. Frieden, "Toward Equality of Urban Opportunity," *Journal of the American Institute of Planners*, 1965, Vol. 31, No. 4, pp. 320–330.

40. L. G. Watts, H. E. Freeman, H. Hughes, R. Morris, and T. F.

Pettigrew, *The Middle-Income Negro Family Faces Urban Renewal* (Boston: Massachusetts Department of Commerce and Development, 1965), p. 79.

41. H. Hughes and L. G. Watts, "Portrait of the Self-Integrator," *Journal of Social Issues,* 1964, Vol. 20, pp. 103–115.

42. White House Conference "To Fulfill These Rights," *op. cit.*

43. Frieden, *op. cit.* A Pennsylvania court decision against the four-acre-per-home zoning requirement of Easttown township may prove a landmark challenge to suburban restrictions. Neil Ulman, "States Move to Trim Local Zoning Autonomy as Criticisms Increase," *Wall Street Journal,* August 15, 1966, pp. 1, 12.

44. Title VI of the 1964 Civil Rights Act requires the cutoff of Federal funds to any program which racially discriminates. The title did not exclude so-called *de facto,* as opposed to *de jure,* segregation, nor did it directly include it. The legal question as to its application to *de facto* segregation arises in part because this condition was specifically excluded by Congress in a number of other titles of the act.

45. Special Commission on Low-Income Housing, *op. cit.*

46. The National Housing Corporation could establish revolving funds to purchase, for resale or rental on a desegregated basis, strategically located existing structures as they become available. J. Tobin, "On Improving the Economic Status of the Negro," in Parsons and Clark, *op. cit.,* p. 461.

47. Below-market interest programs [such as for 221(d)(3) housing] for nonprofit groups are the most noteworthy examples of this approach, though these efforts as yet constitute a bare fraction of the low-cost housing needed. Among the more interesting cooperating groups are the Foundation for Cooperative Housing in Stamford, Conn., Action Housing, Inc., in Pittsburgh, Community Resources Corporation in New York City, and the Housing Development Corporation in Washington, D. C.

48. Allport reviews many of these studies: G. W. Allport, *The Nature of Prejudice* (Cambridge, Mass.: Addison-Wesley, 1954), Chapter 16. The key studies on contact effects between Negro and white Americans in public housing are listed in footnote 13.

49. White House Conference "To Fulfill These Rights," *op. cit.,* p. 58.

50. E. and G. Grier, "Equality and Beyond," *op. cit.,* p. 550.

CHAPTER THREE

RACE AND EMPLOYMENT

Employment presents a slightly brighter outlook than housing. To be sure, the upgrading of black employment has not kept pace with the upgrading created by automation, nor has it significantly narrowed the gap with white employment; yet definite gains were made during the 1960s, and economic predictions for the 1970s indicate that there is a potential for substantial improvement. In 1967, for the first time over half the nonwhite workers had white-collar, craft, or operative jobs. Nonwhite employment in these jobs had increased by 66 percent between 1960 and 1969; for whites, the increase was 22 percent. The percentage of nonwhites employed as professionals and technicians increased by 109 percent; the percentage employed as clerical workers increased by 114 percent; and the percentage employed as craftsmen and foremen increased by 70 percent.[1]

The size of these percentages is deceptive, however, for they represent increments over small base numbers in the past. Consequently, gains in absolute numbers are less dramatic. The relative increases constituted only 1,947,000 nonwhites in these three key occupational groups by 1969; over seven million black men and women were in the labor force and still poor.[2] Even more troubling is the concurrent picture of Negro unemployment; rates of unemployment for Negro adults and youths have both remained roughly twice those for whites since the Korean War. The tight labor market of 1968, with its total unemployment rate reduced to below 4 percent, still witnessed a rate for Negro adults of roughly 7 percent. Among youths, rates soared as high as 25 to 30 percent for out-of-school Negroes aged 16 to 19 and at least 19 percent for the age group 16 to 21.[3] Rashi Fein sums up the problem: "What is recession for the white (say, an unemployment rate of 6 percent) is prosperity for the nonwhite. . . . Therefore, perhaps, it is appropriate to say that whites fluctuate between prosperity and recession but Negroes fluctuate between depression and great depression." [4]

The statistics from which this picture is drawn actually underestimate the desperate economic crisis of the Negro ghetto for several reasons. First, many blacks listed as job holders are seriously underemployed; they work full-time and throughout the year less often than whites, and less frequently hold positions commensurate with their education. Second, Negroes often do not earn as much as whites in comparable jobs.[5] As a result, the median income of nonwhite families has remained only slightly over half that of white families since World War II, although more members of the nonwhite family are in the labor force.[6] Indeed, nonwhite families with an employed head of household have a lower median income than white families with an unemployed head.[7] A third factor complicating the statistics is withdrawal of Negroes from the labor force. A disproportionately large share of working-age Negroes give up the search for a job, and unemployment statistics enumerate only those who are still actively seeking work. Economists estimate that if those who have despaired of finding employment and those who involuntarily work only part-time were considered, the Negro unemployment rate would approximate 12 percent even during a tight labor market year such as that in 1968. A fourth statistical complication has to do with the imprecise concept of "nonwhite." Japanese- and Chinese-Americans constitute less than a tenth of this statistical category, but their relatively secure overall economic position tends to improve the statistics for nonwhites.[8] Finally, recent economic and social data reveal an ominous trend that is masked by the aggregate statistics: although some Negroes are making significant gains, many others are slipping further behind the increasing prosperity of the most affluent country on earth.[9] Those Negroes less scarred by past deprivations are in a position to take advantage of current racial adjustments, and it is to these more fortunate people that fingers point when "racial progress" is proudly cited. These are the Negro Americans who by 1984 will be not just desegregated but truly integrated into "the affluent society." [10] There is, however, another Negro America which is less fortunate and which we must now consider.

This group, this "other Negro America," now constituting at least two thirds of all Negroes, has not been significantly touched by present racial adjustments. Its hopes were raised in the 1950s; [11] but now it cannot even rationalize personal failure entirely in racial terms, for *Ebony* bulges each month with evidence that the affluent Negro America is making rapid strides. Basic progress in improving the economic position of Negroes depends upon reaching the "other Negro America."

Causes and Consequences

Although blatant racial discrimination is an obvious cause of the other Negro America's economic plight, it is not the sole one. Relative to whites, Negroes more often reside in the South, have received fewer years and a poorer quality of education, and form a younger segment of the labor force, all characteristics apart from race which contribute to economic marginality. Moreover, the central cities of the North and West, where Negroes are concentrated in increasing numbers, are actually losing manufacturing jobs.[12] Implicit in these factors are forms of indirect economic discrimination. For instance, the inability of most Negroes to move to the suburbs puts them at a disadvantage in following the manufacturing jobs from central city to outer ring. Likewise, educational discrimination indirectly fosters economic discrimination. Nevertheless, direct and obvious job discrimination by both employers and unions remains the major barrier, for the economic position of the other Negro America still lags dangerously behind the rest of the country even after these indirect factors are taken into account. Attacks upon blatant discrimination in employment also offer far more hope for short-term effects than the slower, though ultimately necessary, alterations in these indirect contributors.[13]

The urgent need for both short-term and long-term remedial action becomes clear when we survey the consequences of the dire poverty of the other Negro America. At the national level, the annual gross national product (GNP) would be lifted by 5 billion dollars if black unemployment were lowered to the 1966 rate for whites; an additional gain of 22 billion dollars in the GNP would result if the productivity of the Negro labor force equaled that of the white labor force; and gains beyond this annual 27 billion dollars would result if Negroes obtained jobs commensurate with their abilities and training.[14] (Some further investment would be necessary, of course, to achieve these increments in the GNP.)

More important, however, are the social consequences of the other Negro America's poverty. The statistics themselves suggest the dire results of the unemployment pattern, particularly among the young. Early unemployment means that Negro youths are less likely to secure the on-the-job training necessary for more stable, skilled work, and thus they are more likely to be condemned to low-skilled, low-paying, low-seniority jobs, and are more predisposed as adults to join the devastated ranks of the hard-core unemployed. It is these factors which account for much of the grossly higher rate of unemployment of Negro adults.[15] Joblessness among youths also swells the ranks of those "riot-age" ghetto residents with little to lose from mass destruction. Significantly, the total unemployment rates in such strife-torn urban areas as Watts often run as high as 40 percent.

A more subtle consequence has been noted by Daniel Patrick Moynihan, who has documented the close and positive relationship over the years between the unemployment rate of nonwhite men, the percentage of nonwhite married women separated from their husbands, and the number of new cases opened under the Aid to Families of Dependent Children Program (AFDC).[16] Widespread family disorganization in the other Negro America, particularly absence of the father, is unquestionably one of the bitter fruits of economic discrimination. Those urban taxpayers who cry out against rapidly rising welfare budgets but continue to foster employment discrimination against Negroes have only themselves to blame.

Moynihan's data bear another ominous message. The close associations between unemployment and family characteristics break down after 1962. While unemployment among nonwhite men decreased in 1963 and 1964, the percentage of separated nonwhite women and new AFDC cases continued to rise. Although this dissociation of trends could indicate merely a transitional lag before improvements take hold, Moynihan raises the disturbing possibility that we are too late for short-term solutions. Has "the impact of economic disadvantage on the Negro community . . . gone on so long that genuine structural damage has occurred, so that a reversal in the course of economic events will no longer produce the expected response in social areas?" [17] Is the crisis "beginning to create conditions which tend to reinforce the cycle that pro-

duced it in the first instance?" [18] The years since Moynihan wrote this have only increased the concern; father
absence and AFDC cases continued to rise in the late
1960s without a rise in unemployment.

Economic Remedies

As with housing, a successful attack on this economic
situation must be metropolitan, systemic, and interactive.
Fortunately, a range of serious proposals that meet these
three criteria have been made; and the economic background should make them possible once the war in Vietnam ends.

Vigorous economic growth is predicted for the 1970s.
The GNP is expected to increase from one trillion to two
trillion dollars between 1970 and 1980. [19]

The labor force is expected to expand by nearly 20 percent between 1965 and 1975, bringing the total to 93.6 million workers. The increase will be double this percentage
for the age group between 20 and 34. Fifteen million more
jobs than were available in 1965 will have to be created. [20]

The Manpower Report of the President in 1967 projected employment changes by major occupational groups
between 1965 and 1975. The total increase in employment
is expected to be 22.8 percent. Breaking this figure down,
a 63 percent increase is expected in the professional,
technical, and white-collar fields, and a 34.5 percent increase among service workers; farming employment, however, is expected to decrease by 19 percent. Between
1960 and 1969 the nonwhite farm population fell by 56 percent, or 1.35 million. Since people coming from farms to
urban areas to seek employment usually desperately lack
the experience and education required by the urban labor
market, [21] and since the bulk of increased employment will
be in the professional and technical fields, where a high
degree of skill and training is demanded, the situation is
especially grave. Experts predict that in 1975 one third of

the male population under 35 will have less than a high school education. Thus we see the close interrelationship between employment problems and those of the public schools, which will be discussed in Chapter 4.

There will, however, be substantial increases in occupations requiring less training: urban reconstruction is expected to increase by one third; and service jobs and service industries will also experience tremendous increases in the coming years—service industries, such as advertising, maintenance, tourism, and health, expect an increase of 3.8 million jobs. In 1966 the Commission on Technology, Automation and Economic Progress estimated that 5.3 million new public-service jobs should be created to upgrade the following public services adequately: medical institutions and health services, educational institutions, national beautification, welfare and home care, public protection, urban renewal, and sanitation. It is important to note that these would not be make-work jobs. The need for the services to be provided underlies the justification for increased public-service employment.[22]

It is vital to begin now the first steps toward providing the needed public services and creating the jobs upon which they will depend. Harold Sheppard writes: "These first steps include the passage of legislation to create the public service employment jobs at local, state, and national levels of government; a more rational and improved program—with realistic recognition of the intrinsic demand problem—of private industry training and hiring of the hard-core unemployed; and, of course, the maintenance of those fiscal and monetary policies conducive to a 'full-employment' economy."[23] Other needed remedies include metropolitan job councils "to plan, coordinate and implement local programs to increase jobs."[24] These councils should combine business, labor, and government interests, and each council should be made responsible for an entire area's array of programs. The U. S. Department of Labor could supply each council with the basic information for initiating an effort in its area tailored to the needs of the Negro labor market. The councils could also serve as the local authority for administering future Federal and state programs "to guarantee the availability of jobs to able workers who cannot be placed in, or promptly trained for, regular employment." [25]

While urging the necessity of this government-financed employment, one must not overlook the critical importance to the Negro of a tight labor market. James Tobin argues forcefully that only with long-continued full employment can other programs to alleviate the black's economic crisis be successful.[26] Tobin further maintains that we already know how to sustain a tight labor market, although "creeping inflation" would be one cost. More conservative economists argue that inflation defeats the goal, since economically marginal citizens supposedly suffer most from rising prices. As far as the Negro is concerned, however, the historical evidence supports Tobin's analysis. The only times in this century when Negroes have made significant gains relative to whites in employment and constant-dollar income have been during periods of war: the tight labor markets brought on by war made racial discrimination too expensive a luxury.

Tobin urges the creation of nearly full employment without war.[27] A tight labor market, he argues, would mean not only more jobs but more skilled jobs for longer hours and better pay. Not only would it soak up Negro unemployment at roughly twice the rate of white unemployment, but it would return to the labor force many Negroes who had despaired of securing work. A continued tight labor market would attract surplus rural population to higher-paying urban jobs; it would force employers to be more realistic about job requirements, to fashion these requirements to fit the available supply, and to render more on-the-job training; it would prevent the sharp cyclical fluctuations which prevent many Negroes from achieving experience and seniority; and it would subvert policies of racial discrimination.

If it can do all of this, why do we not maintain a tight

labor market as a matter of national economic policy? Tobin answers:

> The vast comfortable white middle class who are never touched by unemployment prefer to safeguard the purchasing power of their life insurance and pension rights than to expand opportunities for the disadvantaged and unemployed. . . . We are paying much too high a social price for avoiding creeping inflation and for protecting our gold stock and "the dollar." But it will not be easy to alter these national priorities. The interests of the unemployed, the poor, and the Negroes are underrepresented in the comfortable consensus which supports and confines current policy.[28]

Together with a tight labor market, broader and more effective legal action is necessary. Title VII of the 1964 Civil Rights Act, the discrimination-in-employment title, looks good on paper, but an understaffed enforcement agency without enthusiastic administration support has not as yet achieved significant gains. Part of the problem is the largely case-by-case, complaint basis of enforcement. As with housing legislation, this nonstrategic, nonpatterned method has repeatedly failed in the many states that have relied upon it.[29]

The Federal government as an employer has set a notable example of what can be accomplished through planning in the hiring and upgrading of black personnel.[30] Title VII will not achieve a similar result generally unless a number of changes are made. Its coverage must be expanded to include employees of state and local governments, private-membership clubs, and educational institutions, and employers and unions with eight or more employees or members. The Equal Employment Opportunity Commission (EEOC) must be authorized to issue "cease and desist" orders, to command payment of back pay to persons suffering financial loss through denial of equal employment opportunity, and to initiate more patterned and strategic actions without complaint. Government contracting authority should be utilized to write new training program requirements into appropriate government contracts. Technical assistance for training and for affirmative desegregation programs must be furnished by EEOC to employers, labor unions, private groups, and governmental staffs. Finally, a greatly increased operating budget must be appropriated by Congress for the commission so that it can realistically enforce Title VII.[31]

The necessity of patterned antidiscrimination enforcement points up again the systemic nature of racial issues in urban America. Gunnar Myrdal emphasized a generation ago the vicious circle formed by discrimination in housing, employment, and education.[32] Successful remedies must break this circle at strategic points, such as special employment, training, and counseling programs for youth. Steps toward a more systemic approach include federalizing the public employment service, expanding the Manpower Retraining Act and the educational potential of the armed forces, designing mass transit networks so that Negro workers have better access to centers of metropolitan employment, and, finally, overhauling welfare programs.

Federalizing the public employment service is long overdue.[33] Although the service is operated by the states, it is totally financed by Federal funds. All too often, state agencies have discriminated in their job referrals and have operated parochially, virtually ignoring the national aspects of the problem. Now that a variety of Federal training functions have been assigned to them, it is imperative that this weak link be federalized, strengthened, and coordinated with the proposed metropolitan job councils.

Retraining programs should be expanded. First, the Manpower Retraining Act should be revised to lower its entrance requirements (it has largely rejected those applicants who need it most) and to furnish relocation funds so that the retrained can move to where the jobs are. Also, the most vital Federal source of job training for Negroes, the armed forces, should be more directly exploited. Except in wartime, the armed forces, like the manpower retraining program, exclude those Negroes who most need training and integrated experience. Lower entrance standards in peacetime are indicated, though the training expenditure per inductee will necessarily rise.[34] A start in this direction has been made in the U.S. Army's Project One Hundred Thousand.

Since black workers are more dependent upon mass transit than white workers, the new designs for urban transportation systems assume special importance. Present urban transit systems usually form an additional barrier between the ghetto dweller and the across-town job. Until recently in the Watts area, for instance, many workers had to travel for two hours, transfer several times, and pay fifty cents each way to commute to jobs or to visit employment agency offices.[35] With industry gaining admittance to the suburbs faster than Negroes, improved transit routing is essential.

Finally, there is widespread agreement that present welfare programs have failed, that they foster dependence and act as disincentives for employment. Developing a new approach, however, is a matter of sharp debate. Although reactionaries suggest virtual abandonment, more concerned critics point out specific deficiencies and suggest plausible modifications. Tobin, for example, emphasizes two particularly negative aspects of the present approach to welfare, the means test and the exclusion of families with an able-bodied employed male in the household.[36] "In a society which prizes incentives for work and thrift," he comments wryly, "these are surprising regulations." [37] The means test in effect taxes earnings at a rate of 100 percent, and it discourages savings by limiting property holdings. The exclusion of families with an employed male denies assistance to more than half the poverty-stricken children of the nation.[38] It also encourages absence of the father.

A new approach must offer the incentives for work, saving, and family stability now lacking. It must also be simpler to administer, avoid the indignities of present procedures, and discontinue the exclusion of significant segments of the poor. Such criteria strongly suggest a system of basic income allowances similar to what has unfortunately been tagged "a negative income tax." All Americans would file an annual income tax statement, but those falling below stated poverty levels would receive graduated funds from the government. Tobin has demonstrated that such an equitable system could easily be designed to encourage employment and thrift by taxing the income of welfare recipients at fair rates rather than the present 100 percent.[39]

In addition to metropolitan and systemic criteria, consideration of positive interracial contacts on the job must be a part of effective employment remedies. The other Negro America desperately requires jobs, but it also requires experience and involvement in the mainstream of American life. We will consider interracial contact in detail in later chapters.

Employment will offer, in the immediate future, more opportunities for favorable contact than housing, education, or any other area of activity. That this is so is an essentially negative comment about other realms of American society. Nevertheless, this is a critical point for American race relations in the near future, and we shall return to it in Part Five.

Footnotes

1. U. S. Depts. of Labor and Commerce, *The Social and Economic Status of Negroes in the United States* (Washington, D. C.: U. S. Government Printing Office, 1970), p. 41.

2. *Ibid.;* H. L. Sheppard, *The Nature of the Job Problem and the Role of New Public Service Employment* (Kalamazoo: The W. E. Upjohn Institute for Employment Research, 1969), p. 4.

3. White House Conference "To Fulfill These Rights," *Council's Report and Recommendations to the Conference* (Washington, D.C.: U.S. Government Printing Office, 1966), pp. 5–6.

4. R. Fein, "An Economic and Social Profile of the Negro

American," in T. Parsons and K. B. Clark (eds.), *The Negro American* (Boston: Houghton Mifflin, 1966), pp. 114–115.

5. E. Ginzberg and D. L. Hiestand, "Employment Patterns of Negro Men and Women," in J. P. Davis (ed.), *The American Negro Reference Book* (Englewood Cliffs, N. J.: Prentice-Hall, 1966), p. 231. Among men in 1960, for example, the median income of nonwhite professionals was only 69 percent that of white professionals; of salesmen, 57 percent; of craftsmen, 66 percent; and of operatives, 71 percent. The only reversal to this pattern, interestingly, is among private household workers, where for both sexes nonwhites earn slightly more than whites.

6. A. Brimmer, "The Negro in the National Economy," in Davis, *op. cit.,* pp. 258–260. By the late 1960s, this figure had risen to roughly 60 percent. U. S. Depts. of Labor and Commerce, *op. cit.,* p. 14.

7. D. P. Moynihan, "Employment, Income, and the Negro Family," in Parsons and Clark, *op. cit.,* pp. 148–149.

8. *Ibid.,* p. 143. Moynihan points out that in 1960 there were only 192,00 nonwhite managers, officials, and proprietors; over a fourth of these were Asian Americans.

9. Brimmer, *op. cit.,* pp. 266–271, provides the economic confirmation for this income differentiation through 1960. Thus, the bottom two fifths of nonwhite families in terms of income accounted for 15.0 percent of total nonwhite income in 1947, but only 13.5 percent in 1960; the top two fifths accounted for 69.3 percent of total nonwhite income in 1947 and 70.1 percent in 1960. These figures reveal a sharper income differentiation than among whites, for in 1960 the bottom two fifths of white families acquired 17.4 percent and the top two fifths 64.7 percent of total white income. Some slight improvement had occurred by 1968, when the nonwhite percentages were 15.3 and 68.2 and the white percentages were 18.7 and 63.7. A. F. Brimmer, "Economic Progress of Negroes in the United States" (unpublished speech, Tuskegee Institute, Tuskegee, Alabama, March 22, 1970).

10. Progress for "the affluent Negro America" is, of course, not inconsequential. Successful middle-class Negroes offer needed models of achievement for the Negro community; they can effectively obliterate racial barriers by being "the first of the race" in previously all-white situations; they help eliminate the Negro stigma by providing a constant contradiction between class and caste; and they furnish the great majority of protest leaders. But middle-class Negroes remain only a minority of the group.

11. Pettigrew, *A Profile of the Negro American* (Princeton, N. J.: Van Nostrand, 1964), pp. 184—185.

12. Moynihan, *op. cit.,* p. 142.

13. Fein, *op. cit.,* pp. 112, 119—121. See also O. Duncan, "Patterns of Occupational Mobility among Negro Men," *Demography,* 1968, Vol. 5, No. 1, pp. 11—22.

14. White House Conference "To Fulfill These Rights," *op. cit.,* p. 6. This 27 billion dollars represents roughly 3 percent of the total GNP, about the real gain annually during the 1960s. The degree of investment requirement is difficult to estimate but would probably not be substantial relative to the long-term gain.

15. They do not account for all of the higher rate, however. Unemployment rates for Negroes remain higher at each level on the occupational scale. Ginzberg and Hiestand, *op. cit.,* pp. 234—235.

16. Moynihan, *op. cit.,* pp. 147—158. This article is a more scholarly treatment of the basic theme of the much-criticized "Moynihan Report." For a copy of this original report, together with a discussion of the heated controversy it aroused, see: L. Rainwater and W. Yancey, *The Moynihan Report and the Politics of Controversy* (Cambridge, Mass.: M.I.T. Press, 1967).

17. Moynihan, *op. cit.,* p. 155.

18. *Ibid.,* p. 147.

19. Standard and Poor, *Outlook,* October 20, 1969, Vol. 41, No. 42, p. 556.

20. Sheppard, *op. cit.,* p. 12.

21. *Ibid.,* p. 12; and U. S. Depts. of Labor and Commerce, *op. cit.,* p. 41.

22. Sheppard, *op. cit.,* pp. 14—15.

23. *Ibid.,* p. 30.

24. White House Conference "To Fulfill These Rights," *op. cit.,* p. 11.

25. *Ibid.,* p. 19.

26. J. Tobin, "On Improving the Economic Status of Negroes," in Parsons and Clark, *op. cit.,* pp. 451—471.

27. Tobin points out that economic progress of Negroes is extremely sensitive to general economic growth. If nationwide per-capita personal income is stationary, median family income for nonwhites declines by about 0.5 percent annually; a per-capita-income increment of 5 percent leads to nearly a 7.5 percent gain for nonwhite families. *Ibid.,* p. 452.

28. *Ibid.*, pp. 458—459.

29. L. Mayhew, *Law and Equal Opportunity: A Study of the Massachusetts Commission Against Discrimination* (Cambridge, Mass.: Harvard University Press, 1968).

30. John Hope II and Edward E. Shelton, "The Negro in the Federal Government," *Journal of Negro Education, 1963 Yearbook,* 1963, Vol. 32, No. 4, pp. 367—374.

31. Many of these items were recommended by the White House Conference "To Fulfill These Rights," *op. cit.,* p. 25.

32. G. Myrdal, *An American Dilemma* (New York: Harper, 1944).

33. White House Conference "To Fulfill These Rights," *op. cit.,* p. 27.

34. Discussion of the social psychological advantages of armed forces training is contained in: Pettigrew, *op. cit.,* pp. 175—176. On the necessity of dealing expensively with the "hard-core" problem individuals, see Chapter 11 of this book.

35. White House Conference "To Fulfill These Rights," *op. cit.,* p. 27.

36. Tobin, *op. cit.,* pp. 462—469.

37. *Ibid.,* p. 463.

38. White House Conference "To Fulfill These Rights," *op. cit.,* p. 30.

39. Tobin, *op. cit.,* pp. 462—469. Moynihan and others have argued for another type of transfer-of-payments plan, namely a family allowance. But general application of such an allowance would be highly inefficient, since more than half of the funds would go to families that are not poor. Nor does it contain the valuable incentive features of the negative income tax. Yet the Nixon administration opted for the family allowance in its so-called "welfare reform" proposals of 1970.

CHAPTER FOUR

RACE AND EDUCATION

No institution is more crucial to the full inclusion of Negroes in American society than Horace Mann's "balance wheel of the social machinery"—public education. Yet problems mount faster than progress in this realm. The plain truth is that American education is failing in its critical task and shows at present few signs of becoming more effective.

The Extent of Segregated Education

"Racial isolation in the schools," concludes the U.S. Commission on Civil Rights, ". . . is intense whether the cities are large or small, whether they are located North or South." [1] The data shown in Figures 1, 2, 3, and 4 bear this out. Thus, in the fall of 1965, 65 percent of all Negro pupils in the first grade of public schools and 48 percent of all those in the twelfth grade of public schools were enrolled in schools with student bodies 90 to 100 percent Negro. Moreover, 87 percent of all Negro pupils in the first grade of public schools and 66 percent of all Negroes in

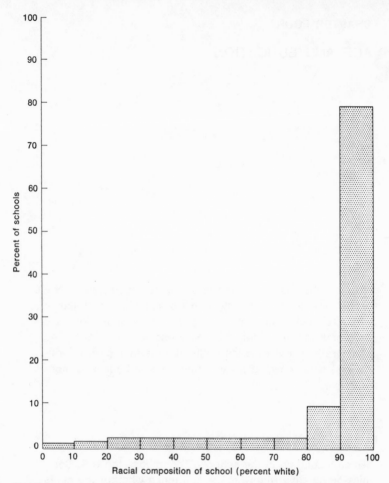

Figure 1. Percent of white students in public schools of differing racial composition: all regions, grade 1. Source: J. S. Coleman *et al., Equality of Educational Opportunity* (Washington, D.C.: U.S. Government Printing Office, 1966), p. 4.

the twelfth grade of public schools were enrolled in predominantly Negro schools.

Regional discrepancies do differ in magnitude, but this does not change the picture significantly: 97 percent of

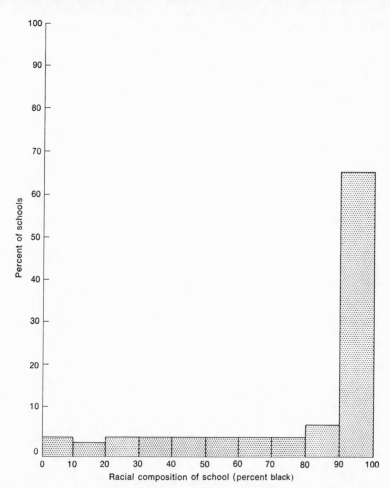

Figure 2. Percent of black students in public schools of differing racial composition: all regions, grade 1. Source: J. S. Coleman *et al., Equality of Educational Opportunity* (Washington, D.C.: U.S. Government Printing Office, 1966), p. 5.

Negro first-graders in the public schools of the urban South attended more-than-half-black schools in 1965; for the urban North, the figure was 72 percent. White children are even more segregated. In the fall of 1965, 80 per-

Race and Education

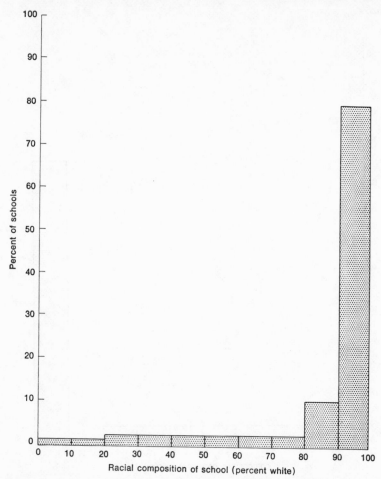

Figure 3. Percent of white students in public schools of differing racial composition: all regions, grade 12. Source: J. S. Coleman *et al., Equality of Educational Opportunity* (Washington, D.C.: U.S. Government Printing Office, 1966), p. 6.

cent of white children in both the first and twelfth grades in public schools were in schools 90 to 100 percent white.[2]

Moreover, the separation is increasing. In Cincinnati in

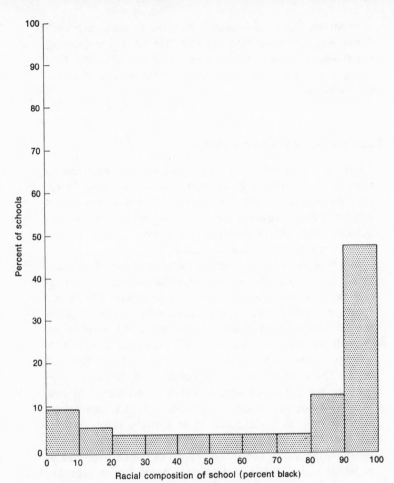

Figure 4. Percent of black students in public schools of differing racial composition: all regions, grade 12. Source: J. S. Coleman *et al., Equality of Educational Opportunity* (Washington, D.C., U.S. Government Printing Office, 1966), p. 7.

1950, for example, seven out of every ten Negro children in the elementary grades attended more-than-half-black schools; by 1965, nine out of ten did so. And while enrollment of Negro children in elementary school had doubled

Race and Education

over fifteen years, the number enrolled in these predominantly Negro schools had tripled.[3] This pattern of growing separation is typical of American central cities, the very cities where black Americans are concentrated in greatest numbers.

The Causes of Segregated Education

There are at least four major causes of this growing pattern of *de facto* school segregation: (1) trends in racial demography, (2) the anti-metropolitan nature of school-district organization, (3) the effects of private schools, and (4) intentional segregation similar to the older problem of *de jure* segregation.

The first two of these factors become apparent as soon as we compare public school organization and current racial demographic trends. There are approximately 25,000 school districts in the United States, with almost all of the recent consolidation of districts limited to the rural areas. Thus, there are over 75 school districts in the Boston metropolitan area alone, and 96 in the Detroit metropolitan area.[4] There is pitifully little cooperation between central-city and suburban school systems; and there are vast fiscal and social disparities between districts—especially between central-city and suburban districts. Now consider the fact that over 80 percent of all Negro Americans in metropolitan areas live in central cities, while over half of all white Americans in metropolitan areas live in suburbs; the racial separation by districts becomes apparent. And as we have just noted, housing trends are not encouraging; they offer no hope for substantial relief of educational separation in the next generation.[5] Consequently, America would face an enormous problem of *de facto* school segregation by district even if there were no patterns of separation by race within districts.

But, of course, the nation does face the task of overcoming sharp racial segregation within school districts. Thus, 90 percent or more of the black children enrolled in elementary schools in central cities in 1968 were in schools 90 to 100 percent Negro in the following cities: Richmond, Atlanta, Little Rock, Memphis, Gary, Omaha, Washington, D.C., Tulsa, Oklahoma City, Baltimore, and Chicago. In cities with large Roman Catholic populations, this segregation within districts is increased by the absorption of many white children into the parochial system. Since only about 6 percent of Negro Americans are Roman Catholics,[6] a large parochial school system necessarily limits the available pool of school-age white children for a central-city public school system. In St. Louis and Boston, about two of every five white children go to private (largely parochial) schools; and in Philadelphia, roughly three out of every five white children go to private schools.

In addition, the Hickses and Wallaces in American political life worsen the problem of segregation within districts by openly advocating separation, careful misplacement of new facilities, distorting attendance zones, and refusing to take those measures which would at least begin to ease the problem. The Civil Rights Commission provides in its report two pointed examples from Chicago and Cincinnati of "de facto" segregation by design.[7] And resistance to racial change from schools acting in bad faith is, of course, blatantly demonstrated in much of the rural South—where almost one-fifth of all Negro Americans still live. We shall return to the Hicks and Wallace phenomena in Chapters 9 and 10. But although the public resistance of anti-Negro political figures gains the headlines, the more important structural barriers (demographic trends, anti-metropolitan school district organization, and effects of private schools) are often the more critical factors.

Results of Integrated Education: Federal Studies

The widespread pattern of *de facto* public school segregation throughout the nation has serious consequences for any attempt to provide equal educational opportunity for this generation and later generations of American children. In racial terms, the complex concept of "equal educational opportunity" translates into *"effective integrated schooling."* That anything less than this has not proven to be truly equal opportunity for black American children is a demonstrably harsh fact of the current scene—and there is reason to believe that the same holds true for white American children as well. There are many reasons for this translation, some of which receive considerable support from the extensive data gathered in the Coleman Report by the U.S. Office of Education as required by Congress under Title IV of the 1964 Civil Rights Act. This brief summary will utilize analyses of the data from the 1966 Coleman Report itself [8] and the 1967 U.S. Commission on Civil Rights Report, *Racial Isolation in the Public Schools.*[9]

The most significant school correlate of achievement test scores uncovered by the Coleman study is the social-class climate of the school's student body. This variable is measured by the social-class origins of all of a school's students; and it appears most critical in the later grades and somewhat more important for Negro than white children. Put bluntly, children of all backgrounds tend to do better in schools with a predominant middle-class milieu; and this trend is especially true in the later grades where the full force of influence of the peer group is felt. This basic finding of the Coleman Report has been vigorously challenged by a number of methodological critics, but none of them seem aware that the identical finding had been attained by four other studies which employed measures and samples sharply different from those used by Coleman. Interestingly, three of these replications were in print several years before the appearance of *Equality of Educational Opportunity* in 1966. The importance of this key conclusion warrants further mention of these supporting studies. In a research paper published in 1959, Alan Wilson demonstrated the special significance of the social class of schools in determining college aspirations in eight high schools in the San Francisco—Oakland Bay area of California.[10] He found higher percentages of college aspirants in higher-status schools even after controlling for other determinants of college aspirations: father's occupation and education, mother's education, median academic grade, and intelligence-test score. For example, among those boys whose fathers and mothers were high school graduates and whose fathers held manual occupations, 60 percent in upper-status schools wanted to go to college, as compared with 54 percent in the medium-status schools and only 32 percent in the lower-status schools. Likewise, among those boys with a modest academic grade record ("C"), 72 percent from upper-status schools aspired to college, in contrast to only 55 percent from medium-status schools and 41 percent in lower-status schools. Finally, for those with IQ scores in the 100 to 119 range, 93 percent in the upper-status schools, 72 percent in the medium-status schools, and 51 percent in the lower-status schools aimed for college.

Differences in college aspirations are not the only outcomes of school social class uncovered in this Wilson study. Controlling for father's occupation, he found that both occupational aspirations and political party preferences are also influenced. Hence, among boys whose fathers occupied manual positions, 44 percent in the upper-status schools wanted to be professionals and 50 percent preferred the Republican Party, compared with 31 percent and 32 percent, respectively, in the medium-status schools and 27 percent and 24 percent in the lower-status schools.

A second early attack on the problem was mounted at Harvard University, though it substituted the social-class level of nine Boston suburbs for a direct measure of the schools' social-class levels.[11] Controlling for father's occupation, the researchers found that boys from the higher-status communities were more likely to go to college. Community status, which determined the status level of the schools, had its crucial impact only at the high school level, the level at which Wilson was working. Consequently, community status predicted neither elementary school grades nor entrance into the college preparatory courses in high school from junior high school, a finding that resembles the Coleman result that the social status of schools gained in predictive value in the secondary school grades.

The most definitive early study was conducted by John Michael.[12] He analyzed the aptitude-test scores (on a test not unlike those used by Coleman) as well as the career and college plans of 35,436 seniors in a nationally representative sample of 518 American public high schools. Michael classified the students on an index of family social class, using such information as the father's occupation and education and whether older siblings had attended college. He classified the high schools into five status ranks according to the percentage of seniors in each school who fell into his two top family-status classifications, a method similar to Coleman's measures of school social class.

The first finding showed that with family status controlled, the higher the status of the school, the higher the average score on the scholastic aptitude test. Further analysis revealed that the variation in the percentages of students scoring above the national average on the test was roughly equally attributable to the individual and school social-class indices. But the variation in the percentages scoring in the top quarter was considerably more related to individual social class than school social class—a result directly in line with Coleman's finding that school social class is most important for the more deprived students and in line with the Commission's reanalysis finding that among whites in the metropolitan Northeast, school social class was least important for the highest-status students.[13] The little-known research by Michael, then, provided early evidence for many of the major conclusions of the Coleman Report.

On the matter of plans to attend college, the study by Michael, like the investigations by Wilson and Harvard, demonstrated that school social class makes a difference. But Michael's larger sample allowed deeper analysis and, as did Coleman's analysis, revealed that these effects are strongest for students from lower individual class backgrounds. Consider first those seniors who score in the top quarter of the aptitude-test distribution. Among these talented youngsters from the lowest individual social-class group, only 44 percent who attended the lowest-status high schools planned to go to college, as compared with 57 percent who attended the highest-status high schools. By contrast, among the talented seniors from the highest individual social class group, 80 percent who attended the lowest-status high schools planned to go to college, as compared with 86 percent who attended the highest-status high schools. In other words, the high-status school exerts a far greater influence on college plans among talented lower-status than talented higher-status students.

Much the same phenomenon is true for Michael's entire sample. The percentage differences in college plans between individual social-class groups is essentially the same at each type of school; but the percentage differences in college plans between scholastic-aptitude-test levels is far higher in the high-status than the low-status high schools. Put simply, attendance at a low-status school does not deter seniors from upper-status families in planning for college, but attendance at a high-status school is an important aid to able seniors from lower-status families.

These three early investigations, however, suffered from two interrelated methodological weaknesses that also limit Coleman's survey: the results are neither longitudinal nor corrected for initial achievement and aspirations upon entering school in the primary grades. These limitations open the studies to the possibility that their findings are merely the result of special selection biases. That is, lower-class children in predominantly middle-class schools may achieve more and aspire higher not because of the school climate but only because they are as a group brighter and more ambitious to begin with than lower-class children in general.

Robert Nichols has been a particularly vehement critic of the finding of the Coleman Report on social-class climate, on precisely these grounds of possible selection biases.[14] He and other critics apparently choose to ignore a fourth replication of Coleman's result reported at length in the U.S. Commission on Civil Rights report.[15] Wilson, in a follow-up to his earlier research, studied the social-class-climate variable on a probability sample of junior high and senior high school children in California's Bay area. He had the advantage of longitudinal data and initial scores upon entering school, thus overcoming Nichols' objections. In this study, Wilson finds a strong effect of the social-class context at even the elementary school level. After carefully "allowing for individual differences in personal background, neighborhood context, and mental maturity at the time of the school entry," he notes that the social-class level of elementary schools has a significant effect upon subsequent academic success at higher grade levels.

The racial significance of this finding of the Coleman Report becomes obvious as soon as we recall that, at most, only about one-fourth of the black American population can be accurately described as "middle-class." Apart from strictly racial factors, then, extensive desegregation is necessary to provide Negro pupils with predominantly middle-class school settings. On these class grounds alone, Negro children in interracial classrooms would be expected to achieve more than similar Negro children in all-Negro classrooms, and these expectations are supported in Coleman's data. Negro children from classrooms more than half white score higher on both reading and mathematical achievement tests than other Negro children; and this effect is strongest among those who began their interracial schooling in the early grades.[16] In addition, Negro students in classrooms more than half white yield as a group higher standard deviations in test scores than Negroes in classrooms with fewer whites—that is, desegregated Negroes reveal a wider spread in test performance.[17]

But are these achievement benefits of the interracial classroom *completely* a function of the social-class climate? Or are factors of racial composition independently related *in addition?* The text of the Coleman Report is equivocal on this point; it speaks of the desegregation effect being "largely, perhaps wholly, related to," or "largely accounted for by," other characteristics of the student body.[18] The Civil Rights Commission's re-analysis of these data, however, focuses further attention upon this particular question and finds that there *is* indeed a critical racial-composition correlate. The re-analysis uncovers relatively large and consistent differences in favor of those twelfth-grade blacks who are in classrooms more than half white even after the two major factors of the Coleman analysis have been controlled—family social class and school social class.[19] The apparent benefits of interracial classrooms are not linear; in other words, Negroes in predominantly white classrooms score higher on the average, but those in classrooms less than half white do no better than those in all-Negro classrooms. Once again, this effect of improved performance appears greatest for those Negro children who begin their biracial training in the early grades. Moreover, this is not a zero-sum game; that is, performance of whites in predominantly white classrooms does not decline as performance of Negroes rises. The achievement scores of white children and biracial classes which are more than half white average just as high as those of comparable children in all-white classes.[20]

The Commission Report also makes a crucial distinction between a merely desegregated school and an integrated one. Desegregation involves only a specification of the racial mix of students—in general, more than half white. It does not include any description of the *quality* of the interracial contact. Merely desegregated schools can be either effective or ineffective, and can boast genuine interracial acceptance or suffer intense interracial hostility. In short, a desegregated school is not necessarily a "good school." Recall the greater spread of test scores of Negro children in desegregated classrooms. Many of these children are doing extremely well, but others are not doing nearly as well. What accounts for the difference? The Commission's re-analysis of the Coleman data suggests that the explanatory intervening variable is *interracial acceptance.* In the schools which can truly be described as "integrated," where most teachers report no racial tension whatsoever, Negro students evince higher verbal achievement, more definite college plans, and more positive racial attitudes than comparable Negro students in tense, merely "desegregated" schools.[21] Desegregation, then, is a necessary but not sufficient condition for integration, for integration involves, in addition to racial mix, a climate of interracial acceptance.

However important, high achievement-test scores are surely not the sole goal of education. Indeed, many advocates of integrated education argue only in terms of the nonacademic benefits of diverse contacts. Preparation for the interracial world of the future, they insist, demands interracial schools today for both white and black youth. Coleman's data speak to this issue, too. The Coleman Report itself shows that white students who attend public schools with Negroes are the least likely to prefer all-white classrooms and all-white "close friends"; and this effect is strongest among those who begin their interracial schooling in the early grades.[22] Consistent with these results are data from Louisville, Kentucky, on Negro pupils. In an open-choice situation, Negro children are far more likely to select predominantly white high schools if they are currently attending predominantly white junior high schools.[23]

A survey by the Civil Rights Commission of urban adults in the North and West suggests that these trends continue into adulthood. Negro adults who themselves attended desegregated schools as children tend to be more eager to have their children attend such schools and do in fact more often send their children to such schools than comparable Negro adults who attended only segregated schools as children.[24] They are typically making more money and are more frequently in white-collar occupations than previously segregated Negroes of comparable origins. Similarly, white adults who experienced integrated schooling as children differ from comparable whites in their greater willingness to reside in an interracial neighborhood, to have their children attend interracial schools, and to have Negro friends.[25] It appears, then, that desegregated schooling does in fact prepare its products—both blacks and whites—for interracial living as adults.

Most discussion of these results to date has centered upon their immediate implications. But of greater psychological significance are the questions they raise concerning the actual dynamics of the interracial classroom and the precise individual processes which undergird these crude aggregate findings. A number of fascinating clues concerning these psychological processes are provided in the Coleman Report, two of which deserve special mention: "fate control" and "social evaluation." The former is essentially Rotter's "internal-external control of reinforcement" variable; [26] the latter refers to the cross-racial comparisons made possible by the interracial classroom.[27]

Student personality variables are surprisingly strong independent correlates of test performance in Coleman's data for all groups of children, though different measures predict achievement for whites and for Negroes. An "academic self-concept" variable (measured by such items as "How bright do you think you are in comparison with the other students in your grade?") proves more significant for performance of whites. But a brief scale of "fate control" (indicated, for example, by disagreeing with the statement "Good luck is more important than hard work for success") is much more important for performance of Negroes. Not surprisingly, this sense of internal control among Negroes tends to be greater in desegregated schools—a vital finding that contradicts those who would distort the results regarding "fate control" to support the idea of separate all-black schools.

Clearly, these findings result from tapping a complex process involving a two-way causal pattern. Not only do those Negro children with a sense of internal control subsequently do better in school, but those who do well in school undoubtedly begin to gain a sense of internal control. Nevertheless, it is tempting to speculate with Coleman that each child faces a two-stage problem: first, he must learn that he can, within reasonably broad limits, act effectively upon his surroundings; and, second, he must then evaluate his own relative capabilities for mastering the environment. The critical stage for white children seems to be the second stage, concerning the self-concept; the critical stage for Negro children seems, realistically enough, to involve the question of manipulating an often harsh and overpowering environment. In any event, more detailed experimental work along the lines of Rotter's research and Coleman's speculation appears warranted.

A number of theoretical considerations from social psychology suggest a broad hypothesis: *Many of the consequences of interracial classrooms for both Negro and white children are a direct function of the opportunities such classrooms provide for cross-racial self-evaluation.* It follows from such a hypothesis that the more opportunities for cross-racial self-evaluation a school provides, the greater the consequences. And it also follows that those children for whom peers of the other race become referent should evince the largest changes.

These predictions are consistent with the analyses of the Coleman and Commission reports and with the conceptual framework and experimental results on biracial performance of Irwin Katz.[28] Hence, the repeated indications of the special potency of desegregation in the early elementary grades fit well with the view about self evaluation; young children have less rooted self-concepts and have not yet adopted uniracial school cliques as their chief peer referents. So, too, do Coleman's conclusions that the most significant school correlate of test scores is the social-class climate of the student body and that this factor is especially important for Negro children. Schools with a middle-class milieu furnish higher comparison levels for achievement and aspirations; and these higher levels will be especially influential for disadvantaged Negro youngsters whose referents otherwise might well have lower levels. And the special efficacy of classrooms and schools more than half white, particularly those characterized by cross-racial acceptance, is also consistent with these predictions. The integrated class and school are unique in the range of opportunities they provide Negro children for maximal self-evaluation against higher comparison levels.

The inclusion in Coleman's student schedules of a question about cross-racial friendships makes possible direct tests of the hypothesis proposed above. All students tested in the sixth, ninth, and twelfth grades were asked: "Think now of your close friends. How many of them are white? None, less than half, about half, more than half, all." Assuming "close friends" to be referent, our hypothesis predicts that the major consequences of interracial schools for both Negroes and white will be found among those who report "close friends" of the other race. The published analyses employing the "close friend" variable confirm this hypothesis. Thus, with the variables of family and school social class controlled, Negro children with close white friends far less often prefer all Negro friends and an all-Negro school than other Negro children, regardless of the racial composition of their classrooms.[29] Classrooms half or more than half white relate strongly to these interracial preferences solely because Negroes in them more often have close white friends.[30] In addition, blacks who participate in extracurricular activities more frequently report having close white friends.[31]

Achievement scores and college aspirations of black students present a slightly different picture from the data regarding attitudes. Having close white friends is related neither to higher scores nor to aspirations in all-Negro classrooms. But in classrooms "more than half" white, Negro students with close white friends tend to have both higher achievement scores and college aspirations.[32]

Friendship operates in a similar fashion for white students. Hence, with father's education controlled, having close Negro friends is strongly and positively related to preference for an interracial school.[33] And, as noted, white pupils who begin their interracial schooling in the early grades are more likely to have close Negro friends when they reach the ninth and twelfth grades.[34]

In short, integrated education in the early grades seems to have important benefits for both Negro and white children in terms of improved interracial attitudes and preferences—not an unimportant consequence in a nation torn by racial strife and bigotry. And if processes of social evaluation during interracial contact are as critical to these benefits as they appear in these data, even the most academically successful "compensatory programs" in ghetto schools cannot rival genuine integration.

A final word needs to be said concerning the Equality of Educational Opportunity Survey. Let it be clearly stated that Coleman and his associates achieved a landmark contribution in an amazingly short time. Though not without its problems of sampling, nonresponse, and analysis, this massive and ambitious study should influence educational research and practice for years to come. It is of necessity a broad-gauged, aggregate survey of what exists now in American public schools. It could neither detail precise learning processes nor test what American public schools could potentially become in the future. The Coleman Report outlined the gross facts of American public education today; now, the precision of the limited experiment is needed to detail the underlying processes that go unseen by the survey. From fate control to social evaluation, the results of the Coleman Report are rich and suggestive for fruitful experimentation. In the meantime, the implications of the Coleman Report for practical school policy are reasonably clear: equal educational opportunity for both black and white children requires socially and racially integrated, not merely desegregated, schools.

Toward a Solution: The Metropolitan Educational-park Plan

Can we really desegregate our public schools? Is it possible to achieve student bodies effectively balanced racially and socioculturally? Are there any "ultimate solutions" for our big city school systems? Isn't integration really a nice but impossible notion? What about Washington, D.C.? Harlem? South Side Chicago?

Initially, we must make a clear distinction between *small-ghetto* and *big-ghetto situations,* for what is possible and useful in small ghettos may well be counter-productive in big ones. The small-ghetto situation generally involves a city with less than a seventh or so of its public-school population Negro. Its high schools and often even its junior high schools are naturally desegregated, and with good faith it can correct segregation in elementary schools *within* its borders. There are many such communities throughout the United States and together they account for a surprisingly large minority of Negro children. They should not be confused with the Washingtons and Harlems, although segregationists often make this confusion.

The elementary schools in these cities with small ghettos can usually be desegregated by a plan modified for the particular system, utilizing a unique combination of the following intradistrict methods: (1) the district-wide redrawing of school lines to maximize racial balance (positive gerrymandering); (2) the pairing of predominantly white and Negro schools along the borders of the Negro ghetto (the Princeton plan); and (3) a priority for and careful placement of new and typically larger schools outside the ghetto (the rebuilding plan). If there is a need to desegregate at the junior high or senior high levels, two other devices are often sufficient: (4) the alteration of "feeder" arrangements from elementary grades to junior highs and from junior highs to senior highs in order to maximize racial balance (the "balanced-feeder" plan); and (5) the conversion of more schools into district-wide specialized institutions (the specialized-school plan). Controversy is typically minimal because the small-ghetto situation can usually be accommodated without the widespread transportation of students (busing).

The real problems of implementation occur in the big-ghetto situation. The devices used in cities with small ghettos are generally far too small in scope for the city with a substantial and growing percentage of Negro students. Thus, pairing schools along the borders of a ghetto would have to be repeated every few years as the ghetto expanded; a new school built outside of the ghetto one year might become a nearly all-Negro school within the ghetto the next year. Even in Boston, with only about thirty percent nonwhites in its public school system, a sophisticated redistricting plan for elementary schools would have only minor effects. In a computer-assisted system analysis, the ultimate limit of redistricting was tested with the rules that children in grades 1 through 3 would not be assigned more than half a mile from their homes and children in grades 4 through 6 not more than three-quarters of a mile. By this plan, the proportion of Boston's nonwhite elementary students attending predominantly nonwhite schools would be reduced only from 78 percent to 66 percent; for nonwhite junior high school students, the reduction would be only from 65 percent to 50 percent.[35] Clearly, for Boston—not to mention New York, Philadelphia, Washington, Chicago, and Los Angeles, the cities with really enormous ghettos—more sweeping measures are required.

If the criteria for these sweeping measures are specified, the form and direction of future efforts begin to take shape. And these criteria were suggested earlier, in the discussion of the causes of "de facto" school segregation. In planning for desegregation in big-ghetto situations, larger educational complexes drawing their attendance from wide areas will be essential. These attendance areas will generally have to include both central-city and suburban territory in order to ensure the optimal stable racial mix. The sites for these facilities not only must be convenient to the mass transit network but also must be on racially "neutral turf." Such locations would avoid public labeling of the school as "white" or "black."

Racial specifications are by no means the only criteria for future remedies. Public schools in our largest cities have lost their former eminence as the innovative educational leaders. Berkeley, California; Newton and Brookline, Massachusetts; and a host of other smaller communities are now the pace-setters. Plans for the future of public schools in large cities should accent and facilitate innovation. Indeed, future public schools should possess facilities which could rarely be duplicated by expensive private schools if they are to compete effectively for the children of advantaged parents. Such arrangements, of course, will cost considerable money; thus, a final criterion must be significant Federal support of capital costs.

Several designs would meet these criteria; but let us consider one design as illustrative. Ringing a major city with educational parks, each of which would serve students from both inner city and suburbs, offers one basic plan—*the metropolitan educational park plan.* Parks could be located on "neutral turf" in an inner-ring suburb or just inside the boundary of the central city; [36] and they could be so placed that the same spoke of the mass transit system would bring both outer-ring suburban children into the park and inner-city children out to it. The attendance area of each park could ideally be a pie-slice of the city, containing a minimum of 12,000 to 15,000 public school students, with the thin end of the slice in the more densely populated central city and the thick end in the more sparsely populated suburbs.

But what incentive could generate the metropolitan co-operation necessary for such a plan? A number of systems have considered educational parks, but they usually find the capital costs prohibitive. Moreover, many systems are currently hard-pressed for expansion funds—especially as referenda for school-construction bonds continue to be defeated throughout the nation. Federal funding on a massive scale, then, will obviously be needed, though it must be dispersed in a far more careful and strategic manner than by the 1965 Elementary and Secondary Education Act, which was based on the "river and harbors bill" principle—"everybody gets his cut." As long as alternative Federal funding for capital costs is available, many school systems—particularly those acting in bad faith—will not choose to join a metropolitan educational park plan. Therefore, future Federal construction grants must meet the following conditions: (1) The construction must involve more than one urban district, and the consortium must always include the central city. (Note that any one park would not require the entire metropolitan area to join the proposal, though some coordination would be necessary, perhaps through review by each area's metropolitan planning commission. Nor would any one park require the consolidation of urban school districts.) (2) Racial and social desegregation—and, hopefully, integration—must be required in every school involved (metropolitan involvement makes this requirement feasible). (3) Alternative routes for Federal building funds must be excluded (though if the first two criteria are met, the proposal need not adopt the metropolitan educational park plan as the only model).

An educational park for 15,000 students, costing 40 to 50 million dollars, 90 percent of it paid by the Federal government, would be a powerful inducement. But is such Federal funding possible in the near future? The answer, as with many other domestic questions, rests with the termination of the war in Vietnam. Once the conflict ends, economists will urge domestic spending to take up the slack from, hopefully, some cutback in defense expenditures. Nothing like the costs of the war, of course, would become available for domestic purposes. Yet, once the war ends, a yearly 2-billion-dollar school-construction program—enough for building roughly forty educational parks annually—would not be unreasonable. Here lies both a great opportunity and an equally great danger. If the money is distributed in the easy fashion of the 1965 Education Act to individual school districts, the effects could go against metropolitan cooperation and be disastrous for both race relations and public education. Federal building money spent in such a manner would further insulate aloof suburbia and institutionalize *de facto* school segregation in the inner city for at least another fifty years. Money for school construction is likely to be made available by the Federal government after the war. The vital question is: What will be its form and effects?

The educational park idea is not a panacea; there can be elegantly effective and incredibly ineffective parks. Yet ample Federal funding combined with the nation's planning and architectural genius should be able to set a new standard and direction for public schools. This combination has successfully been applied to public facilities ranging from interstate highways to magnificent airports. Now the combination should be applied to the benefit of children.

Educational parks themselves can be planned in a variety of ways, from high-rise structures to multiple-unit campuses. The most widely discussed design would involve a reasonably large tract of land (80 to 100 acres as a minimum) and no fewer than fourteen or fifteen schools serving grades from kindergarten through high school. One educator has visualized a campus design for 18,000 students consisting of two senior high schools, four junior high schools, and eight elementary schools.[37] If the park were to serve an especially densely populated section, it might be best if it did not include the entire grade spectrum, so that it could still cover a reasonably expansive and heterogeneous attendance area. In general, however, an educational park would resemble a public university. Both include a variety of educational programs for a large group of students of varying abilities. And like public universities in our major cities, some parks could consist of high-rise structures and some could develop a more spacious campus atmosphere with numerous buildings. Hopefully, the metropolitan park could usually follow the campus model since sufficient space would generally be obtainable at locations in the suburban ring.[38]

Apart from offering remedies for racial segregation, the educational park concept has a number of distinct advantages. First, considerable savings accrue from consolidation; there could be centralized facilities, such as a central kitchen, rather than duplication in each of the park's units. Savings on capital costs, too, would accrue from building many units at one location simultaneously. These savings, however, do not necessarily mean that the total construction and operating costs would be less than those for the same student capacity spread out in traditional units. The advantage is that for essentially the same cost educational parks could provide significantly better facilities than traditional schools. Consequently, each child would be receiving far more per educational dollar.

The improved centralized facilities of the park should maximize innovations and individualized instruction. It is difficult to institute new approaches to learning in old settings. A crucial finding of research on social change is that new norms are easier to introduce in new institutions. The educational park offers a fresh and exciting setting that should encourage new educational techniques and attract the more innovative members of the teaching profession. In addition, the park presents a rare opportunity for designing innovation into the physical and social structures of the schools. This, of course, would include the latest equipment for aiding the teacher and the student. Centralization can enhance this process—for example, by providing efficient concentration of all electronic information storage, retrieval, and console facilities. Yet such centralization of equipment should not be viewed as leading inevitably to a wide assortment of frightening Orwellian devices cluttering the school. Poor planning could lead to this result, but the accent should be on individualized instruction as the unifying and positive theme—a theme far more possible in the park design than in the present pattern of scattered "little red schoolhouses."

Social innovations made possible by the educational park extend far beyond the provision of equipment. For instance, the teaching profession today suffers from being one of the most undifferentiated by rank of all professions, a characteristic which discourages life-long work in the field. The medical profession, for example, has a graded rank order from intern and resident to chief of a service; teachers, on the other hand, must either enter administration and become principals or shift to more prestigious schools in order to move up the ladder. By concentrating a large number of teachers in a relatively small area, far more differentiation of roles becomes possible. Thus, a teacher might progress from an apprentice in a team-teaching situation, to a master teacher in a team, to a supervisor of master teachers, and so on. Concentration of faculties also allows more intensive, across-school in-service training and the formation of departments across schools with rankings within departments as in universities (e.g., a junior high school history department consisting of all history teachers in the four or five junior highs of one park).

Consider, too, the innovative possibilities for guidance counselors. One of the central role conflicts within this profession has pitted psychological therapy against academic and occupational counseling, treatment against advice and direction. The park presents an opportunity to alleviate this conflict by differentiating the roles involved. Academic and occupational direction could continue to be the focus of guidance counselors working within the schools themselves, while therapy for disturbed youngsters could be centralized together with an extensive health facility made possible by the larger scale. Indeed, public health facilities for children might well be attracted to the park and run in close collaboration with the schools.

Concentration of students also allows a wider range of courses to be offered. Specialized classes, from playing the lute to seventeenth-century English literature, become economically possible when the students electing them are gathered from units throughout a park. Moreover, concentration makes possible some remarkable facilities that can be shared by all of the park's units—e.g., an Olympic-size swimming pool, and extensive auditorium and theatrical equipment. These special facilities could far surpass what is now available in all but the most affluent districts, become a source of pride to the students and the community, and provide an advantage over private schools. They also would be used efficiently, whereas expensive facilities in single schools now are only minimally used.

The educational park offers unusual opportunities for an effective liaison with a local university or college. Nova, an earlier form of an educational park near Fort Lauderdale, Florida, even plans to include college and graduate work right on its campus. But direct contiguity is not necessary to develop a mutually beneficial coordination.

An important cause of public school segregation in many central cities, it will be recalled, is the enrollment of large percentages of white children in parochial schools. This fact suggests closer cooperation between public and parochial schools; and the metropolitan educational park plan could facilitate such cooperation under optimal conditions. Most parochial systems are currently in serious financial difficulties, and tapping a park's superior facilities should prove attractive to them. Roman Catholic educators point out that items costing the most—physical science laboratories, gymnasiums, and stadiums—tend to be least related to the "moral training" that they believe to be the distinctive feature of their schools. Having public and parochial schools at scattered sites and making "shared time" and other cooperative arrangements is awkward at best; and when parochial students come to take their public school class as a group, such segregation often reaps its usual harvest of tension and hostility. A recent idea from Vermont introduces a more promising possibility. At the time of planning a large educational park, Roman Catholic educators are given the opportunity of buying an adjoining plot of land and constructing a new facility of their own. As long as the land price is consistent with its true value, no constitutional infringements appear to be involved. The new parochial facility need concentrate only on courses directly needed for "moral training." Parochial pupils would be free as individuals, not as separated groups, to cross the park's grass, not urban streets, and attend public school courses in physical education, science, etc., when these fit their schedules. The Vermont Plan offers construction and operating savings to hard-pressed parochial systems; and it offers to hard-pressed public systems a greater balance of races and classes among the student body.[39]

Cost efficiency, educational innovations, more individualized instruction, a wider variety of courses, special facilities, and coordination with universities and parochial schools—all these advantages of the well-designed educational park are features that parents, white and Negro, would welcome in the schools of tomorrow. This is politically critical, for desegregation efforts of the past have seldom come as intrinsic parts of a larger package promising an across-the-board improvement in education for *all* children.

In addition to the natural resistance to change, four major objections have been raised to the educational park concept: (1) excessive capital costs; (2) the phasing out of existing schools; (3) the problem of impersonalization in the large complexes; and (4) the loss of neighborhood interest and involvement in the school. Each is a serious objection and deserves comment.

The park *is* expensive, and major Federal funding is necessary. Furthermore, mistakes in design and location could be disastrous. A park is an enormous commitment of resources, and, if poorly conceived, it could stand for years as a major mistake in planning. This is precisely what would happen if parks were operated totally within central-city systems, for demographic projections prove the folly of building parks for a single central-city system as a desegregation device.[40] It is for this reason that the parks of the future must be *metropolitan* in character.

Present schools were expensive, too; this raises the problem of phasing them out. For many urban districts this is not a problem; they already have overutilized schools with double shifts and rising enrollments or old schools long past their usefulness. But some urban districts have many new schools and would be hesitant to join a park consortium. The program, however, is a long-term one. Hopefully, by the late 1970s most of the nation's leading metropolitan areas would have one or more parks; these in turn could serve as models for completing the park rings during the following decade. Moreover, enrollments of elementary and secondary students will rise rapidly—from 48.4 million in 1964 to a projected 54.9 million in 1974 and 66 million in 1984.[41] Metropolitan parks, then, could be phased in as older facilities are phased out and enrollments rise.

Such a process would be ideal nationally, but there will be special problems in localities with "planned *de facto*" school segregation. These are cities, such as Chicago, which purposely built new schools in the heart of their black areas in order to maximize racial separation. If racial progress is to be made in these cities, recent structures will have to be converted to new uses—perhaps to much-needed community centers.

The third objection to parks centers upon the impersonalization which presumably comes with organizational bigness—the "Kafka problem." Indeed, much of the description of an educational park—15,000 students, a staff approaching 1,000, the latest electronic equipment—has a frightening ring; and one can easily imagine how an ill-designed park could justify these fears. But such a prospect is not inherent in the park plan; nor is bigness a problem of parks alone, for many of today's huge urban high schools accommodate many thousands of students in a single unit and arouse the same uneasiness. In fact, imaginatively designed parks could act to counter the urban trend toward ever-larger public school units. *Smaller* schools at each level can be economically built as units within a park; and careful planning can afford a reasonable degree of privacy and autonomy for each unit while still providing access to the shared facilities of the park.

Some critics are particularly concerned about the loss of neighborhood interest and involvement. But this criticism assumes that most urban public schools today are neighborhood-based, and that they generate considerable neighborhood involvement. Serious doubts can be raised about both assumptions: we may well be worrying about the loss of something already lost. In any event, there is no evidence to indicate that only a neighborhood-based school can generate parental concern, or that an educational park could not duplicate this feat, or that there is a close and negative association between the size of the attendance area and involvement.

The criticism does raise an important planning issue: How can the park be initiated and planned to heighten parental and community interest? Certainly, the special facilities, the liaison with a university, and cooperation with parochial schools could help generate a community's pride and interest. So could smaller schools and a park school board of parents with wide authority short of taxing power. Furthermore, widespread use of the park for adult education, community affairs, and the like, would also contribute to public involvement; indeed, the special facilities of the park lend themselves to such adult use more readily than does the typical school today.

Finally, one might ask how such a metropolitan educational park plan fits with other widely discussed possibilities such as "decentralization" and "community schools." First, it should be noted that decentralization and community control are typically advanced either apart from integration considerations or as outright alternatives to integration. The "Bundy Report" for New York City, for instance, called for a large number of small, separate districts that could potentially institutionalize racial segregation for generations to come. Yet there is an obvious need in large and unwieldy systems such as New York's and Chicago's to decentralize authority, as well as a general need to increase parental and community involvement in public education. Like compensatory education, however, these possibilities acquire force and meaning when they *accompany* the drive for integration rather than substitute for it. Thus, effective decentralization need not take the form of isolated social-class or racial islands, but should assume the pie-slice shapes described earlier as ideal attendance areas for metropolitan educational parks. New York City's schools *could* be organized along the lines suggested by the "Bundy Report" in such a way as to help rather than hinder integration.[42]

Those who say there is nothing we can do about the educational segregation of our major cities, then, are, fortunately, wrong. This is not to say that the desegregation process will be easy, or even that we will do what is necessary to achieve progress. But it is to say that potentially we *can* do it for a significant number of urban Americans, white and black.

Summary

Public schools in urban America today are highly segregated by race and rapidly becoming more so. The causes of this *de facto* separation are apparent: (1) trends in racial demography; (2) the anti-metropolitan nature of school-district organization; (3) the effects of private schools; and (4) intentional segregation similar to the *de jure* segregation in the South. The consequences of this dismal trend are shown by considerable research to be negative for both white and Negro children. Among other possibilities, the metropolitan educational park plan illustrates the type of remedy which responds to each of the key causes of school segregation.

We shall return to these issues in later chapters, but discussion of the Federal studies of education raises a more general question concerning the contribution, potential and realized, of the social sciences to race relations in the United States. We turn now to considering this question for the two disciplines with which the writer is identified—sociology and social psychology.

Footnotes

1. This section constitutes in large part a terse restatement of Chapters 1 and 2 of: U. S. Commission on Civil Rights, *Racial Isolation in the Public Schools.* Vols. I and II (Washington, D. C.: U. S. Government Printing Office, 1967). The quote is taken from Vol. 1, p. 7.

2. J. S. Coleman *et al., Equality of Educational Opportunity.* (Washington, D. C.: U. S. Government Printing Office, 1966), pp. 3–7.

3. U. S. Commission on Civil Rights, *op. cit.,* Vol. 1, p. 8.

4. *Ibid.,* p. 17.

5. K. E. Taeuber and A. F. Taeuber, *Negroes in Cities* (Chicago: Aldine, 1965).

6. N. Glenn, "Negro Religion a.nd Negro Status in the United States," in L. Schneider (ed.), *Religion, Culture and Society* (New York: Wiley, 1964), pp. 623–639.

7. U. S. Commission on Civil Rights, *op. cit.,* Vol. I, pp. 48–49.

8. Coleman *et al., op. cit.*

9. U. S. Commission on Civil Rights, *op. cit.*

10. A. B. Wilson, "Residential Segregation of Social Classes

and Aspirations of High School Boys," *American Sociological Review,* 1959, Vol. 24, pp. 836–845.

11. S. Cleveland, "A Tardy Look at Stouffer's Findings in the Harvard Mobility Project," *Public Opinion Quarterly,* 1962, Vol. 26, pp. 453–454.

12. J. A. Michael, "High School Climates and Plans for Entering College," *Public Opinion Quarterly,* 1961, Vol. 25, pp. 585–595.

13. U. S. Commission on Civil Rights, *op. cit.,* Vol. 1, p. 85.

14. R. C. Nichols, "Schools and the Disadvantaged," *Science,* Dec. 9, 1966, Vol. 154, pp. 1312–1314.

15. U. S. Commission on Civil Rights, *op. cit.,* Vol. 2, pp. 165–206.

16. Coleman, *et al., op. cit.,* p. 332.

17. *Ibid.,* p. 333. The scores of the few Negroes with only white classmates have the highest SDs of all, though smaller cell sizes are involved.

18. *Ibid.,* pp. 307 and 330.

19. U.S. Commission on Civil Rights, *op. cit.,* Vol. 1, p. 90.

20. *Ibid.,* p. 160.

21. *Ibid.,* pp. 157–158.

22. Coleman, *et al., op. cit.,* p. 333.

23. U.S. Commission on Civil Rights, *Civil Rights USA: Public Schools, Southern States, 1962* (Washington: U. S. Government Printing Office, 1963).

24. U.S. Commission on Civil Rights, *op. cit.,* Vol. 1, pp. 111–113.

25. *Ibid.*

26. J. B. Rotter, "Internal versus External Control of Reinforcement," *Psychological Monographs,* 1966, Vol. 80, No. 609.

27. T. F. Pettigrew, "Social Evaluation Theory: Convergences and Applications," in D. Levine (ed.), *1967 Nebraska Symposium on Motivation* (Lincoln, Neb.: University of Nebraska Press, 1967).

28. I. Katz, "Review of Evidence Relating to Effects of Desegregation on the Performance of Negroes," *American Psychologist,* 1964, Vol. 19, pp. 381–399.

29. U.S. Commission on Civil Rights, *op. cit.,* Vol. 2, pp. 97–99.

30. *Ibid.,* p. 103.

31. *Ibid.,* p. 102.

32. *Ibid.,* pp. 100–101.

33. *Ibid.,* p. 141.

34. Coleman, *et al., op. cit.,* p. 333.

35. Joint Center for Urban Studies of M.I.T. and Harvard,

"Changes in School Attendance Districts as a Means of Alleviating Racial Imbalance in the Boston Public Schools," unpublished report, August, 1966.

36. Other convenient and racially neutral sites would be appropriate to specialized metropolitan educational parks. Sites near the art museum, the science center, the music center, and colleges and universities, rather than near the central city and suburban boundary, could possess enough appeal and status to attract suburban children into the central city despite the longer commuting required.

37. G. Brain, "The Educational Park: Some Advantages and Disadvantages," in N. Jacobson (ed.), *An Exploration of the Educational Park Concept* (New York: New York Board of Education, 1964), p. 16.

38. In some of the thickly populated metropolitan areas, especially the older cities of the East, ideal sites are already scarce and rapidly disappearing—hence the present need for park-site land banks.

39. The old stereotype of parochial school students as children of working-class immigrants is just that—an outdated stereotype. Roman Catholic children who are the students in the Church-operated educational systems tend as a group to be distinctly higher in socioeconomic background than Roman Catholic children who attend the public systems. Thus, inclusion of parochial pupils in public school courses and programs is likely to facilitate social-class balance as well as racial balance.

40. The Philadelphia Urban League, in proposing nonmetropolitan parks for a central-city system whose student body is already more than half nonwhite, has advanced just such a plan.

41. F. Keppel, *The Necessary Revolution in American Education* (New York: Harper and Row, 1966), p. 19.

42. Private communication from Professor Dan Dodson of New York University. Of course, *no* decentralization and redistricting plan in New York City can solve the problem of desegregation alone. The point is only that it can be made to seal in racial and class segregation or to improve the situation slightly, depending on how it is accomplished. See also: T. F. Pettigrew, "School Integration in Current Perspective," *The Urban Review,* January, 1969, Vol. 3, No. 3, pp. 4—8.

"Be involved!" "Become relevant to the society's pressing problems!" These calls to academia in general and social science in particular have become so common in the mass media and from the platform that they are virtually clichés—simple clichés, at that; for "involvement" and "relevancy" pose contradictions and dilemmas that go largely unexplored in newspapers and speeches.

The same pragmatic orientation which demands "practical" research and ready solutions that "work" also leads to a deep suspicion of "experts" and "scientists." A social issue seems less abstract than nuclear physics, and no one without special training assumes he is conversant with nuclear physics; but since we all are human beings, we can all think of ourselves as lay-psychologists by definition, and since we all live in society, we can think of ourselves as lay-sociologists, too. Consequently, if social scientists reach practical conclusions that are in conflict with vested interests, and "common sense," it is not difficult to retort, "What do they know

PART TWO

SOCIAL SCIENCE AND RACIAL CHANGE

about it?" Similarly, the challenged practitioner's refrain —not without some merit—is: "You have to be on the firing line to know what the score really is."

This conflict often places social scientists in a painful dilemma. On the one hand, we are told to get involved, be relevant, come down from the ivory tower; on the other hand, if we become involved, we are told that we are biased and unobjective and that therefore our contribution is "suspect." The point was driven home to me forcefully by an editor of the Los Angeles Times. He rejected summarily a piece on an election which had been requested by the Times for its Opinion section on the grounds that it was "suspect," since an academic associate had been peripherally involved in the election under analysis. By calling for more involvement of academics in social issues on its editorial pages and simultaneously deploring it on the adjoining opinion page, the Los Angeles Times reflects a more general contradiction in American society.

A significant case study is provided by the public reception of The Equality of Educational Opportunity, the 1966 report of the U.S. Office of Education, written by James Coleman and his associates and discussed in Chapter 4. From the day it was quietly released on the Fourth of July weekend, the Coleman Report found itself treated less as a scientific document than as a political football. Those who liked its findings hailed it as a landmark study; those who disliked its findings sought out criticism to validate their claim that it should not be taken seriously by policy makers. Soon a speculative and shrill criticism was informally sent out widely by two young economists to persons in and out of government; and this criticism became the last word among those who cared considerably less about techniques of regression analysis than about the politics of education.

The Coleman Report did indeed have its methodological and theoretical weaknesses, some of which were mentioned earlier. But the necessarily charged political atmosphere into which it was released made the usual procedures of responsible criticism and retesting virtually impossible. The final verdict on the Coleman Report and its influence on American public education is not yet in. Re-analyses of the original data and additional research studies inspired by the report are still under way. Yet a future study of the political history of this report will offer an excellent opportunity to learn more about the complexities created by "involvement" and "relevancy."

It is the contention of this book that the most important contribution of the universities will be made through the full use for major social problems of their scholarly tools for gathering and assessing relevant data in a broader view than the myopia of today's headlines. In so applying their skills, academics need to brace themselves for society's ambivalence toward "experts" and the political perspective within which their work will be judged, used, disused, and misused. "It's hot in the kitchen," maintained Harry Truman; but it is precisely for that reason that academic tools for collection and analysis of data are so desperately needed.

Calls for mere "involvement" and "relevancy," without an appreciation of the kitchen's heat, then, are not enough. Just as the Council of Economic Advisers plays a critical role for economics, and the National Science Foundation for the physical and biological sciences—in much the same way sociology, social psychology, anthropology, and political science could benefit greatly from the establishment of agencies to play middleman roles for them. Two have been proposed in Washington. One would be a Council of Social Advisers reporting directly to the President; the other would be a National Social Science Foundation to balance the National Humanities and Science Foundations, since the latter has never managed to represent social science with the vigor it employs for natural science.

But the rest is up to social scientists themselves. And

here the record in race relations over the past two dec-
ades has not been especially noteworthy. Chapter 5
explores the reasons for this situation in sociology, and
is followed by an example of the potential contribution of
social psychology to understanding racial change in the
South.

CHAPTER FIVE

SOCIOLOGY IN THE DESEGREGATION PROCESS: ITS USE AND DISUSE

with Kurt Back[1]

Pick up almost any segregationist tract or newspaper editorial, and the chances are high that there will be at least one hostile reference to sociologists and sociology. For example, take the assertion of Wesley George in his tract *The Biology of the Race Problem:* "When the justices of the Supreme Court embraced the error of Myrdal without critical examination, they contributed to their own deception and deprived the people of the United States of their right to a firm foundation of truth for anything that purports to be the law of the land."[2] Or the charge of Virginius Dabney in an editorial in his newspaper, the *Richmond Times-Dispatch,* that "the violence at Little Rock . . . never would have happened if nine justices had not consulted sociologists and psychologists, instead of lawyers, in 1954, and attempted to legislate through judicial decrees."[3]

A naïve reader of such statements might understandably conclude that sociologists are dangerously powerful people and that sociology is making critically sinister contributions to the process of racial desegregation. The truth is, however, that sociologists have been neither dangerous nor powerful, and sociological contributions to this key process of contemporary American society have been neither critical nor sinister. The *disuse,* rather than the use, of sociology is more apparent; the attacks of segregationists upon the field are perhaps flattering in their assumptions, but they are simply not valid. To paraphrase Churchill, seldom have so many abused one profession for so little.

Segregationist critics have two specific phenomena in mind. They recall the influential sociological works of the *pre*desegregation era, like Myrdal's *An American Dilemma,* Drake and Cayton's *Black Metropolis,* and the numerous writings of Parks, Wirth, Odum, Charles Johnson, Guy Johnson, Frazier, and others. And they bristle over the quotation of some of these studies in the famous footnote 11, the social-science footnote to the Supreme Court's school desegregation opinion in 1954.[4] But the concern of this chapter is the use of sociology in American race relations since 1954. What is the promise of sociological theory in this area? What uses have been made of sociology and sociologists so far in the process? Why has the potential of sociology been barely tapped?

What Is the Promise of Sociological Theory?

From the perspective of the sociologist, the problem of segregation can be stated as follows: a set of physical characteristics, principally color of the skin, and a degree of ancestry with similar characteristics are used to make socially meaningful and invidious distinctions.[5] The sociologist as scientist investigates under what conditions these characteristics become salient, how the distinctions are maintained in socially patterned responses, and when these distinctions become socially relevant or irrelevant. Once structured in this fashion, problems of race and desegregation can be usefully approached from four different realms of contemporary theory: theories dealing with

(1) the self, self-presentation, and symbolic interaction; (2) balance and equilibration; (3) stratification and structural-functional systems; and (4) social change.

The use of race as a measure of social distinction involves the inference of moral and social worth based on physical characteristics. The social import of bodily characteristics thus has consequences for both the definition and the limitation of the self as perceived by the victim of discrimination and for perceptions between the victim and those with whom he interacts. Both of these consequences are dealt with in philosophy and social psychology. The philosophical question "Who am I?" goes back traditionally to Descartes. The definition of the self as a psychological problem goes back to William James' classical chapter on the self in *Principles of Psychology*. Likewise, the conditions of social and person perception have been traditional topics of psychology from the early theories of the recognition of emotions to the current theory of Fritz Heider and social experimentation on this topic. This work provides the raw material that sociologists must consider in determining the social patterns of interpersonal interaction. Cooley and Mead initiated such theorizing in sociology, leading today to Erving Goffman's treatment of behavior in social situations.

Goffman's notion of stigma appears particularly relevant.[6] He defines "stigma" as a physical characteristic from which moral and social worth can be derived. Prime examples of stigmas include physical deformities and deficiencies, such as illnesses, sensory or motor defects, and injuries. Some conspicuous social characteristics, such as race, sex, and age, can also become stigmas, if perceptions of them lead to socially invidious differentiations.[7] One practical outcome of this thinking is a new perspective on the definitions of racial integration and desegregation. Integration, in these terms, is achieved when the physical characteristics accompanying race are no longer a definition of the self. Desegregation, by comparison, occurs when society fully recognizes the stigma, but no longer assigns disabilities to those possessing the stigma. From this vantage point it becomes clear that desegregation can be accomplished by law as well as other social action, while integration requires additional processes.

Extending these leads from the theory of the self, sociology could make significant contributions to the racial scene by concentrating empirical attention on the subtleties of interactions between blacks and whites. Up to this point little field data exist on this vital topic beyond the general descriptions of "racial etiquette" which are rapidly becoming outmoded. Interracial situations, such as children's summer camps, have been studied, but this work has had more success in measuring such gross aspects as preferences and the amount of interaction than in teasing out the more intricate aspects of conduct.[8] In other words, research so far has concentrated on the study of desegregation rather than integration. More pertinent approaches to the problem come from work on the bias introduced by the use of Negro and white interviewers in survey situations and from rigorous laboratory experimentation.[9]

A second approach concerns the manner in which one's stigmatized characteristic is combined with other types of characteristics. Two general tendencies stand out. On the one hand, people try to obtain the highest possible "status score" through a summing up of characteristics; on the other hand, they evince a certain strain for consistency by minimizing the variability of their various characteristics. Both of these tendencies operate simultaneously and explain many of the strains and directions of the desegregation process.

The desire to define one's own status at as high a level as possible naturally causes the individual to select among his characteristics, rather than to add them all up. Thus, in maximizing his status, he has two choices. Either he can rely on the highest status he has accorded to any characteristic, or he can choose the highest ranked group to which he belongs. Reference-group theory has been developed to explain the consequences of choosing a particular group as a referent anchor, but little has been done to explain the choice of the specific reference group itself.

Some of the initial reference-group research highlights the practical importance of this body of theory for race relations in the United States. In their classic World War II studies of *The American Soldier,* Samuel Stouffer and his associates compared the morale of Negro troops stationed in the South with that of Negro troops stationed in the North.[10] Surprisingly, they found morale roughly the same in the two regions, despite the South's severe restrictions on the Negro soldier's off-base activities. The key to understanding this result is provided by reference-group theory and its companion concept of relative deprivation. Racial characteristics provided the reference group for the Negro in the Southern camp, for, as Stouffer wrote, "the psychological values of Army life to the Negro soldier in the South *relative to the southern Negro civilian* greatly exceeded the psychological values of Army life to the Negro soldier in the North *relative to the northern Negro civilian.*" [11] This is an instance where a reference group is chosen in which the individual has relatively high status, but the group itself has low status. Had the Negro soldiers chosen other soldiers as the relevant reference group, they would have felt considerably more deprived in the South. During World War II, however, racial characteristics continued to provide the strongest reference group.

The choice of the highest-status reference group leads to a different constellation. If the ascribed racial characteristics become less important to his self-image, a black of high achieved status should feel sharply deprived because of the discrimination the racial stigma continues to elicit. Such a person would make an effort to gain equality with people of the same educational and occupational levels—people to whom he now refers himself. Thus, the relaxation of racial barriers and improvement of the minority group in other statuses are precisely the conditions which should lead to greater relative deprivation and a more forceful push for equal rights. It should not be surprising, then, according to sociological theory, that a moderate amount of desegregation does not satisfy the minority group, but only whets its appetite for more rapid and sweeping social change.

While reference-group behavior reflects consistency in the relation of the individual to his surrounding world, a similar striving for consistency occurs within the individual.[12] The concept of status consistency is the internal equivalent of reference-group behavior; and many of the theoretical and empirical uses of this concept parallel the perspectives on race relations gleaned from reference-group theory. Resolution of the stress generated by status inconsistency can result in neurotic symptoms or attempts to alter the environment.[13] Elton Jackson has shown that the type of resolution depends on the type of status inconsistency.[14] Those individuals of high ascribed status but low achieved status, such as white "Old Americans" with only a grammar-school education, seem especially disposed to psychoneurotic symptoms; those of low ascribed status but high achieved status, such as college-educated Negro Americans, seem especially willing to change the social system.

At the practical level, these considerations provide insight into the nationwide black protest for change in the 1960s.[15] The actual gains of Negroes—in business, education, employment, health, housing, income, and voting —have been occurring faster since 1940 than during any other period of Negro American history. Yet these gains are relative to previous conditions of the Negro. When contrasted with the typical conditions of white Americans today, the position of Negro Americans assumes a desperately deprived character. The advances of past years have raised but not kept pace with the aspirations and expectations of Negroes; the result is keen relative deprivation and a ringing demand for "all, here, now!" Furthermore, in Jackson's terms, the advances have led to higher achieved status for many Negroes, producing the inconsistent status pattern—low ascribed status, high achieved status—which often is accompanied by a willingness for change. Indeed, it was the best-educated Negro generation in the South's history that ignited the protest in 1960 with the sit-in demonstrations against racial discrimination at lunch counters.[16] We shall return to these considerations in Chapter 7 when we discuss in detail why black unrest reached major proportions in the 1960s.

The desire for consistency in status and belief is only one force operating in society. Sociological theory has always recognized a second principle: structural and functional differentiation. Durkheim was one of the earliest theorists to categorize social organization according to whether it was dependent on balance or distinction, contrasting mechanical and organic solidarity.[17] Through this route, sociologists learned to distinguish certain characteristics of the social system, one of which is similarity and the other differentiation. In more recent theoretical work derived from balance theories, James Davis has shown the dividing point at which the principle of differentiation begins to operate.[18]

Social-system theory, and the principle of differentiation in particular, is invaluable in identifying and understanding the social supports and resistances in the desegregation process. Desegregation occurs not only because of the individual needs identified in balance theories but in accordance with the strains and instabilities which can be delineated in the social system.

The "Black Belt" areas of the Deep South offer a case in point. These rural, traditional counties with relatively high percentages of Negroes in their populations form the hard core of segregationist resistance from the Eastern shore of Maryland to East Texas. The question thus becomes: Why do these areas provide such stubborn barriers to racial change? The standard answers, of course, are true enough as far as they go. These are the areas where the deepest Negrophobia is harbored,[19] where the historical events of the past three centuries have left an imbedded legacy of white supremacy.[20] But there are, in addition, fundamental answers based on social-system theory. The Black Belt is far less structurally differentiated than the rest of the South.[21] For example, there is considerably less differentiation between the "public" and "private" sectors of life. Hence, distinctions are not clearly drawn between, say, a lunch counter in a variety store and the dining-room table, or between the school as a public educational center and the school as a community social center. This lack of differentiation is also manifest in the ambivalence often shown toward public education in many Black Belt areas. Apart from racial considerations, schools can be seen as an unwelcome intrusion upon home instruction, as vehicles for implanting new and potentially dangerous ideas in both Negro and white youth; in short, as a threat to what is euphemistically called in these areas "the Southern way of life." This factor is responsible in part for the readiness of many "dead-end" segregationists to abandon public education altogether, rather than to allow biracial public instruction. Indeed, one Black Belt county involved in the original 1954 Supreme Court ruling, Prince Edward County in Virginia, actually did close down all its public schools.

Here, too, Parsons' pattern variables can be usefully applied.[22] The Black Belt is still basically characterized by ascriptive, diffuse, particularistic, and affective orientations, though Morton Rubin has shown that change in these realms is under way.[23] In sharp contrast, racial desegregation and the absence of racial discrimination thrive in situations marked by precisely the opposite orientations: achievement, functionally specific, universalistic, and affectively neutral orientations. Thus, the interracial harmony of such groups as athletic teams and industrial unions—groups largely dominated by achievement and by specific, universalistic, and affectively neutral orientations—tends to be dramatically superior to that of such counterpart groups as fraternities and craft unions—groups marked by orientations more approaching those of the Black Belt.[24]

The barriers to racial change erected by the Black Belt, then, go beyond such distinctly racial phenomena as anti-Negro attitudes and a history of plantation slavery. Social-system theory provides the insight that these barriers are also rooted in a less differentiated structure—a structure typified by orientations which run directly counter to those which most facilitate the desegregation process.

Analyzing the alteration of social systems over time, sociologists have long sought a theory of social change. Here it is the scope of the theory that presents problems. It is often difficult to determine whether any particular change is an extremely long-term turn of history, a brief fluctuation, part of a determined evolutionary trend, or some other manifestation of a radical change.

The desegregation movement can be analyzed within several frameworks. Evolutionary, equilibrium-strain, conflict, and social-movement models all offer useful perspectives. Thus, desegregation can be envisaged as a small part of a sweeping evolutionary process which is presently overturning national cultures and civilizations,[25] or as an equilibrium reaction of American society to a long-term, festering strain,[26] or as the reaction to a rapidly escalating conflict between truly divergent interest groups,[27] or as the outcome of efforts by a series of loosely linked social movements.

Once again, these various theories are not mutually exclusive and often converge. This point is questioned, however, by a number of observers of the racial scene of the 1960s. Once the push for desegregation spread from the confines of the legislative and judicial halls to the streets, the usefulness of the Simmel-Coser contentions about conflict became more readily apparent.[28] And some writers assume that these contentions are not only exclusively preferable but directly counter to theories, such as that of equilibrium-strain, which concentrate primarily on consensus and societal stability.[29] Louis Coser cogently answers such reasoning:

> Peace and feuding, conflict and order, are correlative. Both the cementing and the breaking of the cake of custom constitute part of the dialectic of social life. One is hence ill-advised to distinguish sharply a sociology of order from a sociology of conflict, or a harmony model of society from a conflict model. Such attempts can only result in artificial distinctions. The analysis of social conflicts brings to awareness aspects of social reality that may be obscured if analytical attention focuses too exclusively on phenomena of social order; but an exclusive attention to conflict phenomena may obscure the central importance of social order and needs to be corrected by a correlative concern with the ordered aspects of social life. We deal here not with distinct realities but only with differing aspects of the same reality, so that exclusive emphasis on one or the other is likely to lead the analyst astray. Perhaps we need return now to Charles Horton Cooley's statement: "The more one thinks of it the more he will see that conflict and co-operation are not separable things, but phases of one process which always involves something of both." [30]

The theory of the development of social movements is also part of the explanation of social change. This theory, of course, is especially valuable in analyzing some of the groups which have become organized and active in instituting or resisting racial change. Studies of the black Muslims and the Ku Klux Klan have been done within this framework; [31] but studies of other and more influential movements need to be undertaken as well—movements such as the Congress on Racial Equality (CORE), the National Association for the Advancement of Colored People (NAACP), the White Citizens' Councils (WCC), and the Black Panthers. At this point, the direct links between the historical change of the large-scale system and the values and motivations of the individuals within movements for change become obvious. The circle closes; considerations of social movements highlight the necessity and importance of all four types of theory discussed.

It is encouraging that in all four realms sufficient theories have developed for studying this process and that segregation, desegregation, and integration are areas which require the combined use of these theories. It is a further sign of the maturity of the science of sociology that none of these theories has become an exclusive explanation. The promise of sociological theory for understanding racism and change, then, is a rich one, offering an attack which utilizes a variety of developed theoretical approaches.

How May Sociology Be Used in the Desegregation Process?

If the promise of sociological theory is great, one can properly ask what use has been made of these ideas in the desegregation process to date. Disuse of sociology is more immediately apparent than use of it, but sociology and sociologists have contributed to this salient issue in a number of ways and capacities. Three interrelated uses will be sampled here: sociologists as (1) predictors of trends, (2) interpreters of specific events, and (3) consultants on desegregation.

One of the potentials of sociology is the ability to make "educated" predictions of future and significant trends in race relations in the United States. This potential can be illustrated by the broad qualitative predictions concerning desegregation made before the Supreme Court's 1954 decision and by the more specific quantitative predictions regarding the county-by-county pattern of formal school desegregation within Southern states.

A. L. Coleman has examined the predictions about desegregation made by social scientists and published between 1950 and 1955.[32] His first finding was simply that few people had been willing to stick their necks out in this fashion in print. Finally, he located relevant predictions in ten articles and books by eight social scientists: Kenneth B. Clark, Guy Johnson, Charles S. Johnson, Herman Long,

George Mitchell, Alwin W. Rose, Margaret Ryan, and Robin Williams. Most of these forecasts were shrewd projections from data collected on desegregation in border states that took place before the Court's major ruling. How well did they do? One can judge by comparing events of the process to date with the following composite version of their predictions, each point of which was generally advanced by a number, though not all, of the venturesome prognosticators:

Desegregation will occur. There will be a gradual and uneven acceptance of it both between and within communities; and it will come first in the Appalachians and the Upper South, last in the plantation and Black Belt areas. Acceptance and adjustment will be correlated inversely with the percentage of Negroes in the population and with the degree of prejudice in the area—but only loosely so, since other factors, especially firm leadership, will often be more crucial. For the most part, no mass mingling of the races in the public schools will result during the first few years. Violence and extreme tension will sometimes occur, but they will not inevitably or usually accompany desegregation. There will be, however, considerable evasion, litigation, confusion, and turmoil. A wide range of plans, solutions, and adjustments will be forthcoming. Where the authorities adopt a definite policy of desegregation, implement it without delay, and stand firm on the policy, there will be little trouble. Gradual plans will not necessarily be more effective than "immediate" change and may, in some instances, allow greater resistance to develop. Moreover, desegregation in one institution or area of life will not necessarily facilitate desegregation in other institutions or areas of life in the same community. But once desegregation does take place in a given school, official norms of equal treatment will soon develop. Nevertheless, equal status contacts between whites and Negroes will often remain rare, especially in social functions. Negroes will participate strongly in school activities where competence is determining (i.e., where universalistic standards apply, as in athletics).[33]

It appears that these early predictions have proved amazingly accurate and could have been helpful if policy makers had given them more careful consideration.

Also possible are more detailed predictions as to the precise pattern in which desegregation unfolds. As previously noted, the desegregation process has been any-thing but random. When one reviews its history since 1954, clear ecological patterns emerge both between and within subregions and states. In fact, the same ecological pat-terns have emerged previously in research on a wide variety of social phenomena in the South, ranging from the readiness to secede from the Union in 1860–1861 through lynching to current political behavior.[34] Generally speak-ing, desegregation has come first to the border and middle South, to the cities, to areas with relatively small percent-ages of blacks, and to localities less steeped in tradition.

One ecological investigation set out to develop predic-tions for patterns of racial change within states.[35] To forecast the county-by-county initiation of at least token school desegregation, three key census variables were employed: the percentages of urban dwellers, nonwhites, and white women in the labor force.[36] The prognostica-tions derived from these data for border states can be ap-plied to three Southern states—Florida, North Carolina, and Tennessee—since by 1963 these had sufficient educa-tional desegregation to provide an adequate test.[37] As re-vealed in Table 1, significant relationships exist between the three-variable predictions and the unfolding patterns of racial change in the educational systems of these three states. Particularly is this the case with Florida; while al-most three out of four of the counties designated as the easiest to desegregate had biracial schools by 1963, none of those designated as most resistant had such schools. In other words, the earlier ecological pattern of educational desegregation noted in the border South continued to hold true for states farther South.

Such county-by-county predictions, once they achieve greater precision, would have considerable practical value. Consider, for example, the administration of the Civil Rights Acts of 1964 and 1965. Not all provisions of these Acts can be enforced simultaneously throughout the South; some selection of target areas is necessary. Rea-sonably accurate predictions as to the degree of segregationist resistance and integrationist insistence likely to be encountered in various areas would allow the planning of particular strategies, such as moving first in "compliant" areas so as to register early success, or tackling "resistant" areas first so as to demonstrate uncompromising intent, or employing some mixed strategy which combines these alternatives.

Often sociologists can contribute to the understanding of the desegregation process by providing a "sociological perspective" in the interpretation of current situations. One outstanding example of this involves the white response to racial change in the 1960s which the mass media incorrectly labeled "backlash." A range of sociological and social-psychological considerations suggests that a more accurate description for the response is "polarization," that is, an activation and hardening of already existing racial attitudes both pro and con. A full discussion of this phenomenon will be given in Chapter 8, which discusses trends in anti-Negro and anti-Jewish attitudes since World War II.

At the most practical level, sociologists can make their contributions as consultants. One member of the profession, for example, advised a public school board of a medium-sized city in the middle South for two years before it initiated the desegregation of schools. The board was quite anxious to avoid the strife and bad publicity engendered by desegregation efforts in Little Rock, Charlotte, and New Orleans. The adviser pointed out that these cities had compounded social-class and racial conflicts. All three had limited their initial steps to one or two lower-status schools; thus, later disturbances were motivated not only by racial antipathy but also by a feeling that upper-status white leaders were selectively ignoring the interests of the less prosperous segments of the white community. The consultant urged his clients not to make the same mistake, but to begin the process in a large number of public schools which covered the social-class spectrum. His advice was followed and may have contributed to the calm acceptance of the event by the community.

Table 1 PREDICTED AND ACTUAL SCHOOL DESEGREGATION *

State	All Counties	Predicted Order of Desegregation First Third	Middle Third	Last Third	Kendall rank-order correlations between predicted and actual desegregation Tau's	p
		Percentages of desegregated counties by fall of 1963				
Florida	28.4	72.7	13.0	0.0	+.50	<.001
	(19/67)	(16/22)	(3/23)	(0/22)		
North Carolina	30.0	48.5	29.4	12.1	+.24	<.01
	(30/100)	(16/33)	(10/34)	(4/33)		
Tennessee	34.9	46.4	33.3	25.0	+.18	<.01
	(29/83)	(13/28)	(9/27)	(7/28)		

* Prediction formulas were originally presented in T. F. Pettigrew and M. R. Cramer, "The Demography of Desegregation," *Journal of Social Issues*, 1959, Vol. 15, pp. 61–71. This table originally appeared in T. F. Pettigrew, "Continuing Barriers to Desegregated Education in the South," *Sociology of Education*, 1965, Vol. 38, pp. 99–111.

Another consultation in a large Southwestern city involved a social psychologist who helped to set up an elaborate mass-media campaign appealing for "law and order." The campaign was apparently successful. In a city renowned for its violence, desegregation of public schools began without incident. Consultations have also occurred in a number of key northern cities. In Chicago, a number of sociologists, including Robert Havighurst and Philip Hauser, have played highly publicized consulting roles on problems related to *de facto* school segregation in that city. Dan Dodson has often served in a similar way for communities throughout the New York metropolitan area.

Applied surveys in key situations have proved to be an additional tool of value in sociological consulting on the desegregation process. Thus, J. K. Morland has on three occasions demonstrated the merit of such surveys for interested organizations. In 1955 he studied a student strike over desegregation in White Sulphur Springs, West Virginia, for the National Association for the Advancement of Colored People; in 1960 he studied the lunch-counter sit-in protests in Corpus Christi, Galveston, and San Antonio, Texas, for the Southern Regional Council; and in 1962 he surveyed the needs of Southern educators for professional consultation on desegregation for the Potomac Institute.[38] In this third survey, incidentally, Morland discovered a surprising desire for and willingness to use professional help.

Kenneth Lenihan, at Columbia University's Bureau of Applied Social Research, is attempting to demonstrate the utility of survey data in reducing pluralistic ignorance.[39] Confirming previous research, he found that approximately two-thirds of his sample of white homeowners in suburban "Blissville" are not opposed to a Negro family living on the same street. Yet only one in five is willing to sell his home to a Negro, largely because he incorrectly perceives most of his neighbors to be against residential desegregation. Though only a third of the town actually oppose interracial living, 56 percent believe a majority opposes it, with 20 percent even thinking that 80 to 100 percent oppose it.

Lenihan has discussed his findings with the mayor and town council of Blissville and publicized the results in the community. Follow-up surveys will test to see if pluralistic ignorance can in fact be reduced in this manner.

On other occasions, sociologists have voiced their opinions more directly. Some have served as expert witnesses in court cases dealing with desegregation and as consultants in the preparation of legal briefs concerning desegregation.[40] And two sociologists who specialize in race relations even registered their expert views on *de facto* segregation as elected public officials: the late Arnold Rose, of the University of Minnesota, was a state legislator; and Mel Ravitz, of Wayne State University, is a Detroit city councilman.[41]

These examples, unfortunately, are exceptions, not the rule. Sociologists have not often been called upon in consulting capacities. Lewis Killian remarks, "Sociologists in the South have rarely had the opportunity to set foot inside state capitols—unless they were under investigation!" [42]

Why Has the Potential of Sociology Not Been Fulfilled?

There are, then, many potential uses of sociology in the desegregation process which have been concretely demonstrated: predicting trends, interpreting current situations, and consulting. The question thus becomes: Why has this potential not been fully utilized? Three classes of interrelated factors can be advanced as a tentative answer: (1) the timidity of private foundations and governmental agencies about providing the funds for work in this "controversial" area; (2) an atmosphere of resistance to racial change by stern segregationists that acts to constrain both social-science research and its applications; and, finally, (3) a sociological bias in race relations toward studying the static and segregation-maintaining elements, rather than the dynamic and desegregation-impelling features. Each of these explanations warrants further discussion.

1 The major private foundations and governmental research agencies have been extremely reluctant to support social research on the desegregation process.[43] Despite the obvious practical need for such work, the "controversial" nature of the subject makes it far easier to fund such "safe" areas as business education, the arts, and health research. Stuart Cook, in a 1957 paper on desegregation, first noted this timidity in print,[44] and only by the mid-1960s did this financial constraint begin to ease somewhat.

The effects of this situation on social research have been marked. Large-scale interdisciplinary studies, employing longitudinal designs in a variety of carefully chosen communities, were clearly indicated. Only an empirical attack of such magnitude could have captured the emerging pattern of highly diverse accommodations to the racial change ordered by the Supreme Court in 1954. Compare the potential value of such a broad research effort with the limited case studies that have been possible so far.[45] Low-budget reports on only one community are the rule: many of them are theses or seminar projects; some remain on the descriptive level; all but a few sample only one time period; and there is almost no comparability of instruments and approach. Ironically, the first nationwide survey sampling of opinions of black Americans, long sought by specialists in race relations, was finally executed in the summer of 1963 by a commercial concern financed by *Newsweek* magazine.[46] From the point of view of the lost opportunity to study intensively the beginnings of a unique process of social change, then, the results of funding timidity have been little short of tragic.

The reasons for this timidity are varied. One factor, as noted by Cook, is segregationist Southern congressmen. Some of these national legislators have angrily threatened to withdraw the valued tax-free status from private foundations and have menacingly reviewed governmental financing of social research. Another factor is organized boycotts carried out by some segregationists against products identified with the foundations. Some of these boycotts were quite effective in the 1950s and apparently influenced the strategy of such foundations.

A third factor is more subtle. No simple mechanical device or single research breakthrough is likely to provide simple solutions for the peculiarly complex problems of desegregation. In a topic similarly laden with controversy and conflict, birth control, it has proved possible to appropriate large amounts for the study of the purely technical aspects of reproduction and the development of pills which may aid in easing the population problem. No comparable hope for a pill or similar gadget has ever been suggested for desegregation, and so funding agencies are less able to avoid the emotionally charged aspects of the issue by focusing on such purely technical aspects.

A final factor is as much a product as a cause of the financial drought. Many competent sociologists, who until 1954 had specialized in race relations, chose to enter other areas when their proposals were routinely refused support. In time, this has meant an ever-decreasing number of researchers and proposals seeking money for work on desegregation. In other words, the expectation of funding rejection became self-fulfilling. The foundations and governmental agencies which have altered their policies now complain that they do not receive an adequate number of applications for competent social research on desegregation. Hopefully, as information about the policy changes of these funding agencies becomes more widely circulated, this situation will improve.

2 By no means can the disuse of sociology be charged entirely to financial restrictions. The constraining atmosphere created by segregationist resistance has directly influenced sociologists, as it has foundations and governmental agencies. While it is difficult to assess the limita-

tions imposed by such an atmosphere, it is reasonable to infer that the number of direct refusals by institutions to allow such research has actually been small, even in the South. More likely, the greatest deterrent has been created indirectly by the stifling climate which discourages sociologists from actually testing the limits of research opportunities. Interested as researchers may be in the racial realm, they often decide to work in a less controversial area. Or, if they persist in studying race relations, the perceived pressures severely narrow the range of specific problems they will tackle. Sociologists are, after all, only human, part of the society that they study. They are influenced by the same kind of social phenomena with which they deal. The possible detachment which training and investigation give may enable a researcher to identify these pressures and their effects, but he is still subject to them—just as a physician, though he may better understand disease, still remains subject like other mortals to illness.

Aspects of this phenomenon of constraint can be conveniently discussed under three categories: values in social research; the nonstructural bias; and the nonactivist bias.

Values in social research. Value issues are at least implicit in all realms of sociology; the field shares this feature with all other sciences, physical as well as social. Some of the implications of this fact are discussed elsewhere in this book. Yet this topic deserves special attention here because the value implications of any sociological work on desegregation are especially salient and, in some respects, unique, because of the type of climate in which the work is performed.

There exists within the ranks of social science a real conflict around the role of values in social research. On one side of the issue, Nevitt Sanford argues that the role of social reformer should be a major one for the social scientist; [47] Redfield maintains that value deductions are actually drawn by social scientists from their science itself; [48] and Gouldner, in his now famous 1961 presidential address to the Society for the Study of Social Problems, dismissed the concept of a value-free sociology as a myth.[49]

On the other side, many agree with Conrad Arensberg that social scientists have no other end or purpose as scientists than devotion to science per se.[50] Bierstedt, for instance, believes that normative judgments lie entirely outside the realm of science; in the long run, he believes, a sociologist contributes maximally to society through the development of sound knowledge about society.[51] The implications here, of course, are that a sound knowledge about society cannot be developed as long as values intrude and that *true* science must be value-free. Both of these implications can be challenged. It can be argued that only through the explicit recognition and use of the researcher's values can society be adequately understood. Moreover, nonsocial sciences do not appear deterred from holding forthright values. Thus, biologists have distinct values about the pathogenic organisms they study, and few of them are neutral about cancer or polio; physicists have definite values about the physical matter they study, and few of them are neutral about atomic and hydrogen bombs. Yet these biologists and physicists are not limited in the scope of their research, nor are they poorer scientists for having values. For social scientists to insist that this does not hold for them seems strange; it almost appears as if social scientists have given up the model of rational man for everybody but themselves.

In any event, the question of the relationship between values and science is a social problem in its own right. And it is of immediate importance that the debate on this issue offers a ready-made rationalization to the social scientist who wants to avoid a controversial topic. Much as Little Rock's white liberal clergy avoided the fight by maintaining that controversy was unchristian,[52] social scientists can convince themselves that desegregation is simply too fraught with conflict and emotion to allow the type of dispassionate study which "true" science demands. The danger of such a position is obvious. It would lead to the renunciation by sociology of research into all conflict situations in society when the societal lines of fracture are most clearly exposed—the very type of situations that Samuel Stouffer argued would yield the most valuable insights.[53]

Two Southern sociologists, Lewis Killian, formerly at Florida State University, and Kenneth Morland at Randolph-Macon Women's College in Lynchburg, Virginia, have candidly discussed the difficulties raised by their work on desegregation. Killian aided the Attorney-General of Florida in drafting a desegregation brief for the United States Supreme Court.[54] His research report dealt with opinions throughout the state as to the pace and manner in which the 1954 school desegregation ruling should be implemented. He faced two problems: one involved publicity, the other values. Killian found himself in the hot glare of constant attention from the mass media and noted how such attention affected his political client, his respondents, and himself. The social scientist in such a role, he concludes, "is perforce a public-relations man." The second issue of values presented an even thornier problem. Killian's client had previously argued for segregation before the United States Supreme Court and was preparing to argue for gradualism rather than immediate desegregation. Indeed, Killian's survey found that gradualism was in fact the much preferred alternative of most of the influential respondents questioned. On this matter of values Killian writes:

There is little doubt that, in terms of his occupational ethos, the sociologist is expected to take a position in opposition to "gradualism" if that means simply delay or evasion. Even if he adopts a "gradualist" position, he still risks the charge of suffering from the conservative bias of the southern culture. On the other hand, even gradualism is considered radical by many southern politicians.[55]

In spite of these difficulties, Killian believes that sociologists should assume such a role when offered the opportunity. Government officials do not necessarily exploit social science, he argues, since their best interests frequently coincide with granting the social scientist as much independence as possible. More important, such a role gives the social scientist a chance to bring his theory and findings to bear directly on policy decisions. In the South, such a position may help shift the image of the sociologist from an "agitator" to an "expert." "He can never be sure that [his] theories will be accepted or how they will be used," Killian says, "but he does gain an audience."

Morland has personally participated in desegregation organizations, conducted brief applied surveys and consulted for such organizations, and carried on extensive research on racial acceptance and preference among nursery school children. In a paper given at the 1962 meetings of the American Sociological Association, he presented his rationale for playing these three roles of partisan, practitioner, and researcher:

Whatever else he might do, it is the job of the sociologist to seek to increase the amount of valid and reliable knowledge about human groups. . . . The values held by the particular sociologist may lead him to engage in applied sociology or to reject opportunities to do so. Whatever his choice, however, it can be assumed to be based on non-scientific predilections, just as his decision to enter the field of sociology in the first place. In his role as consultant, the sociologist is required to help solve immediate and practical problems in line with the goals of the organization for which he is working. However, it is assumed that in so far as he acts as a sociological consultant, he suggests the means to particular ends, and cannot on a scientific basis propose the ends themselves. Of course, in choosing to act as a consultant for an organization, the sociologist can indirectly choose the ends for which he wishes to work. Fundamental in the author's assumptions about roles is that the sociological task of the development of systematic knowledge neither demands nor forbids that the sociologist apply his discipline to the area of practical problems. Furthermore, the roles of basic research and practical application have nothing directly to do with the sociologist's choice to take part in partisan activities. The decision to take an active citizen role in race relations, or to refrain from doing so, is a non-rational, non-scientific, moral choice. With these assumptions as a basis of clarification, the author has found it possible to continue three lines of activity in a controversial area with the realization that there are separate and distinct role requirements in each activity.[56]

As might anyone engaged in multiple roles, Morland has encountered role conflicts. Because of his partisan activities as a citizen, the public school system in his community refused him research access to its kindergarten and elementary classes. As a practitioner, he faces pressures for quick results and oversimplified interpretations. As a partisan, he must resist the assumption of the group that the entire discipline of sociology is somehow in league with it because one sociologist is involved. And naturally the three roles make conflicting demands on his time and energy.

But Morland emphasizes that there are important compatibilities as well as conflicts among the three roles. He has found that consulting and applied surveys often offer excellent opportunities for the pragmatic testing of theory and measurement techniques. And his partisan activities have provided insights for sociological research; though emotionally involved, he has nevertheless gained from these activities new notions concerning desegregation leadership and segregationist opposition. Furthermore, his participation as a partisan has opened some doors, especially among the desegregationists, that might otherwise have remained closed. Morland concludes:

A warning of sociologists like Alfred McClung Lee and Alvin W. Gouldner is applicable here, namely that sociologists should guard against rigidity and professionalization. New insights are constantly required to further the discipline, and they can come from many directions. Engaging in the application of sociology and in citizen activities can loosen rigidity and provide stimulation—as long as the role requirement of each activity is kept clearly in mind, and if it is remembered that effectiveness in applied sociology and in citizen activity are dependent upon the development of sound theory of human groups.[57]

The nonstructural bias. An intensification of the problem of values in social research is by no means the only result of the constraining climate of the first generation of desegregation. This climate is also at least partly responsible for the recent failure of sociology to explore the structural and power bases underlying segregation and racial discrimination. Although the sociological works of previous years, from Dollard's *Caste and Class in a Southern Town* to Myrdal's *An American Dilemma,* brilliantly detailed these bases, the relationships between them and current racial change have been largely neglected.

A far more fashionable emphasis of recent years has been on attitude studies, particularly the attitudes of rank-and-file white segregationists. Interesting papers have also appeared on the Ku Klux Klan and other resistance groups.[58] But little work has focused on the sources of conservative power, such as the white Southern "moderates," despite the fact that such racial crises as Little Rock and Birmingham offer clear indications of the vast importance of the resistance from entrenched upper-status whites. A few examples suffice to make the point: many of the members of the mob in the school riot at Little Rock were wage earners granted the day off in advance by two major employers in the area; school desegregation was delayed in Little Rock until an all-new, strategically located pubic high school could be completed to accommodate upper-class and upper-middle-class children in all-white classrooms; and the head of the major industry in the Birmingham area openly supported resistance by extreme segregationists in the city and state.

The sociological research which has been directed toward such structural and power aspects of the desegregation process further points up their importance. The Tauebers, as noted earlier, have shown that residential segregation by race in the nation's standard metropolitan areas, certainly one of the most critical structural bulwarks against racial change, actually substantially increased between 1940 and 1950. Moreover, residential segregation continued to increase in the South, while only slightly moderating in the North, between 1950 and 1960.[59] And Richard Cramer has demonstrated that the relationship between attracting new industry and attitudes toward racial change among Southern business leaders is far more complex and intricate than was formerly supposed.[60]

Failure to exploit fully these peculiarly sociological insights concerning structure and power seems akin to the phenomenon documented by Paul Lazarsfeld and Wagner Thielens in *The Academic Mind*.[61] They studied the effects on 2,451 social scientists of the "difficult years" from 1946 to 1955, a period characterized in the nation at large by an intense interest in internal security and a concomitant concern with the political opinions and associations of college teachers. The chief effects were not gross. Those "permissive" social scientists who were most politically concerned maintained most of their previous associations and continued to subscribe to liberal journals. The actual changes wrought by academic apprehension were more subtle: some academicians toned down their writings; some were more careful in recommending reference material to their students lest it be criticized later as too controversial; others avoided researching potentially controversial problems. Much the same phenomena may well have operated in research on race relations during the particularly "difficult years" of 1954 to 1965.

Gross changes have probably been rare. But more subtle changes have occurred, such as the avoidance of research on the influential sources of power which most effectively resist racial change and the failure to explore the basic structural changes that must take place in American society before the full inclusion of Negro Americans into the societal mainstream is possible. This is not to imply that the scientist consciously makes this choice of topics in order to avoid alienating important interests. But it is to suggest that with limited time at his disposal the scientist will often select topics which seem most fruitful at the moment and can readily be performed in a restraining climate.

The nonactivist bias. The focus of research on low-status white segregationists has led not only to neglect of high-status white segregationists but also to neglect of desegregationist whites and Negroes. Values may intrude here, for, paradoxically, the sparse attention paid to desegregationists may partly reflect the sympathy which social scientists in general feel for desegregation. Such sympathy can lead to the investigation of immediate problems and obstacles, especially those raised by "the other side." Thus, the investigator can freely dissect the white supremacist, expose racist beliefs, and stress the changes necessary to counteract such resistance without feeling embarrassed. The situation becomes far more difficult if the weaknesses to be exposed are those of the side favored by the scientist. For example, conservative tendencies and open resistance to desegregation within the black community present a less inviting topic of research. Indeed, the scientist may feel that exposure of these conditions is itself a socially causative factor and may harm the desegregation effort.

Another result of directing so much attention toward lower-status segregationists, at least during the 1950s, has been the devaluation of desegregation activism. The apparent implicit assumption has been that social change would somehow come by itself if only the opposition of the racist extremists could be silenced. Frequently, of course, the social scientist is himself a member of the nonactive white group. In studying the motives and limitations of silent whites, the social scientist would be forced to perform a difficult feat of self-analysis. It is more conducive to one's self-esteem to study people who are different from oneself, such as racist extremists, and to emphasize the great power of the group attempting to uphold the status quo. This partial view of the picture makes it unnecessary to analyze one's own motivations. Further, unquestioned acceptance of a particular social structure has the dual function of indicating that any direct action is useless and of focusing on a static description of a monolithic system. Again one is reminded of the rationalizations made by the white clergymen of Little Rock for their inactivity during racial crisis; many of the ministers emphasized that there was nothing they could do to counter the extremists and that none of the racist demonstrators were members of their congregations, thus avoiding the necessity of actively supporting the desegregation forces.[62]

A 1964 sociological monograph on desegregation illustrates this potential of the nonactivist bias for rationalizing.[63] White activists for desegregation in the South are portrayed as doomed to certain martydom; it is argued that white liberals who play the "waiting role" are often far more effective. "They also serve," goes the rationalization, "who only stand and teach!" [64] But, the desegregationist might inquire, teach what? The "waiting role"?

These effects of the constraining atmosphere of the years after 1954—intensification of the issue of values in social research, the nonstructural bias, and the nonactivist bias—blend into the third and final reason for the relative disuse of sociology in the desegregation process.

3 Many of the limitations of the sociological analysis of American race relations cannot be attributed entirely to timidity of foundations or pressure from resisting groups.[65] Some limitations have been apparent in the sociological literature itself throughout this century. And the failure of sociology to foresee the present black protest—its form, its growth, and its future direction—is partly a function of the narrowness of its own approach.

Table 2 provides the relevant data, with a content breakdown of the 255 papers on intergroup relations published from 1900 through 1958 in twenty of the most relevant sociological journals. Three classifications are made. The first distinction is between the personal and social systems. The second distinction divides the purely structural-static approach from the active approach which accepts far-reaching changes in the system. From the point of view of the individual, this division separates attitudes from action; from the viewpoint of the social system, this division separates the static from considerations of social change. Finally, a third distinction is drawn according to the focus of the object. Does the paper deal principally with processes which favor integration, those which favor segregation, or both?

A glance at Table 2 reveals that there is some susceptibility to the diverse problems and temper of each decade; yet there is also a general and pronounced trend toward static description and concern with segregation. Seventy-one percent (180 of 255) of the papers focused on static aspects; 58 percent (148 of 255) dealt solely with segregation processes; only 30 percent (76 of 255) dealt solely with integration processes.

Table 2   RESEARCH IN INTERGROUP RELATIONS REPORTED IN MAJOR SOCIOLOGICAL JOURNALS *

System:	Individual						Social					
Topic:	Attitudes			Action			Static			Change		
Focus on Factors Favoring:	Integration	Segregation	Both	Integration	Segregation	Both	Integration	Segregation	Both	Integration	Segregation	Both
Time period												
1900–10	1							7				
1910–20							2	4		2	2	
1920–30	3	3	2		1	2	3	2		1	3	
1930–40	3	3		2	2	1	7	8	1	1		1
1940–50	6	20	4	4	0		14	10	6	8	13	
1950–58	5	39	7	4	8	3	7	9	4	3	14	
Total:	18	65	13	10	11	6	33	40	11	15	32	1

* Originally appeared in K. W. Back, "Sociology Encounters the Protest Movement for Desegregation," *Phylon*, 1963, Vol. 24, pp. 232–239.

The emphases over the years can be traced. The first decade of the century showed a special concentration on the static features of the social system which maintained segregation. This corresponded with a belief in the stability of the society as it then existed and fitted with the popular doctrines of "separate but equal" and "stateways cannot change folkways." The decade of change which followed evinced interest in the social system, static and changing, because of the recognition of the impact on society of World War I. During the 1920s and 1930s, attitude measurement introduced the opportunity of studying intergroup relations on an individual basis. And in the 1930s, the question of extremism in racial attitudes became especially prominent. It was only after 1940, however, that many articles appeared on the relevance and development of negative outgroup attitudes. The breakthrough along these lines was the University of California study on the authoritarian personality.[66] This work presented a theory of intergroup relations on a purely individual level and provided a convenient set of scales that fathered a host of related studies. This advance accounts for the sudden imbalance of papers concerned with the individual over the social system: while the personal system accounts for 48 percent (123 of 255) of the total publications, it accounts for almost two-thirds of the 1950–1958 production. Another major influence of the 1940s and 1950s was the publication of Myrdal's *An American Dilemma,* which in turn led to numerous descriptions of conditions which favored and opposed segregation. After 1954, studies on possible Southern resistance to racial change followed the Supreme Court ruling on school desegregation. But there continued to be a neglect of the forces which could hasten desegregation.

What is striking throughout is the lack of dynamic concerns that would have alerted sociology to the oncoming black protests of the 1960s. Most of the papers which do treat the Negro response deal merely with migration, an action within the social system having only an indirect, long-range effect. The next most frequent topics were planned integration and interracial committees, not actions proposed by the minority group itself. Two less popular topics do touch on possible pressures toward social change. One analyzed types of Negro leaders; the other analyzed the types of persons predisposed to protest.

The great majority of sociological research publications on race relations, however, do not present a picture of individual responsibility and social change. These papers typically assume a constant, undefined pressure for integration in the discussion of the powerful personality factors and social institutions which oppose racial change. Criticism within social psychology in recent years has centered on the neglect of the positive resources of human beings: creativity, health, and self-fulfillment. An analogous criticism can be leveled at sociological work on race relations, with its emphasis on restrictive static forces. Adoption of this viewpoint leads to a complete reliance on slow remedies, such as "education" or gradual institutional change. It omits, for example, the possible results of greatly enhanced pressure for integration.

To be sure, events in this sphere move so swiftly that sociology cannot be reproached for being unable to predict each event as it occurs. Yet this situation argues strongly for an application of the whole range of sociological theory to the study of racial change and racism. Many elements of sociological theory, such as relative deprivation, heralded the racial crisis of the 1960s, but these fruitful leads were not fully exploited. A broader, bolder thrust in the sociological analysis of American race relations seems long overdue. No time has ever been more open for such a thrust than now.

Summary

In the process of racial change, disuse of sociology is more apparent than use of it. This situation has come about in spite of the rich promise of relevant sociological theory and demonstrations by individual sociologists of how useful sociology can be. Four different theoretical emphases —centering upon the self, balance, the social system, and social change—all offer important leads for understanding desegregation. In addition, sociologists have in isolated instances proved their value as predictors of trends, interpreters of specific events, and consultants.

Three interrelated reasons can be advanced to explain why the potential of sociology to contribute to the desegregation process has been barely tapped. First, the timidity of major foundations and granting agencies to support research in such a "controversial" realm caused a funding drought for most of the decade following 1954. Second, the pressures applied by stern segregationist resistance to racial change created a climate that was not conducive to broad-gaged scientific research. And, finally, a traditional overemphasis on static elements which bolster segregation in the sociological study of intergroup relations acted to deter the full exploitation of the sociological potential in this area.

All three of these restrictions have eased. Funding sources reevaluated their earlier positions; direct consultation services on desegregation problems are now explicitly offered by the Federal government in the Civil Rights Act of 1964; and the sharp impact of the street protests of the 1960s has drawn sociological attention to the dynamic factors on the American scene which press toward rapid racial change. It can only be hoped that a great upsurge of research activity directed at desegregation will be forthcoming in the 1970s. At least three considerations make such an upsurge of interest imperative: (1) Racial change is a now-or-never phenomenon; either sociologists will start studying it immediately or the chance will be lost completely. (2) Sociological insights and methods are needed to help in the practical solution of the many complex problems raised by such sweeping social changes. (3) And the process offers sociology a rare opportunity to test many of its theoretical formulations in the field on an issue of maximum salience.

Footnotes

1. Back is currently Professor of Sociology at Duke University.

2. W. C. George, *The Biology of the Race Problem* (New York: National Putnam Letters Committee, 1962), p. 56.

3. V. Dabney, "The Violence at Little Rock," *Richmond Times-Dispatch,* September 24, 1957, Vol. 105, p. 14.

4. The sociological works listed in Footnote 11 were E. Franklin Frazier's *The Negro in the United States* and Gunnar Myrdal's *An American Dilemma.*

5. Race in this context, then, is considered primarily as a social concept, rather than as a biological or psychological one. The definition and importance of racial concepts are dependent on social conditions, and racial distinctions are a function of social necessities. Thus, a division of the population into "white" and "Negro" in the United States sets the problem in a social context which contrasts sharply with that in other countries, where either intermediate groups or a continuous degree of shading is recognized. It would be interesting to trace the progressive disuse of such terms as "mulatto," "quadroon," and "octoroon" in relation to changes in interracial relations (on the relation of color naming and the recognition of shades, see R. W. Brown and E. H. Lenneberg, "A Study in Language and Condition," *Journal of Abnormal and Social Psychology,* 1954, Vol. 49, pp. 454–462). In any event, the utility of treating race as a purely sociological concept is demonstrated by Thompson's observation that race as a stratification dimension tends to be most important in precisely those societies where a class system is not accepted as a normal way of life [see E. T. Thompson, "The South and the Second Emancipation," in A. P. Sindler (ed.), *Change in the Contemporary South* (Durham, N.C.: Duke University Press, 1963), pp. 93–118].

6. E. Goffman, *Stigma* (Englewood Cliffs, N.J.: Prentice-Hall, 1963).

7. A similar view, based on existential philosophy, has been presented by Sartre [*Anti-Semite and Jew* (New York: Grove, 1960)]. In his portrait of the anti-Semite, he discusses the problems of self-presentation of both the minority-group member and the aggressor. Both have the problem

of being defamed by a few traits; but while the anti-Semite may welcome the definition of himself as a person who hates Jews, the problem for the Jew is more difficult. The minority-group member must strike a balance between asserting his existence beyond a prescribed set of traits and complete denial of these traits. This balance is what Sartre calls "authenticity," a concept which has already been applied to the description of Negro Americans (A. Booyard, "Portrait of the Inauthentic Negro," *Commentary*, 1950, Vol. 10, pp. 56–64). The principal difference between Goffman and Sartre lies in the fact that Goffman, in the tradition of the symbolic interactionists, accepts the looking-glass self as a basic fact of social life, whereas Sartre considers it to be a possibly unavoidable tragedy.

8. For example, Marian R. Yarrow (ed.), "Interpersonal Dynamics in a Desegregation Process," *Journal of Social Issues,* Winter, 1958, Vol. 38, pp. 3–63.

9. A review of the literature on bias involving the race of the interviewer is provided in T. F. Pettigrew, *A Profile of the Negro American* (Princeton, N.J.: Van Nostrand, 1964), pp. 49–51, 116–117. This work has focused on the bias encountered with Negro respondents; interesting research is called for on the differential responses of white respondents to Negro and white interviewers (a brief start in this direction is reported in R. E. Rankin and D. T. Campbell, "Galvanic Skin Response to Negro and White Experimenters," *Journal of Abnormal and Social Psychology,* 1955, Vol. 51, pp. 30–33). Some of the most promising laboratory research in this realm has been summarized in I. Katz, "Review of Evidence Relating to Effects of Desegregation on the Intellectual Performance of Negroes," *American Psychologist,* 1964, Vol. 19, pp. 381–399.

10. R. K. Merton and A. S. Kitt, "Contributions to the Theory of Reference Group Behavior," in R. K. Merton and P. F. Lazarsfeld (eds.), *Continuities in Social Research: Studies in the Scope and Method of "The American Soldier"* (Glencoe, Ill.: Free Press, 1950); and S. A. Stouffer, *Social Research to Test Ideas* (New York: Free Press, 1962), pp. 35–38.

11. *Ibid.,* p. 36.

12. E. Benoit-Smullyan, "Status, Status Types and Status Interrelationships," *American Sociological Review,* 1944, Vol. 9, pp. 151–161; G. E. Lenski, "Status Crystallization: A Non-Vertical Dimension of Social Status," *American Sociological Review,* 1954, Vol. 19, pp. 405–413; and J. C. Kimberly,

"A Theory of Status Equilibration," in J. Berger, M. Zelditch, and B. Anderson (eds.), *Sociological Theories in Progress* (Boston: Houghton Mifflin, 1964).

13. E. F. Jackson, "Status Consistency and Symptoms of Stress," *American Sociological Review,* 1962, Vol. 27, pp. 469–480; I. W. Goffman, "Status Consistency and Preference for Change in Power Distribution," *American Sociological Review,* 1957, Vol. 22, pp. 275–281; and Lenski, *op. cit.*

14. Jackson, *op. cit.*

15. Documentation for this paragraph is provided in Chapter 7.

16. Even among college Negroes, those from backgrounds of higher achieved status and who believed they were not mere pawns in an unchanging environment were more likely to participate in the protest demonstrations. See Pearl M. Gore and J. B. Rotter, "A Personality Correlate of Social Action," *Journal of Personality,* 1963, Vol. 31, pp. 58–64; and Ruth Searles and J. A. Williams, Jr., "Negro College Students' Participation in Sit-Ins," *Social Forces,* 1962, Vol. 40, pp. 215–220. See also: D. R. Matthews and J. W. Prothro, *Negroes and the New Southern Politics* (New York: Harcourt, Brace & World, 1966), Chapter 14.

17. E. Durkheim, *The Division of Labor in Society* (New York: Macmillan, 1933).

18. J. A. S. Davis, "Structural Balance, Mechanical Solidarity, and Interpersonal Relations," *American Journal of Sociology,* 1963, Vol. 68, pp. 444–462.

19. T. F. Pettigrew, "Regional Differences in Anti-Negro Prejudice," *Journal of Abnormal and Social Psychology,* 1959, Vol. 59, pp. 28–36.

20. Price has demonstrated that this legacy remains even when the percentage of Negroes in a particular Black Belt county has sharply declined. See H. D. Price, *The Negro and Southern Politics* (New York: New York University Press, 1957), pp. 35–54.

21. Social symptoms of the restricted differentiation of rural America are not limited, of course, to race relations or to the South. For instance, thirteen different national surveys by Gallup, spanning the years from 1941 to 1961 and utilizing a variety of question wordings, have repeatedly shown farmers to harbor views concerning the rights of labor which sharply differ from those held by all other occupational groups, including business employers. Thus, farmers as a group are conspicuous in their disapproval of labor unions, minimum-wage requirements, and four-day work weeks and

in their support of the open shop and the reduction of pay with any reduction in the work week. Moreover, even union members who lived in communities of less than 2,500 persons voted significantly less in 1960 for the labor-backed Democratic Party than other union members. See H. G. Erskine, "The Polls: Attitudes toward Organized Labor," *Public Opinion Quarterly,* 1962, Vol. 26, pp. 283–296.

22. T. Parsons, "Pattern Variables Revisited," *American Sociological Review,* 1960, Vol. 25, pp. 467–482.

23. M. Rubin, "Land and Cultural Change in a Plantation Area," *Journal of Social Issues,* 1954, Vol. 10, pp. 28–35.

24. These examples are taken from Ernest Works, "The Pattern Variables as a Framework for the Study of Negro-White Relations" (unpublished manuscript).

25. K. W. Marek, *Yestermorrow: Notes on Man's Progress* (New York: Knopf, 1961). For sociological considerations of evolutionary aspects of social change, see articles by Parsons, Bellah, and Eisenstadt in *The American Sociological Review,* 1964, Vol. 29, pp. 339–386.

26. For a general discussion of the ability of functional theories to explain social change, see F. Cancian, "Functional Analysis of Change," *American Sociological Review,* 1960, Vol. 25, pp. 818–827.

27. L. A. Coser, *The Functions of Social Conflict* (Glencoe, Ill.: Free Press, 1956); D. Henderson, "Minority Response and the Conflict Model," *Phylon,* 1964, Vol. 25, pp. 18–26; and L. Killian and C. Grigg, *Racial Crisis in America* (Englewood Cliffs, N.J.: Prentice-Hall, 1964).

28. Coser, *op. cit.*

29. Henderson, *op. cit.,* and Killian and Grigg, *op. cit.*

30. L. A. Coser, "Conflict: Social Aspects," in D. L. Sills (ed.), *International Encyclopedia of the Social Sciences, Vol. 3* (New York: Macmillan and Free Press, 1968), pp. 235–236.

31. E. U. Essien-Udom, *Black Nationalism* (Chicago: University of Chicago Press, 1962); C. E. Lincoln, *The Black Muslims in America* (Boston: Beacon, 1961); and J. W. Vander Zanden, "The Klan Revival," *American Journal of Sociology,* 1960, Vol. 65, pp. 456–462.

32. A. L. Coleman, "Social Scientists' Predictions about Desegregation," *Social Forces,* 1960, Vol. 38, pp. 258–262.

33. Adapted from *ibid.*

34. A review of this work is provided in T. F. Pettigrew and M. R. Cramer, "The Demography of Desegregation, *Journal of Social Issues,* 1959, Vol. 15, pp. 61–71. For material specifi-

cally on the 1861 Tennessee vote to secede, see V. O. Key, *Southern Politics* (New York: Knopf, 1950), pp. 75–78.

35. Pettigrew and Cramer, *op. cit.*

36. The percentage of white women in the labor force turned out to be a reasonably effective way to tap traditionalism; that is, a county with a relatively small percentage of white women in its recorded labor force was presumed to be more traditional than others.

37. Also reported in T. F. Pettigrew, "Continuing Barriers to Desegregated Education in the South," *Sociology of Education,* 1965, Vol. 38, pp. 99–111. Further work is now under way to construct more precise predictive formulas.

38. Two of these reports were published: J. K. Morland, "Lunch-Counter Desegregation in Corpus Christi, Galveston, and San Antonio, Texas," *Special Reports of the Southern Regional Council* (May, 1960); and J. K. Morland, *School Desegregation—Help Needed?* (Washington, D.C.: The Potomac Institute, 1962).

39. K. Lenihan, "Attitudes towards Negroes in a New Jersey Suburb" (unpublished manuscript).

40. L. W. Killian, "The Social Scientist's Role in the Preparation of the Florida Desegregation Brief," *Social Problems,* 1956, Vol. 3, pp. 211–214.

41. For examples of the views of these two men on *de facto* segregation, see A. M. Rose, *De Facto Segregation* (New York: National Conference of Christians and Jews, 1964); and M. Ravitz, "Uneven School Progress in Detroit," in M. Weinberg (ed.), *Learning Together* (Chicago: Integrated Education Associates, 1964), pp. 61–67. Ravitz led the City Council race in Detroit's 1969 civic election.

42. Killian, *op. cit.,* p. 214.

43. Smaller foundations which stand out as conspicuous exceptions to this trend include the Marshall Field Foundation, the New World Foundation, and the Taconic Foundation.

44. S. W. Cook, "Desegregation: A Psychological Analysis," *American Psychologist,* 1957, Vol. 12, pp. 1–13.

45. Examples of these limited case studies conducted since 1954 include E. Q. Campbell, *When A City Closes Its Schools* (Chapel Hill, N.C.: Institute for Research in the Social Sciences, 1960); E. Q. Campbell and T. F. Pettigrew, *Christians in Racial Crisis: A Study of the Little Rock Ministry* (Washington: Public Affairs Press, 1959); Killian and Grigg, *op. cit.;* D. C. Thompson, *The Negro Leadership Class* (Englewood Cliffs, N.J.: Prentice-Hall, 1963); and

M. M. Tumin, *Desegregation: Resistance and Readiness* (Princeton: Princeton University Press, 1958). The far more extensive study by Robin Williams, Jr. (*Strangers Next Door* [Englewood Cliffs, N.J.: Prentice-Hall, 1964]), is a report of pre-1954 data.

46. W. Brink and L. Harris, *The Negro Revolution in America* (New York: Simon and Schuster, 1964).

47. R. N. Sanford, "Foreword," in *The Role of the Social Sciences in Desegregation* (Anti-Defamation League of B'nai B'rith, 1958).

48. R. Redfield, "Values in Action: A Comment," *Human Organization,* 1958, Vol. 17, pp. 20—22.

49. A. Gouldner, "Anti-Minotaur: The Myth of a Value-Free Sociology," *Social Problems,* 1962, Vol. 9, pp. 199—213.

50. C. Arensberg, "Values in Action: A Comment," *Human Organization,* 1958, Vol. 17, pp. 25—26.

51. R. Bierstedt, "Social Science and Public Service," paper given at meetings of the Society for the Study of Social Problems, St. Louis, 1961.

52. Campbell and Pettigrew, *op. cit.*

53. Stouffer, *Social Research to Test Ideas, op. cit.,* pp. 224, 231—238.

54. Killian, *op. cit.*

55. *Ibid.,* p. 214.

56. J. K. Morland, "Roles of Sociologist and Citizen in Race Relations in the South," paper given at meetings of the American Sociological Association, Washington, D. C., 1962.

57. *Ibid.*

58. Vander Zanden, *op. cit.*

59. K. E. Taeuber and A. F. Taeuber, *Negroes in Cities* (Chicago: Aldine, 1965).

60. M. R. Cramer, "School Desegregation and New Industry: The Southern Community Leaders' Viewpoint," *Social Forces,* 1963, Vol. 41, pp. 384—389.

61. P. F. Lazarsfeld and W. Thielens, Jr., *The Academic Mind* (Glencoe, Ill.: Free Press, 1958). See also a penetrating review of this volume: H. C. Kelman, "Apprehension and Academic Freedom," *Public Opinion Quarterly,* 1959, Vol. 23, pp. 181—188.

62. Campbell and Pettigrew, *op. cit.*

63. Killian and Grigg, *op. cit.*

64. *Ibid.,* p. 101.

65. This section is taken largely from K. W. Back, "Sociology Encounters the Protest Movement for Desegregation," *Phylon,* 1963, Vol. 24, pp. 232–239.

66. T. W. Adorno, E. Frenkel-Brunswik, D. J. Levinson, and N. Sanford, *The Authoritarian Personality* (New York: Harper, 1950).

CHAPTER SIX

SOCIAL PSYCHOLOGY AND RESEARCH ON DESEGREGATION

What one hears and what one sees of race relations in the South are sharply divergent. Consider some of the things that have occurred in my interviews with white Southerners over the past decade.

"As much as my family likes TV," confided a friendly North Carolina farmer, "we always turn the set off when they put them colored people on." But as the two of us were completing the interview, a series of famous black entertainers performed on the bright, 21-inch screen in the adjoining room. No one interrupted them.

A rotund banker in Charleston, South Carolina, was equally candid in his remarks: "Son, under no conditions will the white man and the black man ever get together in this state." He apparently preferred to ignore the government-sponsored integration at his city's naval installation, just a short distance from his office.

Another respondent, a highly educated Chattanooga businessman, patiently explained to me for over an hour how race relations had not changed at all in his city during the past generation. As I left his office building, I saw a Negro policeman directing downtown traffic—the first Negro traffic cop I had ever seen in the South.

The South today is rife with such contradictions; social change has simply been too rapid for many Southerners to recognize it. Such a situation commands the attention of psychologists.

There are many other aspects of this sweeping process that should command the attention of researchers. To name just two, both the pending violence and the stultifying conformity attendant on desegregation are psychological problems. We might ask, for instance, why it is that violence is produced in some desegregating communities, like Little Rock and Clinton, and not in others, like Raleigh and Winston-Salem. A multiplicity of factors must be relevant, and further research is desperately needed to delineate them; but tentative early work seems to indicate that the violence occurring with desegregation so far has been surprisingly "rational." That is, violence has generally resulted in localities where at least some of the authorities give hints beforehand that they would gladly return to segregation if disturbances occurred; peaceful integration has generally followed firm and forceful leadership.[1]

Research concerning conformity in the present situation is even more important. Many psychologists know from personal experience how intense the pressures to conform in racial attitudes have become in the present-day South; indeed, it appears that the first amendment, guaranteeing free speech, is in as much peril as the fourteenth amendment. Those who dare to break the taboo consistently must do so, in much of the South, under the intimidation of slanderous letters and phone calls, burned crosses, and even bomb threats. Indeed, this chapter will contend that conformity is the social-psychological key to analyzing white resistance to racial change in the South.

Limitations on the Contributions of Social Psychology

In the previous chapter we saw how sociology had not realized its potential for understanding race relations in the United States, partly because of inadequacies in traditional sociological analyses. Much the same point can be made in explaining why social psychology has not made its full contribution. Here the relative neglect of situational variables in interracial behavior, combined with a restricted interpretation and use of the attitude concept, has hindered psychological work in race relations. Let us examine each of these aspects briefly.

Situational variables. The importance of the situation as it affects racial interaction has been demonstrated in a wide variety of settings. All-pervasive racial attitudes are often not involved; many individuals seem fully capable of immediate behavioral change as situations change. For example, in Panama there was a divided street, racially segregated on the Canal Zone side and racially integrated on the Panamanian side. Biesanz and Smith report that most Panamanians and Americans appeared to accommodate without difficulty as they shopped first on one side of the street and then on the other.[2] Another example comes from the coal-mining county of McDowell, West Virginia; Minard relates that the majority of black and white miners followed easily a traditional pattern of integration below the ground and almost complete segregation above the ground.[3] The literature abounds with further examples: Southern white migrants readily adjusting to integrated situations in the North,[4] Northern whites approving of integration of employment and public facilities but resisting residential integration,[5] etc. Indeed, in the South there have been many white Southerners who were simultaneously adjusting to integration of buses and public golf courses and still opposing integration of public schools; or, as in Nashville, accepting school integration but continuing to oppose the integration of lunch counters.

This is not to imply that generalized attitudes on race are never invoked. There were some Panamanians and some Americans who acted about the same on both sides of the street; Minard estimated that about two-fifths of the West Virginian miners he observed behaved consistently in either a tolerant or an intolerant fashion both below and above ground; [6] and some white Southerners either approve or disapprove of all desegregation. But these people —people who behave consistently on a basis of consistent attitudes—are easily explained by traditional theory. Consistent segregationists, for example, probably are characterized by extreme authoritarianism; their attitudes on race are so generalized and so salient that their consistent behavior in racial situations is sometimes in defiance of the prevailing social norms.

On the other hand, "other-directed" individuals—those who shift their behavior to keep in line with shifting expectations—present the real problem for psychologists. Their racial attitudes appear less salient, more specific, and more tied to particular situations. The need for conformity is predominantly important for these people. We shall return shortly to discuss these conformists further.

One complication introduced by situational analysis is that interracial contact itself frequently leads to the modification of attitudes. A number of studies of racially integrated situations have noted dramatic attitude changes, but in most cases the changes involved specific attitudes linked to situations. For example, white employees in a department store become more accepting of blacks in the work situation after integrated contact on an equal-status basis, but not necessarily more accepting in other situations. [7] And *The American Soldier* studies found that the attitudes of white army personnel toward the Negro as a fighting man improve after equal-status, integrated contact in combat, but their attitudes toward the Negro as a social companion do not necessarily change.[8] In other words, for many people experience in a novel situation characterized by equal status leads to acceptance of that specific situation. Situations, then, not only structure specific racial behavior, but they may change specific attitudes in the process. We shall consider this important generalization in more detail in Chapters 11 and 12.

One final feature of a situational analysis deserves mention. Typically in psychology we have tested racial attitudes in isolation, apart from conflicting attitudes and values. Yet this is not realistic. As racial change slowly unfolds in such resistant states as Virginia and Georgia, we see clearly that many segregationist Southerners value law and order, public education, and a prosperous economy above their racial views. Once such a situation pits race against other entrenched values, we need to know what sort of hierarchy these values form in the public mind. Thus a rounded situational analysis requires the measurement of racial attitudes in the full context of other values.[9] We shall return to this point in Chapters 9 and 10.

The attitude concept. A second and related weakness in the psychological approach is the failure to exploit fully the broad and dynamic implications of the attitude concept. Most social-psychological research has dealt with attitudes as if they were serving only an expressive function; but racial attitudes in the South require a more complex treatment.

In their volume *Opinion and Personality,* Smith, Bruner, and White urge a more expansive interpretation of attitudes.[10] They note three functions of attitudes. First, there is the *object-appraisal* function; attitudes aid in understanding "reality" as it is defined by the culture. Second, attitudes can play a *social-adjustment* function by contributing to the individual's identification with, or differentiation from, various reference groups. Finally, attitudes may reduce anxiety by serving an expressive or *externalization* function.

Externalization occurs when an individual . . . senses an analogy between a perceived environmental event and some unresolved inner problem . . . [and] adopts an attitude . . . which is a transformed version of his way of dealing with his inner difficulty.[11]

At present the most fashionable psychological theories of prejudice—frustration-aggression, psychoanalytic, and authoritarian—all deal chiefly with the externalization function. Valuable as these theories have been, this exclusive attention to the expressive component of attitudes has been at the expense of the other components—object appraisal and social adjustment. Moreover, it is my contention that these neglected and more socially relevant functions, particularly social adjustment, offer the key to further psychological advances in research on desegregation.[12]

The extent to which concentration on externalization has influenced the general public was illustrated in the popular reaction to desecrations of Jewish temples. The perpetrators, all agreed, must be juvenile hoodlums, or "sick," or both. In other words, explanations having to do with externalization were predominantly offered.[13] Valid though these explanations may be in many cases, is it not also evident that the perpetrators were accurately reflecting the anti-Semitic norms of their subcultures? Thus their acts and the attitudes behind their acts are forms of social adjustment for these persons, given the circles in which they move.

Some sociologists, too, have been understandably misled by the overemphasis on externalization into underestimating the psychological analysis of prejudice. One sociologist categorically concludes:

> There is no evidence that . . . any known source of "prejudice" in the psychological sense is any more prevalent in the South than in the North.[14]

Two others maintain firmly:

> The psychological approach, as valuable as it is, does not explain the preponderance of people who engage in prejudiced behavior, but do *not* have special emotional problems.[15]

Both of these statements assume, as some psychologists have assumed, that externalization is the only possible psychological explanation of prejudice. These writers employ cultural and situational norms as explanatory concepts for racial prejudice and discrimination, but fail to see that the need for conformity is the reflection of these norms in the personality and offers an equally valid explanation on the psychological level. To answer the first assertion, survey evidence indicates that conformity to racial norms, one "known source of prejudice," *is* "more prevalent in the South than in the North." To answer the second assertion, strong needs to conform to racial norms in the South, for instance, are *not* "special emotional problems." Psychology is not just a science of mental illness, nor must psychological theories of prejudice be limited to the mentally ill.

The Importance of Conformity in Southern Race Relations

Evidence of the importance of conformity in Southerners' attitudes on race has been steadily accumulating in recent years. The relevant data come from several different research approaches; one of these is the study of anti-Semitism. Roper's opinion polls have shown the South, together with the Far West, to be one of the least anti-Semitic regions in the United States.[16] Knapp's study of over 1,000 war rumors from all parts of the country in 1942 lends additional weight to this finding.[17] He noted that anti-Semitic stories constituted 9 percent of the rumors in the nation but only 3 percent of the rumors in the South. By contrast, 8.5 percent of the rumors in the South concerned the Negro, as opposed to only 3 percent for the nation as a whole. Consistent with these data, too, is Prothro's discovery that two-fifths of his white adult sample in Louisiana were quite favorable in their attitudes toward Jews but at the same time quite unfavorable in their attitudes toward Negroes.[18] But if the externalization function were predominant in anti-Negro attitudes in the South, the South should also be highly anti-Semitic. Externalizing bigots do not select out just the Negro; they typically reject all outgroups, even, as Hartley has demonstrated, outgroups that do not exist.[19]

Further evidence comes from research employing the famous F-scale measure of authoritarianism.[20] Several studies, employing both student and adult samples, have reported Southern F-scale means that fall well within the range of means of comparable groups outside the South.[21] Moreover, there is no evidence that the family pattern associated with authoritarianism is more prevalent in the South than in other parts of the country.[22] It seems clear, then, that heightened prejudice against the black in the South cannot be explained in terms of any regional difference in authoritarianism. This is not to deny, however, the importance of the F scale in predicting individual differences; it appears to correlate with prejudice in Southern samples at approximately the same levels as in Northern samples.[23]

The third line of evidence relates measures of conformity directly to racial attitudes. For lack of a standardized, nonlaboratory measure, one study defined conformity and deviance in terms of the respondents' social characteristics.[24] For a Southern white sample with age and education held constant, potentially conforming respondents (i.e., women or church attenders) were *more* anti-Negro than their counterparts (i.e., men or nonattenders of church), and potentially deviant respondents (i.e., veterans or political independents) were *less* anti-Negro than their counterparts (i.e., nonveterans or partisans). None of these differences was noted in a comparable Northern sample. Furthermore, Southerners living in communities with relatively small percentages of Negroes were less anti-Negro than Southerners living in communities with relatively large percentages of Negroes, though they were *not* less authoritarian. In short, respondents most likely to conform to cultural pressures are more prejudiced against Negroes in the South, but not in the North. And the percentage of Negroes in the community appears to be a fairly accurate index of the strength of these Southern cultural pressures concerning race.

Thus all three types of research agree that conformity to the stern racial norms of Southern culture is unusually crucial in the heightened hostility toward the Negro in the South.[25] Or, in plain language, it is the path of least resistance in most white Southern circles to favor white supremacy. When an individual's parents and peers are racially prejudiced, when his limited world accepts racial discrimination as a given of life, when deviance means certain ostracism, then his anti-Negro attitudes reflect not so much externalization as they do social adjustment.

This being the case, it is fortunate that a number of significant laboratory and theoretical advances concerning conformity have been made recently in social psychology. Solomon Asch's pioneer research on conformity,[26] followed up by Crutchfield [27] and others, has provided us with a wealth of laboratory findings, many of them suggestive for research on desegregation. And theoretical analyses of conformity have been introduced by Kelman,[28] Festinger,[29] Thibaut and Kelley; [30] these, too, are directly applicable for desegregation research. Indeed, research on race relations in the South offers a rare opportunity to test these empirical and theoretical formulations in the field on a particularly salient issue.

Consider the relevance of one of Asch's intriguing findings.[31] Asch's standard situation employed seven preinstructed assistants and a genuine subject in a task involving judging the length of a line. On two-thirds of the judgments, the seven assistants deliberately reported aloud an obviously incorrect estimate; thus the subject, seated eighth, faced unanimous pressure to conform by making a similarly incorrect response. On approximately one third of such judgments, he yielded to the group; like the others he would estimate a 5-inch line as 4 inches. But when Asch disturbed the unanimity by having one of his seven assistants give the correct response, the subjects yielded only one tenth, rather than one third, of the time. Once unanimity no longer existed, even when there was only one supporting colleague, the subject could better withstand the pressure of the majority to conform. To make an analogy with today's crisis in the South, obvious 5-inch lines are being widely described as 4 inches. Many Southerners, faced with what appears to be solid unanimity, submit to the distortion. But when even one respected source—a minister, a newspaper editor, even a college professor—conspicuously breaks the unanimity, *perhaps* a dramatic modification is achieved in the private opinions of many conforming Southerners. Only an empirical test can learn if such a direct analogy is warranted.

Consider, too, the relevance of some theoretical distinctions. Kelman, for example, has clarified the concept of conformity by pointing out that three separate processes are involved: *compliance, identification,* and *internalization.*[32] Compliance exists when an individual accepts influence not because he believes in it, but because he hopes to achieve a favorable reaction from an agent who maintains surveillance over him. Identification exists when an individual accepts influence because he wants to establish or maintain a satisfying relationship with another individual or a group. The third process, internalization, exists when an individual accepts influence because the content of the behavior itself is satisfying; unlike the other types of conformity, internalized behavior will be performed without the surveillance of the agent or a salient relationship with the agent. It is with this third process that Kelman's ideas overlap with authoritarian theory.

We have all witnessed illustrations of each of these processes in the acceptance by Southerners of the region's racial norms. The "Uncle Tom" is an example of a compliant Negro Southerner; another example is the white man who treats Negroes as equals only when not under the surveillance of other whites. Identification is best seen in white Southerners whose resistance to racial integration enables them to be a part of what they erroneously imagine to be a Confederate tradition. Such people are frequently upwardly mobile and still assimilating to urban society; they strive for social status by identifying with the hallowed symbols of the South's past. Southerners who have internalized the dictates of the culture regarding white supremacy are the real racists who use the issue to gain political office, to attract membership fees for resistance groups, or to meet needs of their own personalities. Southerners with such contrasting bases for their racial attitudes should react very differently toward desegregation. For instance, compliant whites can be expected to accept desegregation more readily than those who have internalized segregationist norms.

On the basis of this discussion of conformity, I would like to propose a new concept: the *"latent liberal."* This is not to be confused with the cherished Southern notion of the "moderate"; the ambiguous term "moderate" is presently used to describe everyone from an integrationist who wants to be socially accepted to a racist who wants to be polite. Rather, "latent liberal" refers to the white Southerner who is neither anti-Semitic nor authoritarian but whose habits and needs of conformity cause him to be strongly anti-Negro. Through the processes of compliance and identification, the latent liberal continues to behave in a discriminatory fashion toward Negroes even though such behavior conflicts with his basically tolerant personality.

He is at the present time *il*liberal on race, but he has, as far as his personality is concerned, the potentiality of becoming liberal once the norms of the culture change. Indeed, as the economic, legal, political, and social forces that have already been unleashed restructure the racial norms of the South, the latent liberal's attitudes about Negroes will continue to change. Previously cited research suggests that there are today an abundance of white Southerners who meet this description; collectively, they will reflect the vast societal changes now taking place in the South.

Summary

Recognition of the importance of the situation in interracial behavior and full exploitation of the attitude concept can remove inadequacies in the traditional psychological approach to the study of race. In this connection, a case for considering conformity as crucial in the attitudes of white Southerners toward blacks was presented, and a new concept—the latent liberal—was introduced. One final implication of this concept should be mentioned. Some cynics have argued that successful racial desegregation in the South will require an importation of tens of thousands of psychotherapists and therapy for millions of bigoted Southerners. Fortunately for desegregation, psychotherapists, and Southerners, this will not be necessary; a thorough repatterning of Southern interracial behavior will be sufficient therapy in itself.

Footnotes

1. K. B. Clark, "Desegregation: An Appraisal of the Evidence, *Journal of Social Issues,* 1953, Vol. 9, pp. 1–79. Clark predicted this from early integration in border states, and a vari-

ety of field reports have since documented the point in specific instances.

2. J. Biesanz and L. M. Smith, "Race Relations of Panama and the Canal Zone," *American Journal of Sociology,* 1951, Vol. 57, pp. 7–14.

3. R. D. Minard, "Race Relations in the Pochahontas Coal Field," *Journal of Social Issues,* 1952, Vol. 8, pp. 29–44.

4. L. W. Killian, "Southern White Laborers in Chicago's West Side" (unpublished doctoral dissertation, University of Chicago, 1949).

5. D. C. Rietzes, "The Role of Organizational Structures: Union versus Neighborhood in a Tension Situation," *Journal of Social Issues,* 1953, Vol. 9, pp. 37–44.

6. Minard, *op. cit.*

7. J. Harding and R. Hogrefe, "Attitudes of White Department Store Employees toward Negro Co-Workers," *Journal of Social Issues,* 1952, Vol. 8, pp. 18–28.

8. S. A. Stouffer, E. A. Suchman, L. C. De Vinney, S. A. Star, and R. M. Williams, Jr., *Studies in Social Psychology in World War II,* Vol. 1, *The American Soldier: Adjustment during Army Life* (Princeton: Princeton University Press, 1949).

9. A popular treatment of this point has been made by H. Zinn, "A Fate Worse than Integration," *Harper's,* August, 1959, Vol. 219, pp. 53–59.

10. M. B. Smith, J. S. Bruner and R. W. White, *Opinion and Personality* (New York: Wiley, 1956).

11. *Ibid.,* pp. 41–44.

12. Though this chapter emphasizes the social-adjustment function of attitudes of white Southerners toward blacks, the object-appraisal function, equally neglected, is also of importance. Most middle-class whites in the South know only lower-class Negroes; consequently their unfavorable stereotype of blacks serves a class-related "reality" function.

13. Such explanations also serve for many anti-Semitic observers as an ego-alien defense against guilt; that is, "such people are so different from me that it doesn't concern me or my attitudes toward Jews."

14. A. M. Rose, "Intergroup Relations vs. Prejudice: Pertinent Theory for the Study of Social Change," *Social Problems,* 1956, Vol. 4, p. 174.

15. E. Raab and S. M. Lipset, *Prejudice and Society* (New York: Anti-Defamation League of B'nai B'rith, 1959), p. 26.

16. E. Roper, "United States Anti-Semites," *Fortune,* 1946, Vol.

33, pp. 257–260; and E. Roper, "United States Anti-Semites," *Fortune,* 1947, Vol. 36, pp. 5–10.

17. R. H. Knapp, "A Psychology of Rumor," *Public Opinion Quarterly,* 1944, Vol. 8, pp. 22–37.

18. E. T. Prothro, "Ethnocentrism and Anti-Negro Attitudes in the Deep South," *Journal of Abnormal and Social Psychology,* 1952, Vol. 47, pp. 105–108.

19. E. L. Hartley, *Problems in Prejudice* (New York: King's Crown, 1946).

20. T. W. Adorno, Else Frenkel-Brunswick, D. J. Levinson, and N. Sanford, *The Authoritarian Personality* (New York: Harper, 1950).

21. O. Milton, "Presidential Choice and Performance on a Scale of Authoritarianism," *American Psychologist,* 1952, Vol. 7, pp. 597–598; T. F. Pettigrew, "Regional Differences in Anti-Negro Prejudice," *Journal of Abnormal and Social Psychology,* 1959, Vol. 29, pp. 28–36; and C. U. Smith and J. W. Prothro, "Ethnic Differences in Authoritarian Personality," *Social Forces,* 1957, Vol. 35, pp. 334–338.

22. A. Davis, B. Gardner and M. Gardner, *Deep South* (Chicago: University of Chicago Press, 1941); and J. Dollard, *Caste and Class in a Southern Town* (New Haven: Yale University Press, 1937).

23. Pettigrew, *op. cit.*

24. *Ibid.*

25. Similar analyses of data for South African students indicate that the social-adjustment function may also be of unusual importance in the anti-African attitudes of the English in South Africa. See T. F. Pettigrew, "Personality and Sociocultural Factors in Intergroup Attitudes," *Journal of Conflict Resolution,* 1958, Vol. 2, pp. 29–42; and T. F. Pettigrew, "Social Distance Attitudes of South African Students," *Social Forces,* 1960, Vol. 38, pp. 246–253.

26. S. E. Asch, "Effects of Group Pressure upon the Modification and Distortion of Judgments," in H. Guetzkow (ed.), *Groups, Leadership and Men* (Pittsburgh: Carnegie, 1951).

27. R. S. Crutchfield, "Conformity and Character," *American Psychologist,* 1955, Vol. 10, pp. 191–198.

28. H. C. Kelman, "Compliance, Identification, and Internalization: Three Processes of Attitude Change," *Journal of Conflict Resolution,* 1958, Vol. 2, pp. 51–60.

29. L. Festinger, "An Analysis of Compliant Behavior," in M. Sherif and M. O. Wilson (eds.), *Group Relations at the Crossroads* (New York: Harper, 1953); and L. Festinger, *A*

Theory of Cognitive Dissonance (Evanston, Ill.: Row, Peterson, 1957).

30. J. W. Thibaut and H. H. Kelley, *The Social Psychology of Groups* (New York: Wiley, 1959).
31. Asch, *op. cit.*
32. Kelman, *op. cit.*

In Chapters 5 and 6 it was argued that one of the important ways sociology and social psychology can contribute to our understanding of race relations in the United States is through the study of social trends. Seen in the perspective of a broad historical sweep, the dramatic events of today can be more accurately interpreted and more adequately dealt with. Moreover, a thorough grounding in the ongoing racial trends of our society makes possible educated predictions, assuming that the trends will continue. Indeed, we noted in Chapter 5 that a number of sociologists predicted the process of public school desegregation in the South before the ruling of the Supreme Court against de jure separation by race; and their predictions proved extremely accurate.

Social trends occur at both the aggregate level and the individual level, though the distinction between these levels is of heuristic value only. The fact is that broad societal and personal changes must necessarily be inseparably intertwined. We explored in detail in Part One the aggregate trends in American race relations since World

PART THREE

TRENDS IN RACIAL ATTITUDES SINCE WORLD WAR II

War II, noting that significant changes had occurred among black Americans as a group in demography, housing, employment, and education. Now we shall explore what these sweeping changes of the last generation have meant to individual Negroes. What are the personal effects of living in the urban North instead of the rural South, of living in more adequate housing, of coping with a highly skilled labor market, or of having a high school education rather than a grade school education? And what are the effects of these changes upon the racial attitudes of white Americans?

Chapters 7 and 8 offer initial attempts to answer these questions. Chapter 7 asks why black protest reached such feverish proportions during the 1960s and answers this question in terms of the social-psychological consequences upon individual Negro Americans of the social changes under discussion. Viewed in this light, black unrest in the 1960s exemplifies some basic social-psychological ideas about how collective protest is generated among any people in any period of history. In perspective, then, the racial unrest of the 1960s was foreshadowed at least in the previous generation, and it is not likely to subside in the foreseeable future.

Chapter 8 considers the corresponding trend in attitudes of white Americans toward Negro Americans over these same years. To gain a basis for comparison, this trend is related to the similar trend in attitudes toward Jewish Americans. Not only has there been a parallel decline in prejudice toward Negroes and Jews since 1944, but this decline also corresponds neatly to the more obvious institutional changes at the aggregate level. In the atmosphere of despair characterizing recent events, these shifts in attitudes since World War II may come as a surprise; but Chapter 7 documents how these very improvements lead to heightened aspirations and subsequent frustration at any slowing of the pace of change. The reader should, then, recall this process when reviewing the change in attitudes in Chapter 8.

CHAPTER SEVEN

WHY BLACK UNREST IN THE 1960s?

Black Americans have been oppressed for 350 years, first by a unique system of slavery, then by *de jure* and so-called *de facto* racial segregation. And they have protested their plight from the very beginning. Yet the question remains why these protests culminated so forcefully and nationally in the sweeping demonstrations of the 1960s. Why did they not burst forth after Reconstruction? Why not during the Great Depression? Why not decades from now? Why the 1960s?

Actually, the protests of the 1960s provide an almost classic case of *relative deprivation* as an explanation for popular uprisings. According to Davies' model for revolution, the characteristic pattern, repeated throughout history, is a relatively long period of objective economic and social development followed by a short period of sharp reversal.[1] The first portion of the cycle is now underway in the United States; the ominous second stage may be near at hand.

Davies' model appears to fit history well because *improving* conditions typically set off four processes which lead to unrest. Thus, economic progress (1) frequently leads to faster improvement for the dominant group or elite than for the subordinate group, (2) typically creates expectations that rise more rapidly than actual changes, (3) generally leads to widespread status inconsistencies, and (4) often causes a broadening of comparative reference groups.

Living standards of Negro Americans have improved dramatically in absolute terms over the past generation.[2] Indeed, relative to previous gains, the past generation has witnessed the most rapid economic and social advances of any generation of Negro Americans. But these advances have typically not closed the gap between standards of living of whites and blacks:

> Thus, in each interrelated realm—health, employment, business, income, housing, voting, and education—the absolute gains of the 1950's pale when contrasted with current white standards. Numerous spokesmen for the status quo have boasted of the present status of the Negro in glowing international comparisons. Negroes in the United States today, goes one boast, have a consumer buying power comparable to that of similarly-populated Canada. And a larger percentage of Negroes, goes another, attends college than residents of the British Isles. But such glittering statements must not blind us to the fact of greatest psychological importance. Negro American standards have their psychological meaning relative to the standards of other Americans, not of Canadians or the British. The Negro American judges his living standards, his opportunities, indeed, even judges himself, in the only cultural terms he knows—those of the United States and its "people of plenty."[3]

All four of the conditions which set off revolts by improving objective standards were present for Negroes in the United States in the 1960s. First, as was just noted, living conditions of the dominant group are improving more rapidly in a number of realms than living conditions of Negroes. Present discrimination is not necessary to create this situation. Past deprivations handicap many Negroes and deter them from seizing new opportunities: the runner with an initial distance handicap needs more than an equal chance if he is to make a race of it.

Table 3   1954 OPTIMISM FOR THE FUTURE [1]

	Percentage that believe "Life will be better . . . in the next five years"		
	National Negro Sample	National White Sample	White Control Sample [2]
Total sample	64	61	53
By occupation			
Laborer	63	46	. . .
Other blue collar	66	62	. . .
White collar	79	71	. . .
By education			
Grammar school	58	46	. . .
High school	72	66	. . .
College	78	74	. . .
By region			
South	66	55	. . .
Non-South	60	64	. . .

[1] T. F. Pettigrew, *A Profile of the Negro American* (Princeton, N.J.: Van Nostrand, 1964), p. 185.

[2] The white control sample is equated with the Negro sample in terms of age, sex, occupation, geographical region, and years of education.

Second, the expectations of Negroes have climbed faster than actual changes. Even as early as 1954, the year the Supreme Court ruled against *de jure* segregation of public schools, these rising expectations became evident. A large probability sample of Americans was asked by Stouffer in 1954: "On the whole, do you think life will be better for you or worse in the next few years than it is now?" [4] Table 3 shows that, among those with an opinion, 64 percent of the Negro respondents felt life would soon be better, as compared with only 53 percent of a white control sample roughly equivalent to the Negro sample in region of residence, sex, age, years of education, and occupation. Indeed, just as relative-deprivation theory predicts, this heightened optimism of Negroes, relative to that of comparable whites, was especially marked among the most deprived segments of the Negro population: the greatest relative optimism was expressed by Negroes who were laborers, or had only a grammar school education, or resided in the South.[5]

Table 4   1959 AND 1963 MEAN LADDER RATINGS [1]

	"Where do you [does America] stand . . . ?"							
	5 Years Ago		At Present		5 Years From Now		Future-Past Diff.'s	
	1959	1963	1959	1963	1959	1963	1959	1963
Personal								
Negroes	5.9	4.6	5.3	5.2	7.3	6.6	+1.4	+2.0
Whites	6.0	5.7	6.7	6.3	7.9	7.5	+1.9	+1.8
National								
Negroes	6.6	5.3	6.3	6.6	7.2	7.7	+0.6	+2.4
Whites	6.4	6.3	6.7	6.7	7.6	7.3	+1.2	+1.0

[1] These ratings can vary from a low of one to a high of ten. For a full description of this ingenious technique, see H. Cantril, *The Pattern of Human Concerns* (New Brunswick, N.J.: Rutgers University Press, 1965), p. 43.

Cantril provides data from a national survey on his "self-anchoring-ladder" questions for 1959 and 1963.[6] Though the figures for Negroes in Table 4 are based on relatively small samples, a number of the results are suggestive. While personal ratings by Negroes are all lower in 1963 than in 1959, note the sizable shift in 1963 between the past and future personal ratings. This trend is even stronger for the 1963 ratings of the United States by Negroes. The sharp alterations of the data for Negroes, in contrast to the stable data for whites, are partly a function of the larger sizes of the white samples; but the remarkably high hopes of Negroes in 1963 for national progress in the future appear to represent a definite racial difference. In response to open-ended questions about national and personal hopes and fears, Negroes cite far more social goals and aspirations for their nation than whites. On the personal level, white respondents report more hopes concerning health and family, whereas Negroes report more economic hopes.

Table 5 1963 NEGRO OPTIMISM FOR THE FUTURE [1]

	". . . five years from now, do you feel . . . you will be . . ."				
	Better Off	Worse Off	About the Same	Not Sure	Total
Pay	67%	2%	14%	17%	100%
Work situation	64%	3%	15%	18%	100%
Housing accommodations	62%	2%	24%	12%	100%
Being able to get children educated with white children	58%	1%	21%	20%	100%
Being able to eat in any restaurant	55%	1%	31%	13%	100%
Being able to register and vote	42%	1%	48%	9%	100%

[1] Adapted from Brink and Harris, *The Negro Revolution in America* (New York: Simon and Schuster, 1964), p. 238.

Another national survey made by Brink and Harris in 1963 questioned only black Americans.[7] It asked: "Thinking ahead to five years from now, if you had to say right now, do you feel in [your work situation, your housing accommodations, your pay, being able to get your children educated with white children, being able to eat in any restaurant, or being able to register and vote] you will be better off, worse off, or about the same as you are right now?" Table 5 again shows the high aspirations of Negro Americans. Note, too, that only 1 to 3 percent considered a slip backward likely. In response to open-ended queries, many Negroes made it clear that they expected to be better off in five years because of reduced racial discrimination.

Consistent with these expectations, 73 percent of this

national Negro sample expected in 1963 that attitudes of whites toward Negroes would be better in five years, and only 2 percent anticipated that they would be worse. Also, 73 percent thought whites would accept racial change without violence; 33 percent expected "a lot" of integration in the next five years; and 85 percent wanted to own a private house. Though only 23 percent reported that they held white-collar jobs in 1963, 47 percent wanted such jobs and considered themselves qualified. Not surprisingly, then, Brink and Harris find that 51 percent felt in 1963 that "progress on Negro rights" was "too slow." [8]

As uncovered by the analysis of the Coleman Report, a key variable in this process is the Negro's sense of environmental control.[9] Shomer shows that only self-attributed gains lead to higher aspirations.[10] If advances of Negroes in recent decades were perceived as paternalistically "given" by whites, these advances would presumably have had far less psychological impact than they have had in fact—since they are typically seen as "won" by Negroes whose control over their fate is expanding.

A third consequence of rising standards is an increase in status inconsistency. In one sense, status inconsistency increases by definition as gains in education, employment, and income are made by Negroes. At least in Lenski's and Jackson's procedures, the Negro's racial status in America is regarded as low, and all Negroes of high educational, occupational, or income status are classified as "status inconsistents." And, as was noted briefly in Chapter 5, this particular type of inconsistency—low ascribed status combined with high achieved status—is precisely the pattern of inconsistency, among both whites and Negroes, that is associated with strong desires for political change.[11]

But status inconsistency among black Americans is increasing in a more fundamental sense. Census data show that as far back as 1940 educational attainment of Negroes had already exceeded their attainments in employment and income.[12] This form of status inconsistency has increased much further in the past generation.[13] From

1940 to 1960, census data reveal larger percentage gains in years of education for nonwhites than for whites; while over the same years percentage gains for nonwhites in occupation and income have not kept pace with the gains for whites. Though simple "years of education" has different quality meanings for Negroes and whites, and absolute educational gains at the higher levels of education have been greater for whites than Negroes, the rising amount of *status* inconsistency between, on the one hand, education and, on the other, occupation and income is still an important characteristic of Negro America.[14]

The fourth product of long-term prosperity and advances is a broadening of comparative reference groups. Studies in the North and South and on Negroes and whites repeatedly find a more differentiated view of the social stratification system among those of higher status.[15] One has to be reasonably elevated before he can view the entire social terrain. But how have the objective social gains of the past generation altered the referents for Negro Americans? In what senses do white Americans become relevant referents, and under what conditions?

The processes involved in selecting referents are obviously complex. At the extremes of Negro life, white referents can be so strongly employed for evaluation that exaggerated behavior can result. Frazier maintains that a zealous adoption of white upper-middle-class referents as a positive reference group helps explain some of the exaggerated behavior he describes as characteristic of a segment of the expanding Negro middle class.[16] And Lincoln maintains that a zealous adoption of white Christian referents as a *negative* reference group helps explain some of the anti-white and anti-Christian beliefs and behavior of the Black Muslims.[17] The complexity of the problem is further illustrated by the Black Muslims' successful efforts to inculcate middle-class values in its members.

Speculations, at least, are possible. It seems reasonably certain that the living conditions and other external attributes of white Americans serve as comparison levels for black Americans more today than formerly. This is not to imply that white comparisons did not serve an evaluative function previously; but white comparisons are now perceived as the appropriate standards to which Negroes are entitled as American citizens. The anchors of the distribution of American prosperity are less fixed now; and, as the social-comparison experiment by Thornton and Arrowood demonstrates, this shift means that divergent referents are more informative than similar referents.[18]

Note that this subtle shift in the use of levels of whites as standards for comparison could be occurring without any significant increase in contact as equals between Negroes and whites. Indeed, as was noted in Chapter 2, data for such realms as segregation of urban housing suggest that racial separation since 1940 has actually increased.[19] Turner maintains that when evaluations are made using only external attributes of the referent, as in estimating satisfaction or social standing, "taking the role" of the referent is not necessary.[20] The shift does require greater knowledge by Negroes since 1940 of the external attributes of white Americans; and this condition appears to be met through the somewhat higher social positions of many Negroes as well as the explosion in white-oriented mass communication since 1940.

Runciman's distinction between "egoist" and "fraternalist" deprivation, between one's deprived status within the group and the deprived status of the group in the wider society, is useful here.[21] In Table 4, the differences between personal and national hopes for the future in the data for Negroes show that fraternalist aspirations are actually higher than egoist aspirations. In other words, Cantril's results suggest that many Negroes in 1963 expected major gains for their group's status in the total American society during the following five years, but they had somewhat more modest expectations for their own rise in status. Clearly, fraternalistic hopes for an improvement in the entire group's status must of necessity employ white Americans as referent; but it may well be that egoist hopes are typically made relative to similar Negro referents within the larger context of the total group's position. Research is obviously needed on these points, and such work could benefit from the use of Runciman's two types of evaluations.

Popular uprisings are not generally started and led by the most objectively deprived. Relative-deprivation theory leads one to predict that relatively upper-status individuals will initiate protests. They are the people elevated enough to judge the discrimination against their group; they are the ones who have received the most gains within the group and have thereby experienced the most severe status inconsistencies. Moreover, upper-status individuals are secure enough to hold out hope for a better life—an essential ingredient in any movement for social change. Brinton observes:

The revolutionary movements seem to originate in the discontents of not unprosperous people who feel restraint, cramp, annoyance, rather than downright crushing oppression. . . . [They] are not worms turning, not children of despair. These revolutions are born of hope, and their philosophies are formally optimistic.[22]

The sit-ins led by college students provide an excellent illustration of upper-status blacks initiating protest. Matthews and Prothro present data on Negro college students and their participation in sit-ins and other protest demonstrations during the early 1960s.[23] Not only are college students a high-status group within the Negro community, but those students who take part have particularly high status. Only one fourth of the students sampled report personal participation; 85 percent approve of the demonstrations. This active fourth, when compared with other Negro students, are more often from large cities and relatively high-income families whose heads hold white-collar jobs. They are more likely to be either juniors or seniors who major in a "prestige" subject (humanities, natural sciences, or social sciences) rather than a practical subject (vocational, teaching, or business administration). Moreover, the activists are more likely to attend a better-quality private institution, located in a Southern area with a low percentage of Negroes in the population. Activists also differ from the other students in their racial attitudes. While more likely to rate race relations in the South as extremely bad, they nevertheless hold out more hope for change. They *less* often agree that "all white people are prejudiced against Negroes," less often think that half or more of white Southerners favor "strict segregation," and less often feel that their home community is worse than the South as a whole. These results are consistent with those of Gore and Rotter, who find that the Negro college students willing to participate in protest possess a greater sense of environment control.[24]

But what of the future? Race relations in the United States, it seems, remain perpetually in a state of crisis. Yet Davies' model predicts that a particularly critical time will occur whenever there is a period of sudden and sharp reversal in the Negro's struggle for full participation in American society.[25] In some ways, 1966 to 1970, years of slowed civil rights activity and progress, suggest that such a time may be near at hand. Much depends on the duration of the war in Vietnam and the domestic decisions made at its close. Recall that some of the nation's most tragic racial conflicts have occurred during wars or just after their close—the so-called "draft riots" of 1863, the bloody summer of 1919, and the race riots in Detroit, Harlem, and Los Angeles in 1943 are a few examples. This relationship seems to hold true for several reasons: wartime prosperity in jobs and wages, combined with wartime domestic shortages, often raises relative-deprivation levels drastically; the nation's attention becomes so internationally fixed that such domestic concerns as civil rights receive little attention; and at a war's close, there is often an economic recession and too loose a labor market to absorb the veterans who re-enter the labor force.

The close of the war in Vietnam need not repeat this sad history; moreover, the forms that protests assume will be significantly shaped by the circumstances of the national situation at the time.

An Overview

Why black unrest in the 1960s? The data reviewed in this chapter support the view that a strong feeling of *relative deprivation* has supplied the basic psychodynamic behind the Negro push for racial change. But it remains to put this theory in the context of competing theories; and we need, too, to raise further questions, such as these: Why was this unrest channeled into urban rioting in the middle and late 1960s? What altered this pattern of mass rioting at the close of the decade?

In their useful compilation of explanations for civil disorders, Masotti and Bowen contend that all the major theories reduce to four basic themes.[26] The first two of these themes center on the individual level, and both were employed in the view just presented. One theme stresses deprivation, both absolute and relative. For it to operate, inequality must be perceived and must be considered unjust. As we have noted, both of these conditions were met by blacks in the 1960s. The second theme emphasizes high expectations of a restless minority, the so-called "want-get ratio." This notion differs from relative deprivation only in that the perceived inequality is a difference between what you have compared with your previously established expectations rather than with a relevant reference group. In real life, of course, this fine theoretical distinction is generally lost; the first two explanations, then, blend to form the theory put forward in this chapter.

The remaining two themes have to do with broader social levels. One focuses attention upon group conflict and struggles for power. It emphasizes sharp social cleavages, rather than social bonds; it therefore applies with special force when two or more significant cleavages correlate highly. For example, the high association in the United States between skin color and social class should according to this theory, create the conditions for an especially severe power conflict. The theory would further predict that as the Negro middle class grows in numbers, the struggle would subside, because the cross-racial ties of mutual class interest would naturally expand. This idea under certain conditions conflicts with predictions based on relative-deprivation theory, and it does not fit with the fact that the Negro middle class has furnished most of the leadership of the drive for change in recent years.

Masotti and Bowen call their fourth theme the "systemic hypothesis." It places civil disorders on a broad canvas and sees them as the logical consequence of a breakdown of consensual norms and the inability or unwillingness of agencies of social control to restore these norms. This systemic explanation points to sweeping social trends in industrialization, urbanization, and modernization, argues that these trends create new classes of citizens with conflicting perceptions and life styles, and maintains that anomie and alienation are the necessary results of these alterations in the social fabric. This theory, then, would pay special attention to the mass migration of black Americans out of the rural South since 1915. Indeed, we have already seen how many of these broad societal trends fit with the relative-deprivation explanation, though anomie and alienation do not appear to set in until the high hopes for the future within the system are dashed over an extended period.

Within this broader context, we can now pose questions about the pattern of urban rioting into which Negro unrest spilled. Why urban riots? And why did this pattern seem to shift by the end of the decade?

Masotti and Bowen again provide an important framework for considering these queries.[27] They maintain that riots and rebellion are both civil disorders in that they challenge the civil and political order. Race riots, they insist, are not merely magnified crime or an undirected libidinal release, for neither of these popular explanations explain the directly *racial* targets of these urban disturbances. Yet since both forms are civil disorders, older theories of rebellion should still apply to riots.

But why did black frustrations in the 1960s culminate in mass urban rioting and not in open rebellion? Masotti and Bowen supply three answers. First, despite rhetoric to the contrary from the New Left, the perceived legitimacy of the *national government* among black Americans remains high; but the perceived legitimacy of *local* officials is often low. The low esteem in which the urban police are held by Negroes has been considered in detail in Chapter 1; and this situation is fundamental to the suspicion in which local officials are held. Second, riots rather than rebellion result when the capacity of the system for force as well as reform is perceived to be high. And, finally, the legacies of history affect forms of protest. The United States has had a long and bloody history of racial rioting, most of it violence by whites against Negroes; but revolutionary movements have been rare on the American scene since the successful initial one in the eighteenth century.

This plausible explanation for the pattern of urban riots heightens interest in why the pattern began to break up by 1969–1970. Considerations of relative deprivation provide a partial answer. Richard Milhouse Nixon was not the choice of black Americans in the Presidential election of 1968: well over nine-tenths of all Negro voters cast their ballots for Hubert Humphrey, the candidate of the Democratic Party; in fact, black votes constituted one-fifth of Humphrey's total—the highest percentage they ever comprised of a major presidential candidate's total. Nixon ran on a so-called "Southern strategy" (better termed a "segregationist strategy"), and, true to his word, behaved accordingly once in the White House. Negro Americans understandably expected little of him or his administration; and they were not disappointed. This has had the effect of lowering black expectations for short-term racial gains, though several studies in 1970 indicated that long-term personal and group aspirations remained high. Relative-deprivation theory predicts that such a trend would temporarily cool racial protests and disturbances. This is not to argue that Negro Americans were more satisfied during such a time, or that they accepted with equanimity such inevitable results of the Southern strategy as the blatant murders of Negroes by the police in Jackson, Mississippi, and Augusta, Georgia, in May of 1970. But it can reasonably be argued that riots are less likely during a period of low expectations combined with fear of national repression against Negroes in general.

Related explanations of the decline in large-scale urban rioting since 1968 emphasize the negative consequences of mass violence to the black community itself. The victims of the pattern of ghetto rioting from 1965 to 1968 were overwhelmingly Negro. Once a black area had suffered a destructive riot, it was not rich soil for another. "How many times can you burn down the same building?" is the popular statement of this point. The potency of this idea is suggested by the fact that during the 1960s the same ghetto never endured two major disturbances. Consequently, smaller cities, which had not previously known the agony of widespread violence, tended to be those involved in the comparatively few riots from the summer of 1968 through the remainder of the decade.[28] And to the extent the pattern persists into the 1970s, it will center in smaller cities and in the South, where riots have been less prevalent.

Two possible alternatives for violent expression could replace this pattern. One would involve rioting in predominantly white areas well outside the ghetto. The other would involve avoiding mass participation and focusing instead on types of guerrilla action. But either of these alternatives would surely trigger swift counteraction, quite possibly indiscriminate repression against black Americans in general. For some years now, the often-voiced fear in the ghetto has been that politicians and police officials motivated by fear would initiate a wave of repression against black Americans, even to the point of mass internment camps tragically modeled after those for Japanese Americans during World War II. This can hardly be dismissed as collective black paranoia when officials of Mr. Mitchell's Justice Department themselves hint at such possibilities.

Various patterns of racial violence, as well as other expressions of unrest, will persist in our cities for some time, waxing and waning to reflect both the national scene and local scenes. Yet the pattern of mass urban rioting which swept the nation in the 1960s is not likely to be replicated in the 1970s. In addition to the reasons just cited, there is a popular opinion among Negro Americans that the riots of the past decade served their purpose in "waking up white America," in attracting attention to the true conditions and feelings which exist in the bowels of the ghettos. Most Negroes deplored the riots, yet felt that they "did more good than harm" to the cause of achieving racial justice in America. And the dominant black opinion, as surveys throughout the country repeatedly show, is that the positive functions of mass rioting have been served and further reenactments would prove largely counterproductive. Even the tough-talking Black Panthers argue for different strategies, especially efforts in coalition with young whites. Without widespread community willingness to tolerate rioting, the typical mass disturbances of the 1960s would be difficult to mount.

Preventing urban race riots, however, should not and cannot be the chief national goal in American race relations. Affirmative, structural programs directed at the root causes of the unrest are clearly necessary. Specific programs in law enforcement, housing, employment, income, and education were cited in earlier chapters. And we shall consider, in Chapter 12, a more inclusive general strategy for addressing the genuine grievances which underlie black unrest.

Footnotes

1. J. C. Davies, "Toward a Theory of Revolution," *American Sociological Review,* 1962, Vol. 27, pp. 5–19.
2. J. A. Geschwender, "Social Structure and The Negro Revolt: An Examination of Some Hypotheses," *Social Forces,* 1964, Vol. 43, pp. 248–256; and T. F. Pettigrew, *A Profile of the Negro American* (Princeton, N.J.: Van Nostrand, 1964).
3. Pettigrew, *op. cit.,* p. 191.
4. S. A. Stouffer, *Communism, Conformity and Civil Liberties* (New York: Doubleday, 1955).
5. Pettigrew, *op. cit.,* pp. 184–185.
6. H. Cantril, *The Pattern of Human Concerns* (New Brunswick, N.J.: Rutgers University Press, 1965), pp. 42–44, 407.
7. W. Brink and L. Harris, *The Negro Revolution in America* (New York: Simon and Schuster, 1964).
8. *Ibid.*
9. J. S. Coleman *et al., Equality of Educational Opportunity* (Washington: U.S. Government Printing Office, 1966).
10. R. W. Shomer, "Effects of Chance and Skill Outcomes on Expectancy, Recall, and Distributive Allocations" (unpublished doctoral dissertation, University of California at Los Angeles, 1966).
11. G. E. Lenski, "Status Crystalization: A Non-Vertical Dimension of Social Status," *American Sociological Review,* 1954, Vol. 19, pp. 405–413; G. E. Lenski, "Social Participation and Status Crystalization," *American Sociological Review,* 1956, Vol. 21, pp. 458–464; E. F. Jackson, "Status Inconsistency and Symptoms of Stress," *American Sociological Review,* 1962, Vol. 27, pp. 469–480; G. B. Rush, "Status Inconsistency and Right-Wing Extremism," *American Sociological Review,* 1967, Vol. 32, pp. 86–92.
12. R. H. Turner, "Foci of Discrimination in the Employment of Non-Whites," *American Journal of Sociology,* 1952, Vol. 58, pp. 247–256.
13. Geschwender, *op. cit.,* pp. 248–256.
14. S. Parker and R. Kleiner, *Mental Illness in the Urban Negro Community* (New York: Free Press, 1966), p. 293. Parker and Kleiner regard education as an indicator of aspiration, and

occupation as an indicator of achievement. Thus, they maintain that the type of status inconsistency involving high education and low occupation is a direct measure of relative deprivation. And, as with their other measures of relative deprivation, they find it positively related to mental illness among their samples of Negroes in Philadelphia.

15. A. Davis, B. Gardner and M. Gardner, *Deep South* (Chicago: University of Chicago Press, 1941); F. R. Westie, "Negro-White Status Differentials and Social Distance," *American Sociological Review,* 1952, Vol. 17, pp. 550–558; and F. R. Westie and D. H. Howard, "Social Status Differentials and the Race Attitudes of Negroes," *American Sociological Review,* 1954, Vol. 19, pp. 584–591.

16. E. F. Frazier, *Black Bourgeoisie* (Glencoe, Ill.: Free Press, 1957).

17. C. E. Lincoln, *The Black Muslims in America* (Boston: Beacon Press, 1961).

18. D. A. Thornton and A. J. Arrowood, "Self-Evaluation, Self-Enhancement, and the Locus of Social Comparison," *Journal of Experimental and Social Psychology,* 1966, Vol. 2 (Supplement 1), pp. 40–48.

19. K. E. Taueber and A. F. Taueber, *Negroes in Cities* (Chicago: Aldine, 1965).

20. R. H. Turner, "Role-Taking, Role Standpoint, and Reference Group Behavior," *American Journal of Sociology,* 1956, Vol. 61, pp. 316–328.

21. W. G. Runciman, *Relative Deprivation and Social Justice* (London: Rutledge and Kegan Paul, 1966).

22. C. Brinton, *The Anatomy of Revolution* (New York: Prentice-Hall, 1952).

23. D. R. Matthews and J. W. Prothro, *Negroes and the New Southern Politics* (New York: Harcourt, Brace and World, 1966).

24. P. M. Gore and J. B. Rotter, "A Personality Correlate of Social Action," *Journal of Personality,* 1963, Vol. 31, pp. 58–64.

25. Davies, *op. cit.*

26. L. H. Masotti and D. R. Bowen (eds.), *Riots and Rebellion: Civil Violence in the Urban Community* (Beverly Hills, Calif.: Sage Publications, 1968).

27. *Ibid.*

28. The interesting results of John White are consistent with this observation. For race riots during the years from 1963 through 1967, he found three variables most important in distinguishing cities which had had riots from those which had not. All three indicate that the large ghettos in major cities were more

likely to have blown up during these years. Thus, the larger the percentage of nonwhites in a city's population, the greater the city's total population, and the more dense the city, the more likely it was to have had a riot. J. G. White, "Riots and Theory Building," in Masotti and Bowen, *op. cit.*, pp. 157–165.

CHAPTER EIGHT

PARALLEL AND DISTINCTIVE CHANGES IN ANTI-SEMITIC AND ANTI-NEGRO ATTITUDES

A revealing incident occurred in Little Rock, Arkansas, during the city's hectic days in the late 1950s. The vociferous local chapter of the segregationist White Citizens' Council suddenly and summarily expelled one of its principal leaders on the grounds that he was an anti-Semite. "You see," a Council official explained candidly, "we had to throw him out, because we can't afford to be seen as an anti-Jewish organization. Why, we are having trouble enough just being anti-Negro!"

Even for the White Citizens' Council in Little Rock, then, it has become inadvisable to be too explicitly bigoted. Indeed, "prejudice" is now a derogatory term in the United States. Obviously, this is not to say that the nation is free from prejudice; many bigoted groups and individuals are still extremely active. But these generally take pains to maintain that they are not prejudiced.[1] Thus, the White Citizens' Councils stoutly insist that they work, not to keep the Negro down, but only to prevent racial strife. Similarly, in Northern cities, segregationist groups of white parents claim that they are not resisting desegregation but only supporting neighborhood schools.

This phenomenon signals a significant change in relation with American minority groups. The new situation has, perhaps, been captured best in Peter Viereck's concept of "transtolerance":

Transtolerance is ready to give all minorities their glorious democratic freedom—provided they accept McCarthyism or some other mob conformism of Right or Left. . . . Transtolerance is also a sublimated Jim Crow, against "wrong" thinkers, not "wrong" races. . . . It is . . . a strictly kosher anti-Semitism.[2]

There is considerable evidence that transtolerance has its uses. For example, Robert Welch, the leader of the far-right John Birch Society, boasts of his group's Jewish and Roman Catholic members. According to Alan Westin, the Society even has two segregated Negro chapters in the South.[3] Though well-known anti-Semitic and anti-Negro figures are prominent in the organization, Welch insists that it is a "communist tactic to stir up distrust and hatred between Jews and Gentiles, Catholics and Protestants, Negroes and Whites."[4] In the same vein, the Reverend Billy James Hargis, a far-right fundamentalist minister who leads what he calls a crusade against Communism, tells his followers: "We cannot tolerate anti-Semitic statements [or] anti-Negro statements."[5] Transtolerance was widely apparent in the campaigns of the Republican Presidential and Vice-Presidential candidates in 1964—the candidates overwhelmingly supported by far-right organizations. The triple religious nature of the team of Barry M. Goldwater and William E. Miller had a special appeal. "Barry's a Protestant and a Jew, and I'm a Catholic," Miller was quoted as remarking during the campaign. "Anybody who's against that ticket is a damn bigot."[6] Miller's lyrics are different, but the tune is somehow the same.

From data such as these, Seymour Martin Lipset concludes:

. . . The object of intolerance in America has never been as important as the style, the emotion, the antagonism and envy toward some specified other who is seen as wealthier, more powerful, or particularly, as a corrupter of basic values. . . . Anti-elitism oriented toward groups that cannot be regarded as oppressed minorities or victims of bigotry, or anti-Communism directed against the agents or dupes of an evil foreign power, can serve as much more palatable outlets for those who require a scapegoat than "un-American" attacks on minorities. . . . The current crop of radical rightists seems to understand this difference.[7]

Obviously, this shift on the part of the far right reflects a sharp change in public norms concerning minorities in the United States during recent years. Charles Stember's useful compilation of data derived from opinion polls demonstrates conclusively that this change is reflected in reduced prejudice toward Jews.[8] It is the purpose of this chapter to explore further aspects of this critical change in norms. Have the attitudes of white Americans toward Negro Americans also undergone a major change? How do anti-Semitic and anti-Negro attitudes today resemble each other, and how do they differ?

Resemblances between Anti-Semitic and Anti-Negro Attitudes: Responses to Polls

In many ways, attitudes toward Negroes provide the acid test of American tolerance of minorities. From the first landing of Africans at Jamestown in 1619 to the racial crisis of the 1970s, the relations between blacks and whites have been inseparable from the nation's roots and development. Anti-Semitism is not nearly as deeply embedded in American life as anti-Negro sentiment; explicit discrimination against Jews did not begin here until late in the nineteenth century, two centuries after slavery had received legal sanction. Therefore, if we want to learn whether the striking reduction in anti-Semitism between 1937 and 1962 represents a more general trend in intergroup relations, we must see if responses to polls manifesting a hostility to Negroes show a similar reduction over the same years.

Herbert H. Hyman and Paul B. Sheatsley present the relevant data in an analysis of replies to certain questions concerning blacks, which were asked periodically from 1942 to 1963 by the National Opinion Research Center.[9] A look at their results reveals marked parallels with Stember's, both where stereotypes and where discriminatory practices were concerned. Thus, while the percentage of Americans who did not think Jews less honest than others rose from 56 to 82 between 1938 and 1962, the percentage who believed Negroes to be as intelligent as whites rose from 42 to 74 between 1942 and 1963. While the percentage who did not think colleges should limit enrollment of Jews increased from 74 to 96, the percentage favoring racially desegregated schools increased from 30 to 63. Analogous shifts also occurred in attitudes toward heterogeneous neighborhoods: over the same years, the percentage voicing no objections to a Jewish neighbor went up from 75 to 97, and those with no objections to a Negro neighbor rose from 35 to 63 percent.[10]

A further parallel may be found in the high points of animosity against the two groups. Stember shows that during the closing years of the Second World War American anti-Semitism reached its highest point within the last generation; Hyman and Sheatsley note a peak in anti-Negro opinions about the same time. Stember presents evidence of this parallel intensity as of 1944: four groups— Protestants, Catholics, Jews, and Negroes—were named, and respondents were asked: "Against which *one* of these groups, *if any,* do you think prejudice or feeling has increased the most?" Thirty-seven percent named Jews; 31 percent chose Negroes.[11] Anti-Semitic and anti-Negro attitudes, then, have both declined over the past generation from peaks of intensity reached simultaneously during the tense war years.

Such striking parallels raise two questions. Do the changes in responses reflect actual reductions in prejudice? And, if so, are these reductions endangered by the so-called "white backlash"—the widely reported reaction of threatened whites in Northern cities against the blacks' demands for change? Each of these issues deserves discussion, for each might well limit severely the conclusions which can be safely drawn from the data so carefully compiled by Stember and by Hyman and Sheatsley.

With some justification, certain observers doubt whether polling can fathom the full depth of most respondents' anti-Semitic or anti-Negro prejudices. What has decreased from the late 1930s to today, they argue, is not prejudice, but the respectability of prejudice—in this case, readiness to admit bigotry to a poll taker. Yet, even if only this standard of respectability had changed, that would itself be noteworthy. For what is "real" prejudice? A change in verbal behavior is certainly "real" in a most important sense.

In any case, need we be so limiting? No doubt the open espousal of anti-Jewish and anti-Negro attitudes became markedly less respectable during the past generation. But this change would seem to be only one among many symptoms of a deeper, more meaningful lessening of prejudice. Indeed, there are a number of reasons for accepting the major shifts reported by the opinion polls as genuine, at least in large part.

First, rapport in the polling situation is generally far closer than those unfamiliar with the technique realize. A pleasant, attentive stranger who has gone to some trouble to record your opinion on vital issues, and who does not provide any cues of disagreement, is often a much safer confidant than acquaintances.

Second, the remarkable consistency of the trends in attitudes toward Jews and Negroes extends to a wide variety of questions, asked by different polling agencies. Presumably, the questions vary considerably in "respectability bias" (or, to use the parlance of modern testing theory, in "social desirability"); thus, if the results were largely a reflection of "respectability bias," we would not expect the consistency noted both by Stember and by Hyman and Sheatsley.

Third, certain questions concerning Jews and Negroes which appear to involve a built-in "respectability bias" as great as any of Stember's items have *not* changed over the past few decades. For example, the National Opinion Research Center has repeatedly asked representative nationwide samples if they "think most Negroes in the United States are being treated fairly or unfairly." The responses have remained quite stable over the years; in both 1946 and 1956, 63 percent answered, "Fairly." [12]

Fourth, election results have borne out the evidence from polls on intergroup attitudes. Ithiel de Sola Pool and his associates attempted to simulate the 1960 Presidential election using only data from polls gathered before 1959. [13] To predict the crucial anti-Catholic vote against John F. Kennedy, Pool used the simple and straightforward question, "Would you be willing to vote for a qualified Catholic for President?"—surely as frontal a measure of prejudice as any employed to explore attitudes toward Jews and Negroes. Yet, for all its obviousness, the question produced a response that proved remarkably accurate and useful in simulating the actual 1960 election. As the authors state in their intriguing volume:

Millions of Protestants and other non-Catholics who would otherwise have voted Democratic could not bring themselves to vote for a Catholic. In total—so our model says—roughly one out of five Protestant Democrats or Protestant Independents who would otherwise have voted Democratic bolted because of the religious issue. The actual number of bolters varied with the voter-type and was determined in the model by the proportion of that voter-type who had replied on surveys that they would not want to vote for a Catholic for President. What our model tends to show is that the poll question was a good one. The model suggests that the number of people who overcame the social inhibitions to admitting prejudice to a polltaker was about the same as the number who overcame the political inhibitions to bolting their party for reasons of bias.[14]

The final reason for accepting data from polls as an adequate measure of prejudice is the most compelling of all. The sharp diminution of anti-minority responses in the polls is completely consistent with the changes in the treatment of minorities over the same years. Discrimination in a wide range of American institutions has lessened at least as much as verbalized prejudice. This process is a two-way street: on the one hand, reductions of prejudice speed the erosion of discrimination; on the other hand—what is probably more important—the decline of discrimination permits increasing contact between groups on a basis of equality, and thus tends to decrease prejudice.[15]

Of course, none of these arguments implies that discriminatory practices against minorities have ceased in the United States. Roughly two-thirds of the nation's private clubs retain religious restrictions; housing patterns based on religious discrimination continue; and some major law firms, as well as the executive corps of the automotive and utility industries, still discriminate against Jews in their recruitment.[16] Moreover, the most elaborate and debilitating barriers of all—those maintained for three centuries against the Negro—are only now slowly beginning to be dismantled. The polls clearly reflect these remaining barriers, indicating that prejudice is still intense in certain sectors of the society. The actual treatment of Jews and Negroes, then, substantiates findings concerning attitudes toward these groups in two separate respects: it confirms that hostility has markedly diminished during recent years, but it also confirms that hostility remains concentrated in particular sectors.

What about the "white backlash"? Does this much-publicized phenomenon indicate a rise in anti-Negro prejudice? Relevant data strongly suggest that it does not. The concept of a backlash was fashioned by journalists for its sensational flavor, not by social scientists for its heuristic value; the evidence that purports to demonstrate its existence lacks the most rudimentary research controls and safeguards. A more detached view, relying upon controlled data, and free from the pressure of deadlines that characterizes the mass media, leads one to doubt that a significant anti-Negro reaction has swept the nation.

The term "backlash" implies that many whites in the North, once mildly sympathetic to Negro aspirations, have suddenly changed their minds and hardened their resistance to racial change. The term first gained favor in the mass media during 1964, when George C. Wallace, the segregationist Governor of Alabama, made a number of relatively successful political sorties into the North. He entered the Democratic Presidential primaries in Wisconsin, Indiana, and Maryland and, to the surprise of many, polled sizable minorities—from roughly 30 percent in Indiana to 43 percent in Maryland. Many observers inferred from these results that an anti-Negro "backlash" was in full swing. Soon every reasonably large vote for a reactionary candidate anywhere in the North and West was cited as a symptom of the supposed "backlash," and even Lyndon Johnson, who was then President, freely used the term in his conversations with reporters.

But throughout this period, national public-opinion polls conducted by Louis Harris revealed a steadily mounting majority in favor of pending civil rights legislation, though these polls were largely overlooked. In November, 1963, an estimated 63 percent of adult Americans favored the Federal Civil Rights Bill; by February, 1964, the figure had risen to 68 percent, and by May it stood at 70 percent—a steady gain of 7 percent in six months, and a strange phenomenon to be occurring in the midst of an alleged anti-black reaction.

Why, then, did Wallace do so well in the primaries in three Northern and border states? An array of well-established principles of social science suggests a number of answers. For one thing, the mass media emphasized the percentage of the votes won by Wallace without thoroughly considering the size of the total vote. The number of votes cast in the three state elections was considerably above the usual turnouts for Democratic Presidential primaries. The apparent "backlash," then, was evidently caused by large numbers of people who do not normally vote in these primaries, people attracted to the polls by the protest implied in Wallace's candidacy but not necessarily by his position on racial matters. Furthermore, Wallace's candidacy did not have to be regarded seriously, and this is a factor of major importance in protest voting. Hadley Cantril has shown, for instance, that many French and Italian voters find their support of the Communist ticket a satisfying expression of protest, though they are not members of the Communist Party and would not want the Communists to gain control of their governments.[17] "Voting Communist can't hurt me," reasons one Frenchman. "It may help me. Nothing like putting a big scare into the *patron*." [18] By the same token, Wallace made an ideal magnet for protest voters of all varieties, precisely because there was so little chance of his actually becoming President. His relative success in the primaries, then, did not necessarily require or reflect any large-scale changing of minds. The many journalists who reasoned that it did were guilty of a blatant form of the ecological fallacy.[19] We shall return to the "Wallace phenomenon" in Chapter 10, where the basis of Wallace's support in 1968 will be considered in detail.

The analyses by the mass media also assumed, without the benefit of before-and-after comparisons, that the racial attitudes of many white Americans were changing, notably in Northern industrial areas. To be certain that people were generally more anti-Negro in July of 1964 than they had been in 1963, we obviously need to know their attitudes in both years. Yet the media did not provide such necessary evidence.

The nearest attempt to obtain before-and-after data was a city-wide poll administered by reporters for *The New York Times* in September, 1964.[20] This survey employed the risky procedure of asking the respondent in retrospect whether he had changed his mind. In addition, the wording of the questions asked was strongly biased: "Have you been affected in any way by a 'white backlash'? Have you changed your thinking during the last couple of months? Which category [of those detailed below] describes your feelings?" To mention the supposed phenomenon by its familiar name and then to suggest the "backlash" alternative the respondent is expected to select is, of course, contrary to all standards of competent polling. Indeed, it is virtually equivalent to asking a sample of ladies: "Do you like the chic new Parisian fashions which simply everyone is raving about?"

As it happens, New Yorkers are a relatively hardy, independent lot. Only 27 percent of a roughly random selection of the city's whites agreed they were now "more opposed to what Negroes want"; 62 percent insisted they still felt "pretty much the same"; and 6 percent maintained that they actually were "more strongly in favor of what Negroes want" than they had been earlier. Abandoning its usual caution, the *Times* captioned the story, "Results Indicate 'Backlash' Exists"; but, once again, the evidence is hardly conclusive. Many of the persons included in the critical 27 percent may actually have been as hostile to Negroes in 1963 as in 1964, and an undetermined number were undoubtedly swayed by the "loaded" questions.

Fortunately, before-and-after data derived from both elections and polls do exist. In Boston's School Committee elections, for example, a ticket of candidates ran for five positions in 1961, before the issue of *de facto* school segregation had erupted in the city, and a similar group ran again in 1963, after the issue had become important. One of the candidates on both occasions was a militant black; another was a white woman, Mrs. Hicks, who between the two elections had become prominent as an outspoken defender of school segregation. (We shall discuss Mrs. Hicks, her campaigns, and her voters in Chapter 9.) In both contests the Negro candidate ran a strong, though losing, seventh; the segregationist won a seat each time. The mass media emphasized that the segregationist had received a sharply higher percentage of the vote in 1963 than in 1961, presenting this fact as evidence of a powerful "white backlash." Actually, in this case, as in the primaries where Wallace ran strongly, great numbers of voters seem to have come out from under the rocks. About twice as many voters went to the polls in 1963 as in 1961, an increase large enough to account for much of Mrs. Hicks's improved showing. It should be noted that the Negro candidate, too, held or bettered his record in total votes in virtually every precinct.

Relevant data from public-opinion polls have been compiled by the National Opinion Research Center.[21] An intensive study of racial attitudes throughout the United States was conducted in December, 1963. In a follow-up the next summer, re-interviews using the same unbiased questions were held with those white members of the original sample who lived in large Northern industrial areas, where the "backlash" was allegedly occurring. Analyses of the results are instructive. Basic attitudes toward the goals of racial change had not shifted: those whites who had previously favored the desegregation of schools, public facilities, and neighborhoods still predominantly favored it; those who had previously opposed it still opposed it.[22] Nor had voting intentions for the Presidency shifted because of the race issue, except among a minute fraction,[23] as was amply borne out in the November election, when the heralded "white backlash" for Goldwater failed to materialize.

What *was* apparent was opposition to the current form and pace of the civil rights movement.[24] "The Negroes are pushing too hard too fast," went the familiar phrase. But this attitude was not new; polls had consistently revealed it throughout the 1960s, with each new militant technique initially provoking a comparable degree of resistance from whites.[25] Thus, in 1961 a nationwide Gallup poll found that 64 percent of the public disapproved of "freedom rides" and 57 percent believed the rides would "hurt the Negroes' chance of being integrated in the South." [26] In 1963, 65 percent of white Northerners and 73 percent of white Southerners thought mass demonstrations by Negroes were "likely to hurt the Negro's cause for racial equality." [27] It is noteworthy that in each case the resistance of white Americans focused upon means, not ends; throughout all the racial turbulence—in part perhaps because of it—attitudes toward the Negroes' ultimate aspirations have continued to improve.

Finally, a comparison of nationwide Gallup polls taken in 1963 and 1965 affords significant evidence. During these years, when the "backlash" was presumed to be raging, increasing percentages of white parents in the South and North said they would not object to sending their children to a school with Negro children. The most dramatic shifts occurred in the South; the proportion of white parents there who stated that they would not object to having their children attend classes with "a few" Negro children rose from only 38 percent in 1963 to 62 percent by 1965. Consistently favorable shifts also characterized opinions of whites in the North: a school with "a few" Negro children was declared unobjectionable by 87 percent of white parents in 1963, by 91 percent in 1965; a school where the student body was half Negro was acceptable to 56 percent in 1963, to 65 percent in 1965; and a school with a majority of Negro students was unobjectionable to 31 percent in 1963, to 37 percent in 1965. Once again, specific data directly refute the notion of a widespread growth in anti-Negro sentiment among white Americans during the period from 1963 to 1965. But, it may be asked, what happened to these attitudes after 1965? Gallup asked the same questions of white parents in 1966 and 1969, and the same trend continued. For example, by 1969 78 percent of white parents in the South had no objection to token integration of schools, 47 percent had no objection to half-Negro schools (compared with only 17 percent in 1963), and 26 percent no objection to predominantly Negro schools (compared with 6 percent in 1963). Opinions of white parents in the North did not show such dramatic change, but the percentages continued to increase for all three questions by from 2 to 4 percent over 1965, a result which is obviously at odds with the "backlash" theory.[28]

The developments popularly described as a "white backlash," then, turn out, when placed in full scientific perspective, to have been something quite different. Anti-black candidates for political office in the North, conspicuous under the glare of television klieg lights, siezed on the race issue and made it more salient; they drew upon preexisting bigotry and alienation, and they often succeeded, at least for a time, in attracting to the polls many apathetic, alienated, authoritarian, or uninformed citizens who usually do not vote.[29] What followed was the familiar phenomenon of activation in a crisis: persons who favored racial change in the first place became more active, and so did persons who opposed it.

The mass media, interpreting this process as a "backlash," went wrong in ignoring the size of the total vote in elections involving anti-Negro candidates; in disregarding the rising support for the Civil Rights Act of 1964 among whites; in misunderstanding the "out-from-under-the-rocks" quality of protest voting; in neglecting to seek before-and-after evidence of change; in relying upon questions with highly biased wording; in failing to differentiate clearly between attitudes toward the means and attitudes toward the goals of the civil-rights movement; and, because of all these errors, in mistaking activation for a change in opinion. What really happened in the course of the so-called "white backlash" does not contradict the steady and dramatic reduction in anti-Negro prejudice throughout the nation over the past generation.

Basically, the expectation of a simple negative reaction

among whites toward Negroes' recent demands failed because the attitudes of white Americans toward Negro Americans are anything but simple. And here we come to a final parallel between attitudes toward Jews and attitudes toward Negroes in the United States: in both cases, a fundamental ambivalence is at work. Halpern traces the ambivalent feelings of gentiles toward Jews through the years, and Stember presents data from polls that document it for the past generation.[30] A similar ambivalence is to be found in the white American's feelings toward the Negro. But here the parallel ends, for the ambivalence stems from markedly contrasting images, and this is only one among many distinctions between hostility toward Jews and toward blacks.

Distinctions between Anti-Semitic and Anti-Negro Attitudes

Bettelheim and Janowitz, among others, have observed that Americans' attitudes toward the Jew are rooted in concerns having to do with the superego, and their attitudes toward the Negro in concerns having to do with the id.[31] Consider, for example, the adjectives typically applied to Jews by anti-Semites: ambitious, striving, crafty, clannish, shrewd, hyperintelligent, sly, dishonest. And compare these with the adjectives typically applied to Negroes by Negrophobes: unambitious, lazy, happy-go-lucky, irresponsible, stupid, dirty, smelly, uninhibited, oversexed. The psychoanalytic interpretation of these distinctive, though strangely reciprocal, stereotypes is straightforward: animosity toward outgroups is explained as a projection of unacceptable inner impulses. Jews and Negroes serve in part as *alter egos* for the bigot. The bigots own sins of the superego, such as ambition, deceit, and egotism, are personified in the Jew; his sins of the id—sins of the flesh—are seen in the Negro.[32]

The psychoanalytic distinction between superego and id stereotypes is useful in a wide range of cross-cultural situations, because many groups besides Jews and Negroes have evoked these contrasting images. Outgroups that are assigned a superego image are typically alien merchants or middlemen caught between the landed and laboring classes. This, of course, was the typical position of European Jews during the Middle Ages, and the similarity is not lost on people who project superego stereotypes upon other groups: the Chinese merchants of Malaysia and Indonesia are often called the "Jews of Asia," and the Muslim Indian merchants of East and South Africa the "Jews of Africa." The id image is attributed, in many parts of the world, to groups that rank at the bottom of the social structure; in Europe, gypsies and Southern Italians often play this role.[33] Occasionally, the two types of images are fused into a single, contradictory stereotype; in Germany before the Second World War, for instance, the lack of a significant id-type outgroup made it necessary for the anti-Semitic image of the Jew to do double duty as the personification of both id and superego concerns, with the result that Jews were seen as both lazy and overambitious, both oversexed and anemic. In America, however, bigots enjoy the luxury of having a variety of outgroups to choose from, and more specific, differentiated stereotypes have evolved.

These cross-cultural examples suggest some further reasons why the images of Jews and Negroes in the United States are so distinctively different. The two stereotypes are, of course, more than just projections of the bigot's impulses; they also reflect, if only in distorted ways, the contrasting social positions and values of the two groups, and particularly their radically different histories both in and outside America. Anti-Semitism in the United States is derived in large part from the image of the Jew as middleman or "economic man," a stigma originally developed in Europe. Anti-Negro prejudice stems from the far more serious stigma left upon Negroes by the uniquely destructive form of slavery sanctioned in the South, and by the subsequent century of segregation and poverty.[34]

A crucial element in these historically implanted stigmata, in addition to position and values, is the concept of "race." In its distorted popular meaning, the term "race" often carries connotations of innate inferiority, of unalterable distinctiveness, of a biological threat. It is thus not surprising that, as Stember shows, persons who think of Jews as a "race" in this sense are somewhat more anti-Semitic than others; and it is significant that this mode of thinking has sharply declined since 1946: Jews are more often viewed now as either a nationality or a religious group.[35] In attitudes toward Negroes, no such shift is discernible. Though it is estimated that 25 percent of the genes in the total gene pool of Negro Americans is Caucasian in origin,[36] Negroes will probably be viewed as a markedly separate "race" for some time to come.

The very different positions of Jews and Negroes in the American social structure are another determinant of their contrasting stereotypes. Jewish Americans are overwhelmingly middle-class. Disproportionately large numbers of them engage in the professions and other white-collar occupations; their median family income easily surpasses the national median, rivaling that of such wealthy religious groups as the Presbyterians and the Episcopalians. Black Americans, on the other hand, are overwhelmingly lower-class. They are found disproportionately often in the service and blue-collar occupations; their median family income is low, barely three-fifths of the national median, and reflects a degree of poverty unequaled among whites except for such destitute groups as the Appalachian mountain folk. There are, of course, poor Jews of lower-class status and prosperous Negroes of middle-class status, but they represent relatively small segments of their respective groups.

There are also differences in the values held by Jews and by Negroes—a natural outcome of their different histories and social positions. The close similarity of the Jews' values and those of the dominant Anglo-Saxon Protestants has been a striking and important aspect of the Jewish experience in America. To use Florence Kluckhohn's convenient scheme, Jewish and Protestant Americans both tend to hold "man-over-nature," "doing," "individualistic" and "future-time" value orientations.[37] Indeed, research on the so-called "Protestant ethic" often finds Jewish subjects far surpassing Protestants in their devotion to such central components of the ethic as achievement values.[38]

The picture is less clear in the case of Negro Americans. The impact of slavery limited the survival of their uniquely African values, so that their value models from the beginning were typically Protestant American. Yet their experience in this country did little to encourage a "man-over-nature," "doing," "individualistic," "future-time" view of life. To be sure, the first moderately prosperous classes of Negroes did evince the Protestant ethic in its purest form.[39] But continued denial of opportunity and increasing racial separation have fostered countervalues among many of the younger, lower-status, less religious Negroes in today's enormous urban ghettos.

The consequences of these differences between Jewish and Negro Americans are vast. To begin with, attitudes toward intermarriage with members of the two groups are markedly different. Stember shows that in 1962 only 37 percent of a nationwide sample stated they "definitely would not marry a Jew," a diminution of 20 percentage points since 1950.[40] In contrast, attitudes toward intermarriage between Negroes and whites have changed very little over the past decades. On the basis of distorted notions of "race," over 80 percent of white Americans opposed interracial marriage in 1963.[41]

A second consequence is that "old Americans," by and large, have responded to Jews and immigrants generally in one way, to Negroes in quite another. In the case of immigrants, including Jews, assimilation was expected; the problem, it was felt, was how to bring them into the main-stream of American life—though "not too fast." In the case of Negroes, assimilation was opposed; the problem, until recently, was defined as how to keep them out of the mainstream. The two contrasting patterns naturally have affected the personalities of individuals in quite different ways. Immigrants and their children have undergone cultural conflicts, painful adjustments in the second generation, and special strains while striving to become "all-American." Negroes, on the other hand, have suffered unique identity conflicts, agonizing threats to their survival and dignity, and a crushing sense of rejection and defeat.[42] Significantly, mental illness among Jewish Americans is marked by relatively high rates of neurosis and low rates of psychosis, while among black Americans the reverse seems to be true.[43]

Because of the many differences between Jews and Negroes, prejudices against the two groups relate differently to social class. Stember shows, for example, that anti-Semitism is relatively widespread among individuals of higher status, especially when measured by questions which suggest that Jews are a "race," are "more radical than others," or have "objectionable qualities." [44] By contrast, anti-Negro responses in polls come most frequently from lower-status whites. Thus, as Hyman and Sheatsley have shown, the poorly educated respondents in nation-wide surveys favor desegregation of public schools and buses much less often than do the better educated. Apparently, prejudice against Jews or Negroes is most commonly found where a competitive threat is most acutely perceived: anti-Semitism tends to be particularly intense among Christians of a social status similar to that of most Jews, and anti-Negro sentiment is likely to be strongest among whites of a social status similar to that of most Negroes. A revealing exception, however, is to be found in the area of residential segregation: according to Hyman and Sheatsley, the more educated are just as resistant to racially desegregated housing as the less educated.[45]

More surprising are the relationships between group prejudice and political viewpoints, as revealed in attitudes toward Joseph R. McCarthy. A survey conducted in 1954 by the National Opinion Research Center found that persons who favored Senator McCarthy, especially the better educated, were slightly less willing than others to accept Jewish neighbors; [46] on the other hand, a study carried out in the same year by International Research Associates demonstrated that supporters of McCarthy were actually more willing than others to vote for a hypothetical Jewish candidate for Congress. [47] There was, in short, no strong and consistent association between anti-Semitism and McCarthyism. A clearer relationship was evident where attitudes toward Negroes were concerned: a Gallup survey in 1954 noted that opponents of McCarthy approved the recent Supreme Court ruling outlawing segregated schools far more often than did his supporters, [48] though the same poll did not find a consistent relationship between attitudes toward McCarthy and objections to sending children to predominantly Negro schools. [49]

The general tendency of right-wing movements to evince anti-Negro rather than anti-Jewish prejudice became evident again ten years later in the candidacy of Barry Goldwater for the Presidency. Though the candidate, in the new style of "transtolerance," insisted throughout that he was not anti-Negro, he and his spokesmen openly rejected the Civil Rights Act of 1964 and attacked racially integrated housing as well as other objectives of the Negro's drive for first-class citizenship. In contrast, no anti-Semitic appeals were broached.

The Jew, then, is no longer a safe target for public attack, while the black still is—in line with the differences between the two types of prejudice which we have noted. Though both types have sharply declined in recent years, anti-Negro prejudice is still far more prevalent than anti-Semitism in the United States today, as is shown in the responses to questions which apply equally to each group. During 1958, roughly two-thirds of the whites in a nationwide Gallup poll said they would vote for a well-qualified man nominated by their party if he were Jewish; only two-fifths said they would if he were black.[50]

Even sharp differences are found when questions about "social distance" are asked. For instance, surveys of four communities by Cornell University in the early 1950s asked respondents if they would find it "a little distasteful to eat at the same table" with a Negro or a Jew. The percentages of white Christians who said it would be distasteful with a Negro ranged from 50 in Elmira, New York, to 92 in Savannah, Georgia; the percentages saying it would be distasteful with a Jew varied only from 8 in Steubenville, Ohio, to 13 in Savannah.[51] Similar responses were obtained by an additional question about going to a party and finding that most of the people there were Negroes or were Jews. The percentages who disliked the idea of a party attended mostly by Negroes ranged from 80 in Bakersfield, California, to 89 in Steubenville; the percentages for a party attended mostly by Jews ranged from 25 in Steubenville to 34 in Savannah.[52]

More intensive investigations have led to the same conclusion. Bettelheim and Janowitz interviewed in depth 150 white Christians from Chicago, all of them World War II veterans of enlisted rank. Using the same criteria for prejudice against both groups, Bettelheim and Janowitz rated 65 percent of their subjects as either intensely or outspokenly anti-Negro, 27 percent as harboring stereotyped anti-Negro attitudes, and only 8 percent as truly tolerant of Negroes.[53] When it came to attitudes toward Jews, only about half as many were rated intensely or outspokenly prejudiced (31 percent), a similar percentage were rated as holding stereotyped beliefs (28 percent), and five times as many were rated as tolerant (41 percent).[54]

Not only are attitudes toward Negroes more negative than attitudes toward Jews, but they are also far more salient to most Americans. A fairly accurate measure of saliency is provided in polls by the percentage of persons who are uncertain, say they don't know, or otherwise fail to choose one of the offered alternatives. In surveys dealing with prejudice against Negroes, these percentages are generally small; thus, Hyman and Sheatsley report that in four polls from 1942 to 1963, questions on racial desegregation consistently obtained noncommittal responses from only about 4 percent of the samples.[55] With anti-Semitic items, the proportions are generally higher; thus, the 137 percentages of noncommittal replies recorded by Stember range from 1 to 42, with a median of 11.

Anti-Negro and anti-Jewish attitudes, being shaped by somewhat different social forces, do not necessarily rise or fall together. True, both have declined sharply over the past generation in the nation as a whole; but, as is often the case, the South shows a deviant pattern and thereby provides special clues. Anti-Negro sentiments have notably lessened in the South since 1942, actually changing faster in many ways than has been true elsewhere; meanwhile, anti-Semitism seems to have declined at a markedly slower pace in the South than in other regions.

Hyman and Sheatsley's analysis of nationwide surveys from 1942 to 1963 conclusively demonstrates massive shifts in whites' opinions about the Negro in the South.[56] With more room for improvement, the South shows generally higher relative and absolute rates of modification than the North. Thus, the belief of the white public in the equal intelligence of Negroes rose from 21 to 59 percent in the South, and from 50 to 80 percent in the North; support by whites of desegregated public transportation climbed from 4 to 51 percent in the South, and from 57 to 88 percent in the North; and approval by whites of desegregated neighborhoods increased from 12 to 51 percent in the South, and from 42 to 70 percent in the North. In short, the white South, for all its ugly signs of resistance to racial change, is altering its most basic sentiments toward the black.

Anti-Semitism in the South presents a contrasting situation. As was noted briefly in Chapter 6, the South has traditionally been one of the least anti-Semitic regions in the nation, and a considerable body of data suggests that it remained so until the 1940s. Stember shows, for example, that in 1939–1946 Southerners ranked lowest in anti-Semitic responses to six of nine questions.[57] In polls conducted during 1946 and 1947, Roper found the South, together with the Far West, to be among the least anti-Semitic areas of the United States.[58] A study of over 1,000 wartime rumors from all parts of the nation, conducted by R. H. Knapp in 1942, lends further weight to this conclusion.[59] He noted that anti-Semitic stories constituted 9 percent of the rumors in the nation but only 3 percent of the rumors in the South; in contrast, anti-Negro rumors made up over 8 percent of the total for the South but only 3 percent of the total for the nation. Consistent with these data, other inquiries have found large numbers of white Southerners intensely anti-Negro and at the same time highly favorable to Jews.[60]

The last twenty years have witnessed a diminution of anti-Semitism in the South, as elsewhere, but a minimal one compared to other regions. Some institutional indications of the South's earlier relative standing still exist; thus, the Anti-Defamation League of B'nai B'rith, in its exhaustive study of religious barriers in social clubs, found discrimination less prevalent in the South, Southwest, and Far West than in other areas.[61] But Stember's broader data present another picture: in seven of his nine comparisons over time, percentage declines in anti-Semitism between 1939 and 1962 were smaller in the South than in any other region; by 1962, the South ranked slightly above all other areas in anti-Semitic responses to four of the nine questions.[62]

Stember offers a methodological explanation for this regional change. The 1939 survey drew its sample from voters, which limited the participation of Negro respondents, whereas the 1962 survey included Negroes in approximately their true proportion of the adult Southern population. Consequently, Stember suggests, a possible greater degree of anti-Semitism among Negroes might have distorted the results in the South. Additional data, however, cast doubt upon this explanation. The Cornell survey of Savannah, conducted in the early 1950s, found approximately the same percentages of Negroes and whites responding to stereotype questions about Jews in an anti-Semitic fashion.[63] For instance, 44 percent of whites and 48 percent of Negroes agreed that "Jews are dishonest in their business dealings."[64] Questions about "social distance," such as the one about eating at the same table with a Jew, uncovered somewhat larger differences between races, but the Negroes' greater preference for distance is probably a function more of racial taboos than of religious bigotry. In any event, only two of Stember's nine comparisons deal with social distance, and one of these can be tested for racial differences by combining three national surveys which asked the same question during the early 1950s.[65] When asked, "How would you feel if a Jewish family were going to move next door to you?" 8.7 percent of whites and 8.0 percent of Negroes in the South stated they "wouldn't like it at all"; 15.5 percent of whites and 12.9 percent of Negroes said it "wouldn't matter too much."[66] In other words, roughly one of every four whites but only one of every five Negroes in the South had some qualms about a Jewish neighbor.

The inclusion of more Negro Southerners in the 1962 survey, then, apparently does not explain away the relatively slow decline of anti-Semitism in the South between 1939 and 1962. The deviant pattern of the South—faster diminution of anti-Negro attitudes but slower diminution of anti-Semitism than elsewhere—provides suggestive clues about the different social forces underlying the two types of prejudice. As the region's cities grow into major metropolitan centers, and its expanding industries erode the older agricultural economy, traditional institutions and attitudes are inevitably undergoing drastic alteration. Basically, the South is becoming more American and less Confederate. The deviant pattern described here is part of this process of "deregionalization": the white South, formerly unique in its rejection of the Negro and its acceptance of the Jew, is becoming more and more like the rest of the nation.

Numerous studies have revealed that urbanization and industrialization are significantly associated with marked reductions in racial animosity.[67] As white Southerners rise into the middle class, receive more and better education, and develop into acclimated urbanites, the fears and threats traditionally associated with the Negro lose some of their force. But these changes often perpetuate or even heighten anti-Semitism.

To see the full importance of this point, we must consider the traditional position of Jews in Southern life. Though few in number, they have long occupied prominent roles in the region—from cabinet posts in the Confederate Government to current ownership of the major department stores in virtually every large city. Acceptance of Jews was facilitated by the special emphasis which Fundamentalist Protestants placed on the Old Testament. Moreover, the superego stereotype elsewhere reserved for the Jew was in the South largely projected onto the Yankee, who was caricatured by the poor, defeated, and defensive South as crafty, pushy, materialistic, too successful, and not to be trusted. Most significant of all, the German Jews who constituted the bulk of the earlier Jewish population in the South were an integral part of antebellum and Civil War folklore. I remember well the special respect which the leading Jewish family enjoyed in my Southern home town. Though this family included the foremost bankers and jewelers of the city, the usual anti-Semitic stereotypes were never applied; for, after all, the family's social position was solidly grounded on the fame of its brave Civil War ancestor, Colonel Kahn.[68]

The rapid social changes in today's South are weakening much of this tradition-linked protection against anti-Semitism. An increasing percentage of Southern Jewry is not of pre-Civil War German stock and thus is not draped in the Confederate battle flag. In addition, typical forms of anti-Semitism are being fostered by many of the very processes which reduce anti-Negro feeling—for example, the growth of the middle class, immigration of Northerners, and competitive urban life. The inference is clear: Anti-Semitism and anti-Negro attitudes are by no means shaped by identical social forces; hence, they do not necessarily rise and diminish together.

Do prejudices necessarily replace one another? The many distinctions between anti-Jewish and anti-Negro attitudes raise the question of how hostile sentiments toward various minorities are related to one another. Conventional wisdom holds that a reduction in one type of prejudice invariably leads to an increase in another. But is this true? If prejudice against one minority drops, does prejudice against another necessarily rise?

To tackle this central question, a choice must be made between two contrasting conceptions of aggression. Sigmund Freud and later psychoanalytic writers have generally postulated a closed system on the order of a steam boiler, containing a fixed amount of instinctive aggression which if not released through one outlet will seek and find another. According to this view, society's problem is how to channel aggression through appropriate safety valves. Indeed, creative, constructive work is seen as an important means of sublimating fundamentally aggressive instincts. Gordon W. Allport objects to this conception.[69] He argues that no single closed-system model can account for the vast range of phenomena which Freudians classify under the single instinct "aggression" (from individual rage to war) and under sublimation (from counting up to ten to painting the *Mona Lisa*). The model he proposes is an open-system, feedback type. Rather than a finite, instinctual force that demands release, aggression in Allport's view is a variable capacity whose expression is governed by both inner and outer conditions; once it is released, further aggression is more likely, not less likely, to occur. Creative, constructive endeavors, he maintains, are ends in themselves, meeting specific needs, rather than mere reflections of aggression.

How we answer our question depends on which of these rival models we choose. If we accept the Freudian model, we will expect a reduction of prejudice against one minority to cause an increase of prejudice against another, unless the inevitable flow of aggression finds a different outlet altogether. Prejudice, the old saying goes, will always be with us. Allport's model creates markedly different expectations. From this vantage point, there is nothing inevitable about prejudice. In fact, his feedback model suggests that greater tolerance of one minority would improve the chances for greater tolerance of others. Hence, prejudice need not always be with us; both personal and social conditions can be achieved which essentially eliminate this societal liability.

The available evidence tends to support Allport's more optimistic open-system view. Social-psychological studies of prejudice have repeatedly found hostility toward one outgroup to be highly and positively correlated with hostility toward other outgroups; that is, individuals who are prejudiced against Jews also tend to be prejudiced against Negroes, Catholics, and outgroups in general.[70] One ingenious experiment tested attitudes of students toward the peoples of thirty-two nations and races plus three nonexistent groups ("Daniereans," "Pireneans" and "Wallonians"),[71] and found, as the open-system model would predict, that persons who rejected the real groups tended to reject the imaginary ones as well. Unless we assume that the quantities of instinctual aggression, while finite, vary vastly among individuals, it is difficult to see how a fixed-quantity, closed-system model of aggression could easily account for this well-established finding.

Other data provide further evidence. Anti-Jewish responses to questions asked in polls were most intense during the later stages of the World War II—presumably the high point in the nation's release of aggression. More important, Stember's data, together with those of Hyman and Sheatsley described above, prove that anti-Semitic and anti-Negro attitudes have since then undergone a sharp simultaneous decline. A similar conclusion is reached by G. M. Gilbert, who compared the stereotypes of ten groups as held by Princeton undergraduates of similar backgrounds in 1932 and in 1950: [72] Across the board, stereotypes had "faded" and lost their saliency. Data like these are what we would expect if the open-system model of aggression is correct.

Closed-system theorists might challenge such results on the grounds that the studies did not properly allow for substitute channels of aggression. Thus, some individuals might use prejudice against outgroups as their principal outlet for aggression, while others might channel all their aggressive energies in other directions. But research by Ross Stagner casts doubt upon this method of explaining away the findings of Stember and others.[73] Stagner found that students who channeled aggression in one direction were especially likely to channel it in others as well.

Finally, cross-cultural research further confirms Allport's position. S. T. Boggs found positive relationships between individual, group, and ideological aggression within societies; in war-oriented societies, individuals were inclined to behave aggressively toward one another, and myths and legends tended to be aggressive in content.[74]

Though such evidence is not conclusive, it weighs heavily in favor of Allport's open-system, feedback conception of aggression. We may therefore answer our basic question in the negative: available evidence suggests that a reduction in prejudice against one minority does *not* necessarily lead to any increase in prejudice against another. On the contrary, prejudices against different groups, even when shaped by somewhat different social forces, are likely to decline together.

Note that this expectation rejects only the Freudian closed-system or "drainage" theory, not the more limited displacement theory; it still allows for possible substitution of scapegoats. Just as in the South the Yankee long replaced the Jew as the object of superego stereotyping and hostility, so today the political establishment is perhaps substituting for the Jews as a target of animosity on the national scene. The phenomenon of transtolerance and other aspects of the radical right strongly suggest this possibility.[75] Incidentally, any such anti-elite bias would be noteworthy as evidence against the widely held dogma that scapegoats must be weak and vulnerable. In any event, such substitutions are possible, but not, according to the open-system model, inevitable.

The Future of Anti-Minority Prejudice in the United States

The open-system model, together with recent advances in social-psychological research on attitude change, suggests possible future trends of ethnic and religious prejudice in the United States. In brief, long-term alterations in American society are slowly institutionalizing acceptance of minorities and nondiscrimination. These evolving institutional safeguards provide the necessary "outer" conditions for the reduction of group prejudice specified by Allport; many of them also provide the setting for consequent changes in the behavior of individuals. These behavior changes in turn produce the "inner" conditions for reducing group prejudice. Increasingly, Americans accept the *fait accompli* of their new institutions and behavior as "the American way."

This process has been under way since 1945, and there are good reasons for expecting it to continue, with occasional periods of regression as during the Nixon administration.

Slowly evolving institutional safeguards against bigotry are well illustrated in Herbert Hyman's analysis of the toleration of political nonconformists in England.[76] Hyman was intrigued by the fact that since World War II England had seen fewer overt acts against such persons than the United States. There was no obvious reason for this difference, he felt. America's political traditions were originally modeled after English ones of an earlier time; England herself had a long history of ugly overt acts against nonconformists, extending until recent times; and the public's attitudes on the subject did not seem vastly different in the two countries. His persuasive answer to the riddle was that England over the past centuries had slowly evolved distinctive political institutions and mechanisms which restrained latent public intolerance. For example, the English public allows its elite far more privacy and deference than the American public—except for an occasional affair as sensational as the Profumo case of 1963. However, this example also points up a vital qualification to the process outlined above: some institutional safeguards against bigotry merely restrain intolerance without requiring new, positive forms of behavior, and consequently do not by themselves initiate a reduction in prejudice.

In the United States, institutional protections for minorities have so far evolved in various ways. Sometimes they emerge dramatically, as did the Civil Rights Act of 1964; more often they come quietly, without national attention, like the acceptance of minorities in such previously discriminatory sectors as the engineering profession and college social fraternities. But generally the new safeguards have been won, at least in large part, by pressure exerted by the minorities themselves. Witness the desegregation of lunch counters that was achieved by the sit-in protests. The process has been aided by the circumstance that groups of Americans, though usually minorities by themselves, can often be combined into a majority. Thus, the nation's largest political party is a delicately balanced coalition of minorities, including the major share of the country's blacks, Jews, and Roman Catholics. And this party has managed to win seven of the last ten Presidential elections, in part because of what it has done to establish institutional protections of the type under discussion. The momentum of this trend, together with the growing militancy among practically all the nation's minorities, who feel entitled to full citizens' rights and mean to obtain them, afford good reason to expect that the evolution of institutional protections will continue, if slowly and haltingly. But will they evolve during the 1970s? We shall face this pressing issue in Chapter 12.

Institutional safeguards which go beyond mere restraint and prompt new intergroup behavior act to reduce group prejudice directly.[77] Once again, the actual process contradicts conventional wisdom. It is commonly held that attitudes must change *before* behavior does; therefore, the argument runs, intergroup problems can be solved only through what is vaguely described as "education." Yet recent advances in social psychology point conclusively in the opposite direction: behavior changes first, because of new laws or other institutional interventions; after the fact, individuals modify their ideas to fit their new acts, often proving amazingly adaptable in doing so. Indeed, considerable research suggests that this behavior-to-attitude cycle of change is generally easier and more effective than the attitude-to-behavior cycle.

A number of psychological mechanisms are at work in this process. Commitment is one such mechanism. An individual who has publicly behaved in a new manner and been rewarded for doing so is likely to become committed to the change. Acceptance of the *fait accompli* is another. When a person first encounters Negro sales clerks in a department store, busily at work and accepted naturally by others, he is likely to accept the innovation even though he may previously have opposed the idea. If he objected vocally, he would create a scene, and risk being isolated as a bigot without social support. This process is buttressed by the sanction of the "American creed" of equality for all; measures to attain "fair play" for minorities today command a widespread ideological and moral support, such as Prohibition in the 1920s, for example, never enjoyed. We shall consider this important process at greater length in Chapters 11 and 12.

Lest this discussion appear too optimistic about the future, two strong caveats must be emphasized. First, American life retains many deeply rooted institutional supports for group prejudice and many barriers to beneficial inter-group contact, especially with respect to blacks. As long as such high officials as Governors and Presidents openly or implicitly sanction racial oppression, as long as the majority of Negroes remain tightly sealed off in urban ghettos, as long as most young Negroes in both the North and the South remain permanently handicapped by separate and inferior education, as long as the typical Negro family has an annual income barely three-fifths that of the typical white family, anti-Negro prejudice will continue to thrive. It will be a long time before the animosity of whites forward Negroes sinks to the relatively low level which animosity of gentiles toward Jews has reached. Those who would hasten that day would be best advised to help demolish the institutional barriers that still hinder racial progress—such as housing discrimination fostered by real-estate interests with the acquiescence of government, or *de facto* segregated education upheld by citizens who have suddenly become attached to neighborhood schools.

The second caveat concerns the current activities of the radical right, a movement that has proved powerful enough to seize parts of the machinery of the Republican Party. True, the examples of transtolerance which we noted at the outset suggest that explicit anti-minority attitudes are not an essential ingredient of the far right today. In modern parlance, the movement is primarily status-oriented, not class-oriented.[78] Moreover, as Talcott Parsons has stressed, its ideology differs from that of extremists in the 1930s: whereas the Nazis needed the Jew as an ideological link between capitalism and Communism, today's radical right supports its own version of capitalism and has no need of anti-Semitism for this purpose.[79] However, the movement is vehemently opposed to the nation's elite, the sponsors of the trend toward institutional protection of minorities, and it attracts elements known for their previous activities in anti-Semitic and anti-Negro organizations. And it appears that the Nixon administration is to some degree captive to the movement, especially in matters of civil rights.

The rightists' anti-elite ideology is not likely to abate soon—not because of any instinctual need for a perpetual scapegoat, but because of the times in which we live. As Alan Westin observes, the world scene will almost certainly become increasingly complex; America will suffer unavoidable reverses; real threats will continue to plague international affairs. These are the conditions upon which the simple jingoist ideology of the radical right feeds.[80] In addition, as Hyman has noted, the United States—unlike England—lacks the developed political structure needed to restrain such a movement. And the rise of a violent far left also feeds the far right. All told, it would appear that today's virulent far right could well deter the process of institutional change outlined above.

Summary

We have compared anti-Jewish with anti-Negro sentiments against the background of our age of "transtolerance," in which "prejudice" is a derogatory term. According to extensive data from national surveys, both prejudices reached a peak near the close of World War II and have markedly and steadily declined since that time. There are convincing reasons for accepting these data as reasonably accurate reflections of the level of prejudice in American society; and there are equally good reasons for discounting the much-publicized "white backlash" against the Negro, which was presumed by the mass media to have begun in 1964.

The two types of prejudice differ in many important ways. Though anti-Semites and Negrophobes both reveal a strong ambivalence toward their targets, the two stereotypes show sharp differences. The image of the Jew is related to concerns connected with the superego (for example, ambition, intelligence, dishonesty), while that of the black is related to concerns connected with the id (for example, sexuality, uncleanliness, laziness). These contrasting stereotypes can be traced directly to the histories of the two groups; to the significance imputed to racial, as against religious, differences; to the very different positions which Jews and Negroes typically occupy in the American social and economic structure; and to the similarity of the values held by "old Americans" and Jewish Americans.

The consequences of these distinctions are manifold. Jews and others of immigrant stock have been traditionally criticized for failing to enter the mainstream of American culture; Negroes have been traditionally rebuked for wishing to enter it. Anti-Semitism is often widespread among upper-status individuals; Negrophobia is frequently common among persons of lower status. Not surprisingly, then, far higher levels of anti-Negro prejudice than of anti-Jewish prejudice remain in the United States— especially where intermarriage is at issue. Results of surveys also suggest that attitudes toward Negroes are generally more salient to most Americans than attitudes toward Jews. Finally, the special case of the South— where anti-Negro sentiment has declined faster and anti-Semitism slower than in the rest of the nation—highlights the fact that somewhat different social forces underlie the two forms of bigotry, with the result that they do not necessarily rise and decline together.

It also seems clear that a reduction in prejudice against one minority does not necessarily lead to an increase in prejudice against another. The available evidence suggests a feedback, open-system model of aggression, rather than a steam-boiler, closed-system model. According to this open-system view, it is more likely that lessened prejudice against one group will occasion lessened prejudice against other groups.

When the trends of the past generation are projected into the future, it appears that institutional protection of minorities in the United States may continue to advance slowly. But many barriers to progress, especially to improved race relations, remain in our society; and the conflict in Southeast Asia and the current political movement of the radical right present serious threats to this progress. It *is* within our power to construct institutional safeguards that create both the societal and the individual conditions necessary for harmonious intergroup relations in the United States of the future. But will we construct them?

Footnotes

1. A blatant exception is, of course, the Ku Klux Klan, which is still openly anti-Negro, anti-Jewish, and anti-Catholic. But, significantly, today's Klan is a mere ghost of the Klan of the 1920s; it is isolated in numbers and locale, shunned even by the vast majority of Southern segregationists.

2. D. Bell (ed.), *The Radical Right* (Garden City, N.Y.: Doubleday Anchor Books, 1963), p. 168.

3. *Ibid.*, p. 250.

4. *Ibid.*, p. 256. Similarly, Welch was "pleased" to reprint *Color, Communism and Common Sense* by Manning Johnson, a Negro and former member of the Communist Party.

5. *Ibid.*, p. 445.

6. F. Knebel, "Race Riots: Goldwater Boon," *Look,* September 22, 1964, p. 41.

7. Bell, *op. cit.*, pp. 442, 444.

8. C. H. Stember, *Jews in the Mind of America* (New York: Basic Books, Inc., 1966), pp. 31–47.

9. H. H. Hyman and P. B. Sheatsley, "Attitudes Toward Desegregation," *Scientific American,* July 1964, Vol. 211, No. 1, pp. 16–23.

10. Stember, *op. cit.*, pp. 69, 96, 104.

11. *Ibid.*, p. 81.

12. H. G. Erskine, "The Polls: Race Relations," *Public Opinion Quarterly,* 1962, Vol. 26, p. 139. It should be noted that the failure of this item to provoke different response patterns in 1946 and 1956 does not conflict with the earlier finding that there was a sharp reduction in anti-Negro prejudice. The item does not correlate well with known measures of prejudice.

13. I. de Sola Pool, R. P. Abelson, and S. L. POPKIN, *Candidates, Issues, and Strategies: A Computer Simulation of the 1960 Presidential Election* (Cambridge, Mass.: M.I.T. Press, 1965).

14. *Ibid.,* p. 115.

15. G. W. Allport, *The Nature of Prejudice* (Cambridge, Mass.: Addison-Wesley Publishing Co., 1954), pp. 261–282. We shall explore in detail the implications of the latter process in Chapters 11 and 12.

16. See: Anti-Defamation League of B'nai B'rith, "A Study of Religious Discrimination by Social Clubs," *Rights,* 1962, Vol. 4, No. 3; "The Jewish Law Student and New York Jobs," *Rights,* 1964, Vol. 5, No. 4; "Employment of Jewish Personnel in the Automobile Industry," *Rights,* 1963, Vol. 5, No. 2; American Jewish Committee, *Patterns of Exclusion from the Executive Suite: The Public Utilities Industry,* December 1963.

17. H. Cantril, *The Politics of Despair* (New York: Basic Books, 1958).

18. *Ibid.,* p. 71.

19. The "ecological fallacy" is committed when the characteristics or behaviors of individuals (in this case, shifts of their opinion toward being anti-Negro) are inferred from data for groups only (in this case, statewide voting for an anti-Negro candidate). The fallacy is easily recognizable in some instances. For example, when we sample by city-block units, say in Chicago, we will find a high positive correlation between the percentages on each block of adult illiterates and of adult readers of comic books, though these group percentages obviously cannot represent the characteristics of the same individuals. For a thorough discussion of this common fallacy, see W. S. Robinson, "Ecological Correlations and the Behavior of Individuals," *American Sociological Review,* 1950, Vol. 15, pp. 351–357; H. Menzel, "Comment on Robinson's 'Ecological Correlations and the Behavior of Individuals,'" *American Sociological Review,* 1950, Vol. 15, p. 674; H. C. Selvin, "Durkheim's *Suicide* and Problems of Empirical Research," *American Journal of Sociology,* 1958, Vol. 63, pp. 607–619. All three papers may be found in S. M. Lipset and N. J. Smelser (eds.), *Sociology: The Progress of a Decade* (Englewood Cliffs, N.J.: Prentice-Hall, 1961), pp. 132–152.

20. F. Powledge, "Poll Shows Whites in City Resent Civil Rights Drive," *The New York Times,* September 21, 1964, pp. 1, 26.

21. Information kindly supplied by Professor Peter Rossi, then the Director of N.O.R.C., and used with his permission.

22. This was also suggested in *The New York Times'* results,

which showed large majorities of white New Yorkers supporting the employment title of the 1964 Civil Rights Act and stating that they would not be uncomfortable if some "nice" Negro families lived near them. Powledge, *op. cit.*

23. In this particular, too, *The New York Times* poll agreed as far as it went; indeed, a slightly larger majority favored Johnson over Goldwater than had chosen Kennedy over Nixon in 1960.

24. Once again, the findings of *The New York Times* poll agree with those of the more definitive N.O.R.C. study. Fifty-four percent of the New Yorkers interviewed felt the civil-rights movement "should slow down," and 49 percent felt nonviolent demonstrations "hurt the Negro's cause." See also: J. W. Carey, "An Ethnic Backlash?" *The Commonweal,* October 16, 1964, pp. 91–93.

25. For examples of these earlier polls, see S. Alsop and O. Quayle, "What Northerners Really Think of Negroes," *The Saturday Evening Post,* September 7, 1963, pp. 17–21; "How Whites Feel About Negroes: A Painful American Dilemma," *Newsweek,* October 21, 1963, pp. 44–57.

26. Erskine, *op. cit.*

27. American Institute of Public Opinion, press release, July 18, 1963.

28. American Institute of Public Opinion, press release, May 22, 1965. See also: *Integrated Education,* November–December 1969, Vol. 7, No. 6, pp. 51–52.

29. A large body of literature supports the proposition that people who generally do not vote are more apathetic, alienated, authoritarian, and uninformed than those who do. Relevant studies include G. M. Connelly and H. H. Field, "The Non-Voter—Who He Is, What He Thinks," *Public Opinion Quarterly,* 1944, Vol. 8, pp. 175–187; P. K. Hastings, "The Non-Voter in 1952: A Study of Pittsfield, Mass.," *Journal of Psychology,* 1954, Vol. 38, pp. 301–312; and "The Voter and the Non-Voter," *American Journal of Sociology,* 1956, Vol. 62, pp. 302–307; H. H. Hyman and P. B. Sheatsley, "Some Reasons Why Information Campaigns Fail," *Public Opinion Quarterly,* 1947, Vol. 11, pp. 412–423; M. Janowitz and D. Marvick, "Authoritarianism and Political Behavior," *Public Opinion Quarterly,* 1953, Vol. 17, pp. 185–201; S. M. Lipset, *Political Man* (Garden City, N.Y.: Doubleday & Co., 1960), pp. 79–103; F. H. Sanford, *Authoritarianism and Leadership* (Philadelphia: Institute for Research in Human Relations, 1950), p. 168; S. A. Stouffer, *Communism, Conformity,*

      and Civil Liberties (Garden City, N.Y.: Doubleday & Co., 1955).

30.   B. Halpern, "Anti-Semitism in the Perspective of Jewish History," in Stember, *op. cit.,* pp. 273–301; and Stember, *op. cit.,* pp. 31–47.

31.   B. Bettelheim and Morris Janowitz, *Social Change and Prejudice* (New York: The Free Press of Glencoe, 1964).

32.   *Ibid.;* T. W. Adorno, E. Frenkel-Brunswik, D. J. Levinson, and R. N. Sanford, *The Authoritarian Personality* (New York: Harper & Bros., 1950). Each of these studies provides impressive case and quantitative data in support of this psychoanalytic interpretation of prejudice.

33.   Direct evidence on the parallels between the American stereotype of the black and the Northern Italian stereotype of the Southern Italian is provided in M. W. Battacchi, *Meridionali e settentrionali nella struttura del pregiadizio etnico in Italia* [Southerners and Northerners in the Structure of Ethnic Prejudice in Italy] (Bologna: Società Editrice Il Mulino, 1959).

34.   S. M. Elkins, *Slavery* (New York: Grosset & Dunlap, 1963).

35.   Stember, *op. cit.,* pp. 50, 53.

36.   B. Glass, "On the Unlikelihood of Significant Admixture of Genes from the North American Indians in the Crescent Composition of the Negroes of the United States," *American Journal of Human Genetics,* 1955, Vol. 7, pp. 368–385.

37.   F. R. Kluckhohn, "Dominant and Variant Cultural Value Orientations," in H. Cabot and J. A. Kahl (eds.), *Human Relations,* Vol. 1 (Cambridge, Mass.: Harvard University Press, 1953), pp. 88–98.

38.   B. C. Rosen, "Race, Ethnicity, and the Achievement Syndrome," *American Sociological Review,* 1959, Vol. 24, pp. 47–60.

39.   E. F. Frazier, *Black Bourgeoisie* (New York: Collier Books, 1962). However, once socio-economic factors are controlled, there appear to be no sharp value differences between black and white Americans. See: M. Rokeach and S. Parker, "Values as Social Indicators of Poverty and Race Relations in America," *Annals of the American Academy of Political and Social Science,* 1970, Vol. 388, pp. 97–111.

40.   Stember, *op. cit.,* p. 106.

41.   In the Harris poll of whites in 1963, 84 percent objected to a "close friend or relative marrying a Negro," and 90 percent objected to their "own teen-age daughter dating a Negro." William Brink and Louis Harris, *The Negro Revolution in*

America (New York: Simon & Schuster, 1964), p. 148. That these data are largely determined by racial, and not social class, considerations is indicated by similar results of other items which specify upper-status blacks.

42. T. F. Pettigrew, *A Profile of the Negro American* (Princeton, N.J.: D. Van Nostrand Co., 1964), p. 148.

43. *Ibid.,* Chapter IV.

44. Stember, *op. cit.,* p. 227. This is *not* to imply that upper-status individuals tend to be more anti-Semitic across many types of items. In recent years, this trend has if anything lessened, with some studies now showing greater anti-Semitism among lower-status Americans. See: G. J. Selznick and S. Steinberg, *The Tenacity of Prejudice: Anti-Semitism in Contemporary America* (New York: Harper & Row, 1969), Chapter 5.

45. Herbert H. Hyman and Paul B. Sheatsley, "Attitudes Toward Desegregation," *Scientific American,* December 1956, Vol. 195, No. 6, pp. 35–39.

46. Bell, *op. cit.,* p. 416; C. H. Stember, *Education and Attitude Change* (New York: Institute of Human Relations Press, 1961), p. 118.

47. Bell, *op. cit.,* p. 415.

48. Stember, *Education and Attitude Change, op. cit.,* p. 95. This relationship manifested itself strongly among persons with a high school or college education; it was, however, reversed among those with only a grammar school education.

49. *Ibid.,* p. 143.

50. *Ibid.,* pp. 62, 76.

51. R. M. Williams, Jr., *Strangers Next Door* (Englewood Cliffs, N.J.: Prentice-Hall, 1964), p. 52.

52. *Ibid.*

53. Bettelheim and Janowitz, *op. cit.*

54. *Ibid.*

55. Hyman and Sheatsley, *op. cit.* (1964).

56. *Ibid.*

57. Stember, *Jews in the Mind of America, op. cit.,* p. 224.

58. "The Fortune Survey," *Fortune,* February 1946, pp. 257–260; October 1947, pp. 5–10.

59. R. H. Knapp, "A Psychology of Rumor," *Public Opinion Quarterly,* 1944, Vol. 8, pp. 22–37.

60. See, for example, E. T. Prothro, "Ethnocentrism and Anti-Negro Attitudes in the Deep South," *Journal of Abnormal and Social Psychology,* 1952, Vol. 47, pp. 105–108.

61. Anti-Defamation League, "A study of Religious Discrimination by Social Clubs," *op. cit.*

62. Stember, *Jews in the Mind of America, op. cit.*, p. 224.

63. Williams, *op. cit.*

64. *Ibid.*, p. 50.

65. These data are based on a secondary analysis by the writer of three national surveys by the National Opinion Research Center: Studies No. 294 (November 8, 1950), 342 (June 30, 1953), and 365 (November 26, 1954). The writer wishes to thank the Roper Public Opinion Research Center at Williams College and its director, Professor Philip K. Hastings, for making these studies available.

66. With the three surveys combined, these percentages involve 854 white Southerners and 201 Negro Southerners.

67. T. F. Pettigrew and M. Richard Cramer, "The Demography of Desegregation," *Journal of Social Issues*, 1959, Vol. 15, No. 4, pp. 61–71.

68. Not the actual name. Incidentally, this special role of the Jew provides an additional explanation for Ringer's finding that in the South Jews are generally perceived as being far less in favor of racial desegregation than they actually are. See Stember, *Jews in the Mind of America, op. cit.*, Chapter 9.

69. Allport, *op. cit.*, pp. 354–366.

70. *Ibid.*, pp. 68–81; Adorno, *et al., op. cit.*

71. E. L. Hartley, *Problems in Prejudice* (New York: Kings Crown Press, 1946).

72. G. M. Gilbert, "Stereotype Persistence and Change Among College Students," *Journal of Abnormal and Social Psychology*, 1951, Vol. 46, pp. 245–254.

73. R. Stagner, "Studies of Aggressive and Social Attitudes: 1. Measurement and Inter-relation of Selected Attitudes," *Journal of Social Psychology*, 1944, Vol. 20, pp. 109–120.

74. S. T. Boggs, *A Comparative Cultural Study of Aggression* (unpublished honors thesis, Social Relations Library, Harvard University, 1947).

75. Bell, *op. cit.*

76. *Ibid.*

77. T. F. Pettigrew, "Prejudice and the Situation," in J. P. Davis (ed.), *The American Negro Reference Book* (Englewood Cliffs, N.J.: Prentice-Hall, 1966), pp. 714–723.

78. Bell, *op. cit.*

79. *Ibid.*

80. *Ibid.*

Gordon Allport, after a close examination of the relevant data in 1953, estimated that roughly four-fifths of the American population harbor "enough antagonism toward minority groups to influence their daily conduct." [1] *This crude figure varies widely, of course, across regional, age, and social-class groupings; it varies, too, with the research questions and methods employed. Although the survey findings reviewed in Chapter 8 suggest that this estimate should be reduced somewhat, Allport's figure continues to receive support from various sources of data. Furthermore, the "unprejudiced fifth" is apparently matched by an "extremely prejudiced fifth," for whom racism is so salient that they will typically act on it even when it conflicts with other values which they hold.* [2] *This group can be counted on to vote against any civil rights referendum, to give prejudiced responses to most survey questions concerning minority groups, and to favor political candidates with openly anti-Negro platforms.*[3] *It is these white Americans who are the focus of the following two chapters.*

Roughly speaking, three-fifths of white Americans

PART FOUR

RACISM AT THE BALLOT BOX

may well be "conforming bigots." On racial issues that arouse considerable disapproval, such as the busing of children to interracial schools, most of these people join the prejudiced fifth, forming a majority resistant to change. On racial issues that win wide approval—such as the 1964 Civil Rights Act, which was passed after the assassination of President John Kennedy, who had advocated it—most "conforming bigots" will join the unprejudiced fifth, forming a majority favorable to change. Strongly subject to influence by institutional norms and dramatic events, this wavering group is primarily responsible for the breathtaking swings in the national mood on racial change, from the highly favorable mood of 1964 to the unfavorable mood of 1970. These "conforming bigots" differ fundamentally from the "extremely prejudiced fifth"—the hard-core bigots—in that they often place other values above racism when the situation supports other values: that is, their racism is less salient than that of the hard core.

Crude as these proportions must necessarily be, they are accurate enough to order and render understandable a great mass of recent data on race relations.[4] Analysis suggests that persons who are like the "conforming bigots" probably outnumber those who believe and act consistently on race—both the prejudiced fifth and the unprejudiced fifth. Even among white Southerners, as was noted in Chapter 6, "conforming bigots" ("latent liberals") appear to predominate.

Three practical implications flow from this analysis of white racism at the individual level. First, it suggests that the opinions of white Americans about race are more flexible than they sometimes appear. This is consistent with the contention made throughout this book that major institutional changes can effectively counter racist attitudes and beliefs of individuals, and that efforts toward needed structural alterations cannot and should not be deterred by initial opposition from a majority of white Americans.

But the second implication of this analysis is that

*there is a strong possibility that the salient anti-Negro
sentiments of about a fifth of white Americans reflect a
strong personality commitment to racism, and this
should give us pause. Twenty million adult citizens
probably fit this description, or approach it; and they
form a critical mass, a continuing source of societal
conflict. The existence of this group makes it likely
that the Wallace phenomenon of 1968 will be repeated throughout the 1970s. It is important, then, to
look more closely at the individuals making up this group,
and this is done in the two chapters of Part Four.*

*The third implication of this analysis is that a widespread
misconception about racist attitudes must be corrected.
Often, when the spectre of "white racism" is raised in
current discussions, it is described as if it operated in
a psychological vacuum apart from all of the other
attitudes, values, and feelings of human beings. This
psychological model is obviously too simple, and the
danger of it is its implication that white racism is
invulnerable to remedial measures, that it is forever
destined to be part of the American racial scene and
therefore must simply be accepted as an unchanging
fact of American life. Such a view contributes to the
pessimism so prevalent in recent years among people
concerned with race relations. The present analysis
argues that white racism is intertwined with other,
nonracial, attitudes and values. It is true that often these
nonracial concerns support racism. But they also can
come into conflict with racism; it becomes important,
then, to discern precisely which attitudes and values
support racism and which conflict with it, and how these
other attitudes may be influenced in order to alleviate
individual racism.*

*This approach is clearly appropriate to the majority
of white Americans described as "conforming bigots."
The importance of values supporting or conflicting with
racism becomes obvious when apparently inconsistent
racial attitudes and actions crop up among this group. But
even for the minority of white Americans whose racial*

*prejudice is salient and deeply rooted, racism does
not operate in a psychological vacuum. Even for this
hard core, racism must be seen in the context of other
concerns and fears. One method of gaining this broader
perspective is to examine in some detail the social and
psychological characteristics of those who support
blatantly anti-Negro candidates for high office, and it is
this method which is used in the following two chapters.*

*Chapter 9 investigates the supporters of Louise Day
Hicks, who has been a dominant figure in Boston politics
since 1963, when she acquired a reputation as the local
leader of white resistance to racial change. We shall
find consistent patterns of differences between those
voters who support her strongly, those who support her
for lower office only, and those who oppose her. These
patterns suggest that her support is based in the lower
middle class and that her popularity stems from a complex
web of fears and feelings.*

*Chapter 10 reaches similar conclusions in examining
the voters in Gary, Indiana, who supported George
Wallace for President in 1968. Moreover, we will find that
the psychological key to understanding these voters is
the same powerful social-psychological mechanism
discussed in Chapter 7 as the key to understanding black
protest—relative deprivation. Though materially more
comfortable than most Negroes, Wallace's supporters
share much the same sense of being victims of national
neglect relative to other groups of Americans. In an
"age of rising expectations," relative deprivation becomes
an important phenomenon on both sides of the color line.*

Footnotes

1. G. W. Allport, *The Nature of Prejudice* (Cambridge, Mass.:
   Addison-Wesley, 1954), p. 78.
2. Thus, 18 percent of white adults believed in December, 1963,
   that "white people should have the first chance at any kind of
   job"—the most extreme item asked in this survey conducted by
   the National Opinion Research Center of the University of Chi-

cago. At the other extreme, only 27 percent *disagreed* that "Negroes shouldn't push themselves where they're not wanted." P. B. Sheatsley, "White Attitudes Toward the Negro," in Parsons and Clark (eds.), *The Negro American* (Boston: Houghton Mifflin, 1966), pp. 303–324. Similarly, the Harris national survey for *Newsweek* in 1966 found on its four most extreme anti-Negro items that only "the prejudiced fifth" objected "to using the same rest rooms as Negroes" (22 percent), "to sitting next to a Negro in a movie" (21 percent), "to sitting next to a Negro on a bus" (16 percent), and "to sitting next to a Negro in a restaurant" (16 percent). W. Brink and L. Harris, *Black and White: A Study of U.S. Racial Attitudes Today* (New York: Simon and Schuster, 1967), p. 136. Finally, the existence of the "unprejudiced fifth" was revealed in four questions asked in a Gallup national survey in May, 1968. To queries about whether "white people or Negroes themselves" were more to blame for the present conditions of Negroes, only 23 percent of the whites answered "white people"; 19 percent had "no opinion." Likewise, only 17 percent of whites thought that Negroes in their communities were being treated either "badly" or "not very well" (10 percent had "no opinion"); only 18 percent thought businesses in their area discriminated against Negroes in hiring (14 percent had "no opinion"); and only 17 percent thought labor unions in their area discriminated against Negroes in their membership practices (31 percent had "no opinion"). H. G. Erskine, "The Polls: Recent Opinion on Racial Problems," *Public Opinion Quarterly,* Winter 1968–1969, Vol. 32, pp. 696–703.

3. As we shall note in Chapter 10, for example, George Wallace in his 1968 campaign for the Presidency reached a high point of 22 percent (or 25 percent of whites) in the national surveys and secured almost 14 percent (or 16 percent of whites) of the total popular vote cast.

4. Compilations of relevant data from surveys on race relations include: H. G. Erskine, *op. cit.;* "The Polls: Race Relations," *Public Opinion Quarterly,* Spring 1962, Vol. 26, pp. 137–147; "The Polls: Negro Housing," *Public Opinion Quarterly,* Fall 1967, Vol. 31, pp. 482–498; "The Polls: Demonstrations and Race Riots," *Public Opinion Quarterly,* Winter 1967–1968, Vol. 31, pp. 655–677; "The Polls: Negro Employment," *Public Opinion Quarterly,* Spring 1968, Vol. 32, pp. 132–153; "The Polls: Speed of Racial Integration," *Public Opinion Quarterly,* Fall 1968, Vol. 32, pp. 513–524; J. M. Fenton, *In Your Opinion* (Boston: Little, Brown, 1960); W. Brink and L. Harris, *op. cit.;* and *The Negro Revolution in America* (New York: Simon and Schuster, 1964).

CHAPTER NINE

BIGOTRY IN BOSTON: MRS. HICKS AND HER SUPPORTERS

with J. Michael Ross and Thomas Crawford [1]

"I've really got my doubts about all this racial balancing of schools," a white Bostonian remarked to a pollster. "Don't get me wrong—I have nothing against Negroes, and I wouldn't mind having my children go to school with a few Negro children. But I don't like all this busing business." This view and similar views have achieved special importance in recent years as resistance to racial change from whites in the urban North has become more conspicuous. Some observers interpret this resistance as blatant bigotry, different from the Southern variety only in that its idiom is more subtle. Many assert that this bigotry is a "white backlash" produced in response to demands made by Negroes. Others, particularly officeholders who themselves have opposed racial change, insist that this response is not bigotry at all, but merely a strong belief in the educational value of "neighborhood schools."

In order to evaluate these interpretations, we conducted two opinion surveys on the issue in Boston. This old city of liberty and abolition provides fertile ground for such a study: an intense struggle over the racial composition of Boston's public schools began in 1963, and a new political figure emerged as a champion of those who defend the racial, *status quo.* Louise Day Hicks has gained national attention by her forceful rejection of Negro aspirations and her subsequent victories at the polls in elections for a variety of local offices. Indeed, her electoral triumphs make her one of the most politically successful opponents of racial change outside the South. The national significance of her elections lies in the question: Do they mark a new era of explicit resistance by whites to civil rights progress in the urban North?

Mrs. Hicks first ran in 1961 as a reform candidate who wanted "to serve the youth of the city" and "to keep politics out of the School Committee." But by 1963 she had discovered the political value of opposing the moderate requests of Boston's relatively small black community (roughly 15 percent of the city's population). Aided by considerable coverage in the mass media, Mrs. Hicks ran in 1963 as a defender of the *status quo* (that is, "neighborhood schools"), and garnered 69 percent of the vote, easily leading the ticket. After two more years of publicized rejection of requests by Boston's Negroes, in 1965 she received 64 percent of the vote, again easily leading the ticket. In 1967, she received 46 percent of the vote in a losing effort to become mayor of the city. In 1969, she successfully ran for a position on the Boston City Council, once again leading the ticket. And in 1970 she won a seat in the U.S. House of Representatives when the district's liberal vote was split in the Democratic Party primary.

Her triumph in the School Committee election of 1965 evoked a range of reactions. The Roman Catholic Archdiocesan *Pilot* bluntly charged that those who had voted for Hicks had voted ". . . against the rightful claims of the Boston Negro for the education of his children." The defeated black candidate, Melvin King, remarked, "A little bit of democracy died in Boston yesterday." The election results were, he maintained, proof ". . . of the appeal of bigotry and racism in the city." But if Mrs. Hicks's critics see her as a racist, her admirers consider her courageous. They interpreted her victory as a mandate for "neighborhood schools" and against "busing." On election night, Mrs. Hicks observed, "The people are speaking tonight. . . . I am of the people. I don't need any pipelines to know what they want."

The "Hicks phenomenon" has implications that go far beyond the perpetually boiling political pot of Boston. The existence of the Parents and Taxpayers group in New York City, the appearance of politicians in other Northern cities who have attempted campaigns like Mrs. Hicks's, and the approval of pro-segregation housing referenda by large majorities in California, Akron, Detroit, and Seattle —all this indicates a widespread Northern response to racial change. It is appropriate, then, to take a hard look at the elections of this outspoken politician.

Who votes for Mrs. Hicks? Why? And what are the general views of her supporters concerning Negroes and racial change? We set out to answer these questions by selecting nine Boston precincts which provide both middle-class and working-class respondents from each of the city's three major white groups (Irish Americans, Italian Americans, and Jewish Americans). With the able assistance of the National Opinion Research Center, we interviewed a representative sample from each of these nine key precincts. All told, we secured the opinions of 317 white Bostonians in two lengthy interviews conducted nine weeks and one week before the School Committee election of November, 1965.

Our findings cast serious doubts upon many of the facile explanations that have become current. Is it "blatant bigotry"? Not precisely. Our data reveal that support for Mrs. Hicks *is* strongest among the most anti-Negro respondents, but the form their anti-Negro views assume is often not "blatant." Is it a "white backlash"? No. Together with the evidence from throughout the nation which was discussed in Chapter 8, our findings in these surveys show that there is no indication that these anti-Negro opinions have been recently adopted. Is it purely a desire to maintain "neighborhood schools"? Hardly. The idea of "neighborhood schools" is popular, but it is by no means the central issue. In short, white resistance to racial change in the urban North is a much more complex phenomenon than is generally recognized.

Consider, first, the surprising specificity of Mrs. Hicks's electoral support. Her two triumphs in 1963 and 1965, by two-to-one majorities, made her seem unbeatable to many; and her ambition to become Boston's mayor was no longer considered a joke. Yet our surveys revealed that most Bostonians—even among those who supported her for the School Committee—did *not* want to see her become mayor. Disregarding those respondents who had no opinion, only 27 percent of our sample were so pro-Hicks that they both supported her for the School Committee and wanted her for mayor (the designation "pro-Hicks" will hereafter refer to this group). The largest group (43 percent) were only partial supporters; they backed her for the School Committee but did not want to see her become mayor (the designation "partial supporters" will refer to this group). The anti-Hicks group, opposing her for both offices, account for the remaining 30 percent of our sample (the designation "anti-Hicks" will refer to this group). The accuracy of these data for 1965 was proven two years later, when Mrs. Hicks received 28 percent—the same percentage as our pro-Hicks group—in the mayorality primary and went on in the runoff to lose to Kevin White, then the Secretary of State of Massachusetts and Boston's answer to John Lindsay of New York.

The complexity of the phenomenon begins to emerge when we compare these three groups of white Bostonians. In terms of broad social characteristics, the pro-Hicks group resemble their Southern counterparts: these resisters of racial change were, as a group, less educated, poorer, and older than others in the sample. Interestingly, the partial supporters of Mrs. Hicks fell neatly between the other two groups in terms of education, income, and age.

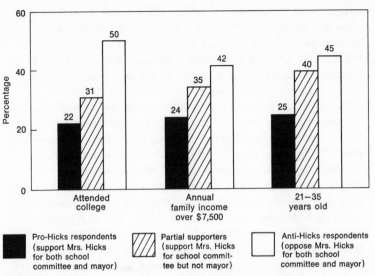

Figure 5. Survey results: Background characteristics of respondents.

The anti-Hicks group were the best educated, richest, and youngest. See Figure 5 for the complete results relevant to this point. But the likeness of this sample to their counterparts in the South ends when one asks them certain direct questions concerning Negroes and racial discrimination. Only 12 percent of the entire sample, for instance, thought Negroes were not as intelligent as whites; only 16 percent admitted that they "disliked Negroes as a group"; and 95 percent believed that "Negroes should have as good a chance as white people to get any kind of job." [2] Nationwide surveys employing these same questions have actually found white Northerners in general to be considerably less tolerant of blacks than this Boston sample.

Indeed, this attitude of the Boston sample extended in part to schools. All 317 of our respondents were asked: "Do you think white students and Negro students should go to the same schools or to separate schools?" Only 7 percent of our full sample preferred separate schools; and even among the pro-Hicks group only 9 percent preferred separate schools. What about parents? Each of the respondents who had children in, or about to enroll in, Boston's public schools was asked if he had "any objection to sending his children to a school where *a few* of the children are Negro." Only 1 percent had any objection.

The real fears and racial antipathies of the sample did not become apparent until our surveys probed beyond abstract principles and views on token integration: 22 percent of the parents said they objected to sending their children to a school where *half* of the student body was Negro; 64 percent objected to sending their children to a school where *more than half* was Negro. Here differences in opinion between the pro-Hicks group, the partial supporters, and the anti-Hicks group became evident. At each level of education, pro-Hicks parents objected to enrolling their children in a predominantly Negro school more than anti-Hicks parents.

We found that subtle anti-Negro sentiments were often evoked by questions concerning the pace and nature of recent efforts for change by Negroes. Sixty-two percent of the entire sample thought that "civil rights leaders are trying to push too fast"; 52 percent thought that the protest actions of Negroes have been "generally violent"; and 48 percent thought that "the actions Negroes have taken, on the whole, *hurt* their cause." In each of these instances, pro-Hicks respondents gave these responses more than comparably educated anti-Hicks respondents; the partial supporters fell roughly midway between the two other groups (see Figure 6).

Questions related to specific aspects of school controversies in the North reveal fundamental inconsistencies. While 65 percent of the total sample realized that "racial imbalance does exist in the Boston public schools" and 45 percent believed that "racial imbalance in schools hurts the education of children," large majorities still favored "neighborhood schools," opposed busing of any type, and insisted that "Negro children are getting equal educational

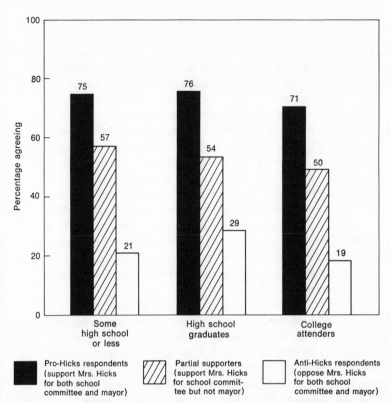

Figure 6. Survey results: Respondents agreeing that "Negroes' actions have hurt their cause."

opportunities in Boston's public schools." For example, two-thirds of our respondents agreed that "children should always go to school in their own neighborhood, no matter what." Eighty-seven percent rejected the busing of white children to predominantly Negro schools; 71 percent rejected busing Negro children to predominantly white schools. These inconsistencies suggest that white Northerners are surprisingly misinformed or uninformed about how interracial education might be achieved. So much of the controversy has focused upon "neighborhood schools"

Bigotry in Boston: Mrs. Hicks and Her Supporters

and "busing" that few of our respondents were aware that "busing" is only one of many methods of achieving racially balanced schools—a method which is, incidentally, not particularly popular among black parents. We tried in pilot studies to explore opinions about other balancing techniques, such as redrawing school district lines, strategically locating new schools, pairing white and black schools, and building large metropolitan educational parks like those described in Chapter 4; but most of the people questioned in our pilot research did not know of such techniques. They failed to see any direct relationship between these actions and the racial balancing of schools, and they simply did not have opinions about them. Nationwide polls have found much the same situation in other cities. This fact points to the possibility that there could be some reduction in white resistance to school desegregation in the North if the public comes to know more about the issue.

To be sure, the political preferences of our sample are consistent with their positions on school balancing as they understand it. The issues do seem to be important; the popularity of Mrs. Hicks is not, as some observers claim, solely a function of her personal appeal as a "courageous mother." Thus, the pro-Hicks respondents most often endorsed "neighborhood schools," opposed "busing," and denied the harmfulness, indeed the existence, of imbalanced schools. Once again, however, the critical middle group, the partial supporters, tended to respond midway between the pro-Hicks and anti-Hicks members of the sample; and among the resisters to change, these are the people who are the most likely to be influenced by reassuring additional information on the issue.

Our data for Boston are consistent with the findings for the nation related to a so-called "backlash," cited in detail in Chapter 8. Since we did not conduct interviews in Boston in 1963, we cannot test directly for voting and attitude shifts over these years. But at least our respondents report marked uniformity in their voting for or against Mrs. Hicks in 1963 and 1965. Moreover, the sentiments we uncovered favoring Mrs. Hicks and racially imbalanced public schools were typically connected with an orientation of personality and a political orientation that extended beyond racial issues. Thus, at each educational level, the pro-Hicks members of the sample most often agreed with such statements as these: "If a child is unusual in any way, his parents should get him to be more like other children." "Things are pretty good nowadays—it is best to keep things the way they are" (see Figure 7). "We should be sympathetic with mental patients, but we cannot expect to understand their odd behavior" (see Figure 8).

It seems unlikely, then, that such fundamental outlooks on life—outlooks repeatedly shown in social-science research to be associated with intergroup prejudice—would have been created recently and suddenly: that is, that they represent a "white backlash." A more plausible explanation is that these anti-Negro attitudes were shaped long

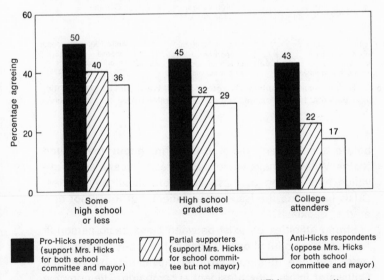

Figure 7. Survey results: Respondents agreeing that "Things are pretty good nowadays—it is best to keep things the way they are."

Bigotry in Boston: Mrs. Hicks and Her Supporters

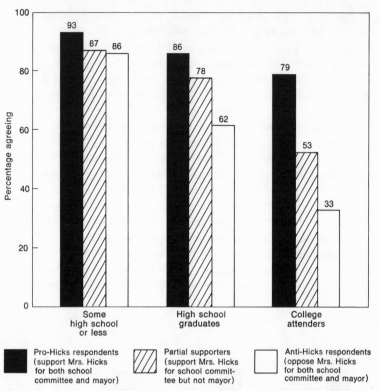

Figure 8. Survey results: Respondents agreeing that "We should be sympathetic with mental patients, but we cannot expect to understand their odd behavior."

before the present racial crisis throughout the United States. What we have witnessed in recent years is an activation and voicing of these long-held racial animosities. Crisis has made the issue more salient, but it has not created a "backlash."

Strong affinities do exist between these basic personality traits and political orientations of the pro-Hicks respondents and the general position advanced by Senator Goldwater in his 1964 presidential campaign. The common core is a general psychological predisposition to resist and condemn the liberal policies of the last four decades. It is a feeling of discomfort and confusion resulting from the inability to understand and cope with the exceptionally fast pace of social change in the urban environment. "There is a stir in the land," noted Goldwater. "There is a mood of uneasiness. We feel adrift in an uncharted land and stormy sea. We feel we have lost our way." Goldwater's ideas revolved around moral deficiencies: "The moral fiber of the American people is beset by rot and decay." Similarly, our pro-Hicks respondents most often agreed that "the facts on crime and sexual immorality show that we will have to crack down harder on young people if we are going to save our moral standards." Likewise, the pro-Hicks supporters with high school and college education typically reflected Goldwater's emphatic rejection of liberal ideology and distrust of the liberal intellectual who "frowns on the policeman and fawns on the social psychologist." [3] They most frequently believed that the government gives "too much" attention to "problems such as housing, unemployment, and education," and that "a lot of professors and government experts have too much influence on too many things nowadays."

As national surveys revealed, Goldwater's stand on specific economic issues and his impulsive attitude toward foreign affairs deterred many voters from voting for him and thus from expressing their feelings of discontent on the national level. When only local issues are involved, however, these dispositions can play a crucial role in determining preference for the candidate who is most vocal in resisting change. This aspect of the Boston scene also appeared in New York City, in somewhat less dramatic fashion, with the vote for William F. Buckley for mayor in 1965 and the protests of the Parents and Taxpayers group; by 1969, it had also appeared dominantly in the elections of right-wingers in major cities such as Los Angeles and Minneapolis. By the time of this writing, it is being seen in the popularity, in some quarters, of the uninhibited speeches of Vice-President Spiro Agnew; in their attacks on the "Eastern establishment," the mass media, and the universities, they closely resemble Goldwater's message of 1964.

This feeling of discontent, then, definitely underlies many of the attempts to resist change that we are seeing in our cities today. It is not the result of any recent "white-backlash"—in fact, racial concerns are only one manifestation of this generalized resentment against social change. Discontent is strongly felt by a sizable minority of the white urban electorate. This minority has some difficulty in mobilizing full support for candidates for high offices, such as the Presidency; but for lower offices, particularly when the candidate is an incumbent, this minority becomes politically important. In the Boston School Committee elections, the pro-Hicks, discontented minority was joined by the larger and less extreme group we have called "partial supporters"; for the higher office of mayor, however, many of Mrs. Hicks's partial supporters deserted her in 1967.

Let us now examine the third popular explanation for white resistance to racial change in urban school systems: the argument that bigotry is not involved at all, that parents of children in public schools are merely expressing strong preferences for "neighborhood schools" and against "busing." We have already seen that the first part of this idea is not confirmed by the data from our survey: bigotry is involved, for at each educational level the supporters of Mrs. Hicks are more anti-Negro than those who oppose her. The second part contains a kernel of truth: "neighborhood schools" are popular, and "busing" is unpopular. Moreover, there are differences between our three groups of Bostonians in the degree to which they use the public schools. Twenty-five percent of the pro-Hicks respondents now send or will soon send children to the city's public schools, in contrast to 16 percent of the partial supporters and 10 percent of the anti-Hicks respondents. If only 25 percent of the pro-Hicks group are parents of public school students, this means that 75 percent of Mrs. Hicks's staunchest supporters are not directly involved with Boston's public educational facilities. Clearly, then, the reasons for their position in the racial crisis lie beyond purely educational issues; in addition to general discontent, what precisely are these reasons?

Our data strongly point to the central importance of opposition to biracial neighborhoods. We believe that the special significance of the sudden devotion in the urban North to the concept of the "neighborhood school" lies more in the adjective "neighborhood" than in the noun "school"; and that the rejection of "busing" is linked to the perception by many whites that "busing" is a harbinger of residential desegregation. This interpretation would explain why the pro-Hicks group in our sample were those most involved with their neighborhoods, most hostile to residential desegregation, and most likely to live in all-white neighborhoods.

The greater neighborhood involvement of Mrs. Hicks's supporters is revealed by their ownership of homes and the importance of their local roots and ties. Half of the pro-Hicks group owned their own homes, compared with only 37 percent of the partial supporters and only 29 percent of the anti-Hicks group. Even more striking, 42 percent of the pro-Hicks group had owned their present homes for more than ten years; 42 percent of the anti-Hicks group had rented their present homes for less than four years. These differences are especially marked among the younger members of the sample. Forty percent of the pro-Hicks respondents under 36 years of age had lived more than ten years in their present neighborhoods, compared with 24 percent of the partial supporters and only 10 percent of the anti-Hicks respondents in the same age groups. Finally, the anti-Hicks respondents least often chatted with their neighbors, least often had nearby relatives, and most often came originally from places outside of Boston.

Where housing is concerned, much of the subtlety which clothes racial prejudice in the North is lost—even among

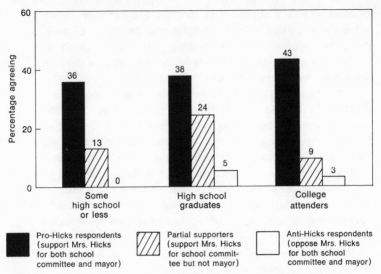

Figure 9. Survey results: Respondents agreeing that "White people have a right to keep Negroes out of their neighborhoods if they want to."

the well-educated. This becomes apparent when we contrast the three groups on questions related to residential desegregation (see Figures 9 and 10). At each educational level, the pro-Hicks group agreed more than others that "it is best to keep [Negroes] in their own districts and schools" and that "white people have a right to keep Negroes out of their neighborhoods if they want to." They also volunteered—more often than comparably educated partial supporters and anti-Hicks respondents—a variety of unfavorable comments concerning the prospect of "a Negro with the same income and education" moving into their blocks. Indeed, of all the questions in our survey, these three questions on housing as a cluster evoked the largest and most consistent differences between our three groups.

Finally, evidence for the special importance of housing desegregation may also be found in a comparison among the groups concerning reported contact with Negroes.

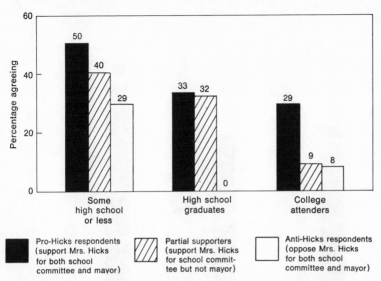

Figure 10. Survey results: Respondents agreeing that "Negroes certainly have their rights, but it is best to keep them in their own districts and schools and to prevent too much contact with whites."

Some of the fear of biracial neighborhoods may well stem from the lack of equal-status contacts with Negroes in the past and present. Thus, at each educational level the pro-Hicks respondents reported far more often than anti-Hicks respondents that they presently live in all-white neighborhoods (see Figure 11). Furthermore, the pro-Hicks respondents were far less likely to "know personally a Negro professional" than similarly educated anti-Hicks respondents.

These close links between attitudes toward school policies concerning racial balance and resistance to residential desegregation pose special problems. Many Northern educators, caught in the crossfire of the current crisis, have argued that school desegregation should logically await housing desegregation. Yet our data suggest that white resistance to interracial neighborhoods is far more entrenched than direct opposition to school desegrega-

Bigotry in Boston: Mrs. Hicks and Her Supporters
225

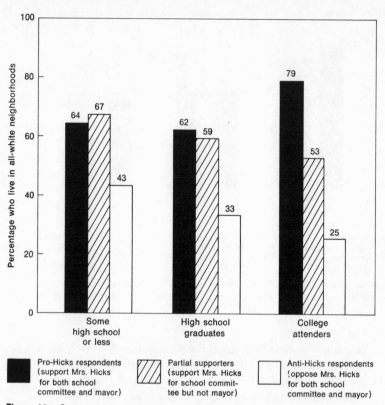

Figure 11. Survey results: Residence of respondents in all-white neighborhoods.

tion. Indeed, it appears that Mrs. Hicks effectively tapped these fundamental fears by tirelessly reiterating the "neighborhood school" theme, with special emphasis upon "neighborhood."

Intense pressure for racial reform in public schools will undoubtedly continue to develop throughout the nation. And residential desegregation is likely to progress at too slow a pace—even with Federal legislation—to aid the schools significantly. Thus, racial change in the public educational systems of the urban North must generally precede, not follow, racial change in housing.

Racism at the Ballot Box

This conclusion indicates that the bitter struggles that have raged over the schools in cities from Boston to Oakland will probably continue. Are there indications of how such struggles might be alleviated, if not avoided, in the future? Data from our surveys offer hope along the same lines that have proven effective in prodding the reluctant South. To put it bluntly, money is the Achilles' heel of bigotry. As was emphasized in Chapter 6, attitudes toward any one issue cannot be viewed in isolation; all attitudes, including those about race, are embedded in a network of other, often conflicting, attitudes. In particular, anti-Negro attitudes and discriminatory practices are frequently pitted against financial considerations. Racial conflict and bad publicity can hurt a city's image and economy, as Little Rock and New Orleans learned too late. In Boston, insistence upon racially imbalanced schools could lead to a rise in local taxes by causing a cutoff of state and Federal funds to the city's schools. In 1965 Massachusetts enacted a statute that empowers the State Commissioner of Education to halt state funds to a school district which insists on maintaining schools of imbalanced racial enrollments. And this power was later invoked against the Boston public schools. Title VI of the 1964 Civil Rights Act gives similar, if less explicit, powers to the United States Commissioner of Education. Such laws pose a threat to Mrs. Hicks and other politicians of similar persuasion. Consequently, we asked our 317 sample members if they agreed or disagreed with the following statement: "Although taxes may go up, it is better to lose state aid to Boston public schools than to bring about racial balance in the schools." Figure 12 shows the results: only 17 percent of our total sample agreed; for the vast majority, lower taxes easily outranked school segregation in importance. Even among the pro-Hicks group, only a minority were willing to pay more taxes for segregated schools. And among the key group, the partial supporters, only one-fifth were willing to pay the price for segregation.

Finances, then, offer an effective lever for social

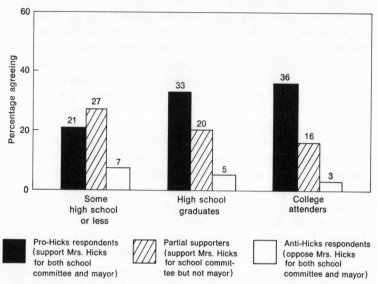

Figure 12. Survey results: Percentage of respondents agreeing that "Although taxes may go up, it is better to lose state aid to Boston public schools than to bring about racial balance in the schools."

change. But granting funds to discriminating school districts and later withdrawing these funds is politically difficult—as is revealed by the lack of enforcement of these statutes to date. Moreover, this procedure places the burden of proof upon understaffed governmental agencies—not on the school district itself. In short, withholding promised school funds is an unpopular and unwieldy "stick" approach, though it is potentially valuable in particularly difficult situations. Other legislation, both state and Federal, could supplement these existing statutes with a variety of financial "carrots." Shifting the burden of proof onto the school systems themselves, these "carrot" statutes could offer funds only for those educational endeavors which definitely produce or further desegregation. For example, new school construction could be financed only after the placement of the proposed schools is shown to contribute significantly to greater racial balance. In Chapter 4 we discussed in detail one such plan, the metropolitan educational park, which we noted required Federal incentive funds to come into being.

Summary

The problem of desegregating the schools of the urban North will be with us for some time to come. Fueled in large part by a generalized discontent and fears of interracial housing, resistance to the process will continue. Efforts toward alleviating the problem by increasing the amount of residential desegregation will help but are likely to be too slow. The directions the evolving solutions must take, however, are becoming clearer. We need the carrot *and* the stick to influence the process through state and Federal funds. And the inner cities desperately need aid from surrounding suburbs if they are to break the deadlock and contribute positively to this acute national problem.

Footnotes

1. Ross is currently a Research Associate in the Social Relations Department of Harvard University; Crawford is an Assistant Professor of Psychology at the University of California, Berkeley.
2. By comparison, 41 percent of white Southerners in 1963 believed Negroes to be less intelligent, and only 81 percent believed Negroes should have an equal chance to secure employment. H. H. Hyman and P. B. Sheatsley, "Attitudes toward Desegregation," *Scientific American*, July, 1964, Vol. 211, pp. 16–23; and P. B. Sheatsley, "White Attitudes toward the Negro," in Parsons and Clark (eds.), *The Negro American* (Boston: Houghton Mifflin, 1966), p. 317.
3. As social psychologists, we were intrigued by Senator Goldwater's going out of his way to specify our small and little-known discipline. In any event, we can assure the reader that no one has actually "fawned" on us lately.

Bigotry in Boston: Mrs. Hicks and Her Supporters

CHAPTER TEN

THE SOCIAL PSYCHOLOGY OF THE WALLACE PHENOMENON

with Robert T. Riley [1]

"Little George" Wallace's [2] nationwide bid for the Presidency of the United States in 1968 represents a full-blown political phenomenon of our times. As Wolfe points out, it was the first time in 112 years that a strong challenge to the two major parties had been posed by a right-wing candidate. [3] Wallace attracted almost 10 million (14 percent) of the votes cast and carried five states. Fifty-eight percent of his popular vote, and all of his votes in the electoral college, came from his native South; but if Wallace's American Independent Party (in 1968, Wallace and the American Independent Party were one and the same) received 30 percent of the South's votes, it also received almost 8 percent of the Northern and Western vote, with only Hawaii and Maine giving him less than 3 percent of their votes. Who are Wallace's supporters? What lies behind the Wallace phenomenon, especially in the urban North?

Some initial answers can be derived from the post-election surveys made by the University of Michigan's Survey Research Center (S.R.C.). [4] In the South, Wallace's supporters disproportionately reside in small towns and on farms. Indeed, they closely resemble the voters for the previous Southern segregationist third-party candidate, South Carolina's Strom Thurmond, who ran in 1948 on the Dixiecrat ticket but was unable to attract any significant support in the North. Both Wallace and Thurmond, for example, ran best in the Deep South, worst in the Upper South.[5] Wallace, however, acquired considerable support in the North in large central cities as well as in some suburbs and open country. In both regions, S.R.C. found that Wallace supporters more often have grown up on a farm, regardless of where they live today. And in spite of numerous speculations to the contrary in the mass media, the Wallace supporters in the North were not typically white migrants from the South.[6]

The rural and small-town base of the American Independent Party's Southern constituency indicates a generalized conservatism going beyond just racial issues. Together with the national election, Virginia had on the ballot in November, 1968, referenda on "liquor-by-the-drink" and state educational bonds. Table 6 shows the correlations between votes for Nixon, Wallace, liquor, and the bonds across precincts for central-city Richmond (excluding eighteen overwhelmingly Negro precincts) and each of three counties surrounding the city. With Humphrey receiving relatively few white votes, the totals for Wallace and Nixon across precincts relate negatively in all four areas. In these Virginia districts, then, two contrasting types of conservatism emerge. One type, found in more prosperous precincts, favored Nixon, liquor by the drink, and more state bonds for public education (a "good government" issue).[7] The second type, found in less affluent precincts, backed Wallace, opposed liquor by the drink, and opposed the educational bonds. The consistently negative correlations between liquor by the drink and Wallace offer evidence of the fundamentalistic religious quality of the Wallace phenomenon in the South.[8] And the consistently negative correlations with the bond issue offer evi-

Table 6 GENERAL CONSERVATISM AND THE 1968 WALLACE VOTE IN VIRGINIA

	Pearson product-moment correlations across precincts between				
	Wallace– Nixon	Wallace–Liquor by the Drink	Nixon–Liquor by the Drink	Wallace–Education Bonds	Nixon–Education Bonds
Central-city Richmond (51 precincts) [1]	–.35	–.71	+.10	–.63	–.16
Henrico County (40 precincts)	–.89	–.85	+.78	–.94	+.84
Chesterfield County (28 precincts)	–.88	–.79	+.80	–.67	+.56
Hanover County (14 precincts)	–.47	–.47	+.54	–.47	+.35

1. Eighteen overwhelmingly Negro precincts omitted.

dence for the "protest against the establishment" which was basic to the phenomenon.

Five social characteristics predominated among Wallace voters: they tended to be (1) white, (2) men, (3) married, (4) relatively young, and (5) working class. Black Americans, needless to say, did not cast their ballots for Wallace, any more than German Jews cast their ballots for Adolf Hitler. For that matter, Negroes rarely voted for Nixon either, and thus accounted for about one fifth of Humphrey's total though they were less than one tenth of the electorate. The sharp preponderance of men among the Wallace following in both the North and the South is noteworthy. Surveys of a variety of polling agencies indicated that at least three out of five supporters of the American Independent Party were men, compared with only about four-ninths of the supporters of the Republican and Democratic parties. Wallace supporters were more likely than others in the electorate to be married and between the ages of 25 and 34. There were very few Wallace supporters among voters over 65 years old, who hold the strongest loyalties to the two major parties. Finally, all the surveys and special studies agree that the basic constituency of the American Independent Party was of lower status, was identified with the "working class," and had only modest education and income.[9] But, as we will note shortly, the very poorest whites in the urban North tended to remain Democrats.

The greater susceptibility of men to an authoritarian candidate who symbolizes protest has often been noted in political studies throughout the world—for example, among neo-Nazi voters in current West German elections.[10] It is interesting, however, that the men who backed Wallace often could not influence their wives to do so. Working-class families are generally characterized by a patriarchal structure and by an expectation that the wife will follow her husband's lead on political and other general matters; this fact makes the wives' resistance to Wallace and his party all the more significant and intriguing.

Not surprisingly, the supporters of the American Independent Party were inconsistent and divided in their orientations to the two major parties. Wolfe reports, on the basis of S.R.C.'s survey data, that Wallace's voters were far more likely to identify themselves as Democrats or Independents than as Republicans; and they tended to vote for Democratic candidates for Congress. But if Wallace had not run, they would have generally preferred to vote for Nixon.[11]

Consistent with their difficulty in aligning themselves with either major party, the Wallace supporters generally stood to the right of those who supported Humphrey or Nixon.[12] They were far more often hawks on the war in Vietnam, yet sharply more isolationist. They were against permitting protest marches and favored using force to "solve" urban unrest. And, of course, S.R.C.'s data reveal them to be consistently and blatantly more anti-Negro and more resistant to racial change on each racial question asked in the survey.

A deep cynicism concerning government, combined with a sense of political powerlessness, seems to have characterized many of the supporters of the American Independent Party. By significant margins, they more often agreed that the Federal government is "getting too powerful," "wastes a lot of money," and "can be trusted [only] some of the time"; that Federal employees often are "not smart" and are "crooked"; and that political "parties don't keep their promises." They most often believed that "public officials don't care how people think"; that "government doesn't pay much attention to people"; that "politics are too complicated"; and that "people don't influence government much." This sense of political alienation detected by S.R.C. in national data may be most widespread among Wallace supporters in the South; as we shall see shortly, data from Gary, Indiana, suggest a more complex picture in the North.

Some observers argue that Wallace successfully appeals to this segment of the electorate by mixing conservatism with a dash of old-time Populism.[13] One of the statements used by S.R.C. to measure cynicism sounds like a Populist slogan of the 1890s—"The federal government is run by a few big interests." Of the Wallace voters, 65 percent interviewed agreed with it, compared with only 39 percent of the Nixon voters and 32 percent of the Humphrey voters. Moreover, on two questions concerning Federal aid, Wallace's supporters reacted more favorably than Nixon supporters (though less favorably than Humphrey supporters): these were questions about Federal medical assistance and Federal employment assistance. We shall discuss later this interesting blend of economic liberalism and racism.

The Wallace Phenomenon in the Urban North

Interesting as these findings from national surveys are, they fail to isolate the distinctively regional aspects of the Wallace phenomenon. In a number of important respects, the constituency of the American Independent Party in the South differs from its constituency in the rest of the country. In the South, as we have noted, the movement had a flavor of regional nationalism, bolstered by the fact that "Little George" had won some acceptance beyond the region.[14] Traditionalism, nationalism, fundamentalism, racism, and a dash of Populism—all these familiar ingredients make up the heady political brew favored by George Wallace's supporters in the Deep South. This is not new; what is new is the 8 percent of the vote he achieved outside his native region, most of it in industrial cities. Let us concentrate attention upon these Wallace supporters of the urban North; for they are a more direct measure of the madness of our times.

We will employ two complementary research approaches to the problem. First, we will look at the precinct results in three Northern cities: Boston, Cleveland, and Gary. At this aggregate level, the key question is, How do precincts in those areas which provided relatively strong support for Wallace differ from those which did not? Second, we will focus upon individual voters, using a special opinion survey similar to the Boston study described in Chapter 9. This survey was conducted just before the election in October of 1968 in Gary, Indiana, where Wallace was reputed to be surprisingly popular.

The precinct analysis of voting patterns is more difficult than it might first appear. To achieve our present purpose, we had to eliminate every precinct whose Negro population exceeded 10 percent in the 1960 census,[15] and to construct the social characteristics for each precinct from the census by a variety of techniques.[16] Only then were we able to test for the differences between relatively pro-Wallace and anti-Wallace precincts.

In general, the findings about voting from our extensive regression analyses are similar across the three cities.[17] The centers of Wallace's electoral strength were typically precincts with relatively low rents and low housing values. The residents of these precincts tended to have limited educations but medium incomes; this disparity between education and income is the most conspicuous and interesting feature of pro-Wallace precincts in all three cities. The poorest white precincts did not report substantial votes for Wallace. In addition, these areas were marked in all three cities by relatively greater instability; that is, many of their residents in 1960 had not lived in the same residence five years before.[18] Strongly anti-Wallace precincts present a contrasting profile: greater affluence, education, and stability.

Aside from these dominant trends, the two types of precincts presented somewhat different patterns in the three cities. Pro-Wallace areas in Boston and Cleveland typically had older homes owned by their occupants, but in Gary they had newer, often rented homes. And in Gary precincts with numerous Polish Americans and Czech Americans tended to vote heavily for Wallace, but this was not the case in Cleveland.[19] Finally, areas with high percentages of first- and second-generation Americans of all nationalities generally cast relatively large votes for Wallace in Cleveland and Gary, but relatively small votes in Boston. Within the overall patterns of social class, then, certain subsidiary neighborhood and ethnic factors varied according to particular social contexts in the individual cities.

We noted in Chapter 8, when discussing the mythical "white backlash," that it is hazardous to make inferences about *people* from data on *areas.* To avoid this "ecological fallacy," we must review data for individuals from a survey in a Northern city. During October, 1968, we interviewed 257 male voters who were representative of nine white precincts in Gary, Indiana.[20] Our overall figures indicate that Gary is indeed the place to study the Northern wing of the Wallace phenomenon. Although 42 percent of the white male respondents favored Nixon and 28 percent favored Humphrey, 30 percent favored Wallace—a percentage twice that found for white men in the North by national pre-election surveys. In the actual election (one month after the survey) the figure for white voters of both sexes in Gary was approximately 22 percent; this can undoubtedly be accounted for by the presence of women in the electorate, who were not interviewed in our all-male study, and by strenuous efforts made for Humphrey by unions in the final weeks of the campaign.[21]

Those who favored Wallace were not in any sense marginal members of the Gary community. Table 7 shows a

Table 7   PERSONAL CHARACTERISTICS AND CANDIDATE PREFERENCE IN GARY, INDIANA, 1968

	Wallace supporters	Nixon supporters	Humphrey supporters	Total
Total Sample (245) [1]	29.8%	42.0%	28.2%	100%
Age				
20–35 (young) (67)	38.8	38.8	22.4	100%
36–55 (middle-aged) (105)	37.1	42.9	20.0	100%
56 + (old) (73)	11.0	43.8	45.2	100%

	Wallace supporters	Nixon supporters	Humphrey supporters	Total
Total Sample (245) [1]	*29.8%*	*42.0%*	*28.2%*	*100%*
Education				
Grade school (45)	18.2	36.4	45.5	100%
Some high school (41)	43.9	26.8	29.3	100%
High school graduate (80)	36.2	40.0	23.7	100%
College (67)	23.9	58.2	17.9	100%
Occupation				
Blue collar (155)	38.0	31.7	30.3	100%
White collar (87)	12.6	62.2	25.2	100%
Union membership				
Yes (142)	38.5	32.5	29.0	100%
No (101)	16.8	56.4	26.7	100%
Income				
Less than $5,000 (37)	8.1	35.1	56.8	100%
$5,000–$7,500 (54)	31.5	38.9	29.6	100%
$7,500–$10,000 (64)	48.5	32.8	18.7	100%
$10,000–$15,000 (56)	28.6	44.6	26.8	100%
$15,000 and over (22)	9.1	68.2	22.7	100%
Religion				
Protestant (111)	36.0	45.0	18.9	100%
Roman Catholic (104)	26.0	38.5	35.6	100%
Party				
Democrats (113)	26.5	22.1	51.3	100%
Independents (81)	42.0	45.7	12.3	100%
Republicans (48)	12.5	85.4	2.1	100%
Subjective social class				
Working (133)	39.8	30.8	29.3	100%
Middle (111)	18.0	55.9	26.1	100%
Class identification				
Strong working (87)	43.7	31.0	25.3	100%
Weak working (45)	33.3	28.9	37.8	100%
Strong middle (69)	14.5	55.1	30.4	100%
Weak middle (39)	23.1	59.0	17.9	100%

1. The numbers in parentheses refer to the absolute number of respondents in each row. Though the total number interviewed was 257, twelve men expressed no candidate preference and are thus excluded from these analyses.

comparison of the backers of the three candidates.[22] Note that Wallace did disproportionately well among the young and the middle-aged, those with some high school training, blue-collar workers, members of labor unions, and those with moderate family incomes. [23] He did poorly among the old and those with either quite low or high family incomes. Indeed, those with annual family incomes between $7,500 and $10,000 were *six* times more likely to prefer Wallace than those with family incomes under $5,000 (48.5 percent to 8.1 percent). By contrast, the truly poor favored Humphrey and the well-off favored Nixon, though both the Democratic and Republican followings ranged far more widely over the social spectrum than that of the American Independent Party. Note, too, that Wallace's support was greater among Protestants and those who considered themselves political "independents." [24]

The findings on "subjective social class," consisting of the social-class identifications which the survey respondents applied to themselves, are of special interest. The results (summarized in Table 7) revealed that not only was Wallace stronger among those who identified themselves as "working class" than among those identifying themselves as "middle class," but he was especially popular among those who "felt close to the working class." At the extremes, a respondent in our sample who strongly identified himself with the working class was three times more likely to prefer Wallace than a respondent who strongly identified himself with the middle class (43.7 percent to 14.5 percent). Clearly, then, the Wallace supporters in Gary were "solid citizens"; this image is similar to the one we have already gleaned from national surveys and precinct analyses.

Consistent with this image of the Wallace supporters is their political involvement. Among those who reported having worn campaign buttons, used a candidate's bumper stickers, donated money to a political campaign, or worked actively for a candidate, Wallace supporters were *over*-represented—a fact which runs counter to the description of these people as politically alienated. Moreover, of the three groups of voters, they reported the *most* interest in local and national politics. Yet as Table 8 shows, on each of the four "political alienation" statements those who agreed were somewhat more likely to be Wallace supporters than those who disagreed. But the contradiction is more apparent than real. To start with, while the differences shown in Table 8 are consistent, they are not as large as those reported for a nationwide sample by Wolfe.[25] And it may well be that by the time of our survey Wallace's candidacy itself had stimulated political activity and interest among his supporters, even though their detachment from "public officials" and "the government" (see Table 8) remained high. In any event, we shall soon see that control of an additional social-psychological variable largely eliminates the differences between supporters of the American Independent Party and other voters on the items listed in Table 8.

Three other psychological variables proved more predictive of support for Wallace: feelings of fear and distrust, anti-Negro prejudice, and relative deprivation. Table 9 summarizes the results on the first of these dimensions. Note that in each of the five statements, those with fearful suspicions were far more likely to favor Wallace than those without them.[26] Thus, disproportionate strength for Wallace is found among those who believed that the assassinations of national leaders are planned by a group, that Communists and other outsiders are chiefly responsible for race riots, that race riots are likely to spread to their neighborhoods, that buses without a policeman are not safe, and that safety on the streets is the most important issue facing the nation. These findings recall the national data indicating a high degree of cynicism among Wallace supporters (see page 235) and the data from Boston on Mrs. Hicks's supporters cited in Chapter 9.

This pattern of perceiving conspiracies and hostility in the surrounding environment occurs frequently throughout the history of American politics. Richard Hofstadter, the

Table 8 POLITICAL ALIENATION

	Wallace supporters	Nixon supporters	Humphrey supporters	Total
Statement Total Sample (245)	*29.8%*	*42.0%*	*28.2%*	*100%*
"Public officials don't care what people like me think."				
Agree (123)	33.6	38.5	27.9	100%
Disagree (122)	26.1	44.5	29.4	100%
"Politics and government seem so complicated that a person like me can't really understand what's going on."				
Agree (172)	32.9	35.9	31.2	100%
Disagree (73)	21.1	56.3	22.5	100%
"People like me don't have anything to say about what the government does."				
Agree (100)	36.4	32.3	31.3	100%
Disagree (144)	25.7	48.6	25.7	100%
"Voting is the only way that people like me can have a say about how the government runs things."				
Agree (183)	33.0	39.6	27.5	100%
Disagree (62)	21.3	49.2	29.5	100%

noted social historian, described the syndrome in *The Paranoid Style in American Politics:*

Paranoid spokesmen in politics see the hostile and conspirational world directed against a nation or culture. . . . His sense of political passions is unselfish and patriotic, in fact, goes far to intensify his feelings of righteousness and moral indignation.[27]

Viewing the world in this way has been characteristic of many marginal political groups in the United States in the past: the Free-Masons, the Know-Nothings, the Populists, the Coughlinites and the [Joseph] McCarthyites.

As Table 10 shows, this analysis can be extended by means of a similar pattern of findings. The fears and sus-

Table 9   FEAR AND DISTRUST

	Wallace supporters	Nixon supporters	Humphrey supporters	Total
Statement Total Sample (245)	*29.8%*	*42.0%*	*28.2%*	*100%*
"Assassination of national leaders is carefully planned by ————."				
A group (173)	36.8	33.5	29.7	100%
Individuals (72)	18.6	52.8	28.6	100%
"The major cause of riots is ————."				
Social conditions (72)	11.1	46.3	42.6	100%
Local Negroes (23)	24.4	51.2	24.4	100%
Communists, outsiders (150)	38.7	37.2	24.1	100%
"Violent riots' spreading to my neighborhood is ————."				
Likely (135)	36.8	36.1	27.1	100%
Very unlikely (110)	21.6	49.6	28.8	100%
"Buses are not safe these days without a policeman."				
Agree (173)	36.6	37.3	26.1	100%
Disagree (72)	17.7	46.8	35.5	100%
"Safety on the streets is the most important issue facing America now."				
Agree (193)	34.0	39.3	26.7	100%
Disagree (52)	15.4	50.0	34.6	100%

picions of Wallace supporters often are focused specifically upon racial concerns. Wallace supporters were more numerous among those who did not believe that Negroes are as intelligent as whites and among those more willing to discriminate against Negroes in housing, schools, and face-to-face contact; furthermore, Wallace supporters are disproportionately found among those who report that they had *not* visited socially with Negroes recently. They were also 2½ times more likely to agree that the "police should shoot to kill" to prevent looting during a riot.

The Social Psychology of the Wallace Phenomenon

Table 10   RACIAL CONCERNS

Statement Total Sample (245)	Wallace supporters	Nixon supporters	Humphrey supporters	Total
	29.8%	42.0%	28.2%	100%
"Negroes are as intelligent as white people."				
Agree (174)	26.8	42.2	31.0	100%
Disagree (71)	40.0	38.6	21.4	100%
"Whites have a right to keep Negroes out of their neighborhoods."				
Agree (145)	37.1	38.6	24.3	100%
Disagree (100)	18.5	45.6	35.9	100%
"It is best to keep Negroes in their own districts and schools."				
Agree (105)	35.2	32.4	32.4	100%
Disagree (140)	25.6	48.8	25.6	100%
"Negroes shouldn't push themselves where they're not wanted."				
Agree (213)	33.8	37.3	28.9	100%
Disagree (32)	9.4	65.6	25.0	100%
"I would object to a family member bringing a Negro friend home to dinner —————."				
Very strongly (91)	41.3	33.7	25.0	100%
Maybe (45)	25.5	42.6	31.9	100%
Not at all (109)	20.8	49.5	29.7	100%
"I would mind if a Negro family with the same income and education moved next door —————."				
A lot (67)	46.4	31.9	21.7	100%
A little (67)	26.5	44.1	29.4	100%
Not at all (111)	21.0	46.6	32.4	100%
"When looting occurs during a riot, the police should shoot to kill."				
Agree (151)	40.4	39.7	19.9	100%
Disagree (90)	15.9	45.5	38.6	100%
Don't know (4)				

Racism at the Ballot Box

The Wallace phenomenon in the North, as in the South, contained a large degree of generalized protest in addition to blatant racism. Only a minority of Wallace's supporters believed he could actually win the presidency. And, surprisingly, many of these men had voted for Eugene McCarthy in the Indiana presidential primary in 1968. Though almost the complete opposite of Wallace in his ideological position, McCarthy offered these threatened men what they wanted—a critic of the establishment with a vague program and a refreshingly different style that broke the old political rules. And Wallace, coming from the other direction, offered them much the same.

This protest element in the Wallace movement led us to predict in print throughout the campaign that in the actual election Wallace would not do as well in the North as he was doing in the national surveys. This prediction proved accurate. Protesting as a respondent in a survey is "safer" than actually voting for a man who will probably not win. This is not a new phenomenon; it has characterized previous third-party candidacies. In 1936, William Lemke, the presidential nominee of Father Coughlin's United Party, achieved as much as 8 percent of the vote in pre-election surveys, but only 2 percent of the actual vote. Likewise, in 1948 Henry Wallace, running as a candidate of a left-wing party, gained 9 percent of the vote in a survey early in the campaign; but later he gained only 2 percent of the actual vote.

George Wallace did much better in 1968 than Lemke and Henry Wallace, in large part because his ticket had a base in the Deep South which held firm. In the North, we anticipated, his support would shrink. Though according to national polls as much as 22 percent of the voters favored him at his high point in the campaign, we correctly guessed his final total as 14 percent on the basis of these considerations. But 14 percent was no mean achievement for a Southern politician running as a third-party candidate. To understand the meaning of such an achievement, and its implications for the future of a democratic society, one must appreciate who Wallace's supporters are and what motivates them. And to gain this appreciation, we must search for yet another characteristic which predisposes these people to extremist politics.

Up to this point in our analysis, the social and psychological characteristics of Wallace's supporters appear in many ways to be in conflict. To recapitulate, the white men of Gary who favored Wallace were people solidly identified with the working class, with a high school education and a better-than-average income. Yet the psychological measures revealed them to be somewhat more politically alienated and considerably more fearful, distrustful, and anti-Negro than those who did not support Wallace—all of which characteristics are generally found most intensely among the worst-educated and most poverty-stricken segments of the population, white and nonwhite. Obviously, some additional social-psychological component is missing from our analysis, a component which would clear up this apparent contradiction by linking the objectively fairly secure social position of the Wallace supporters with their subjectively insecure personality tendencies.

We believe that this missing link is a heightened sense of *relative deprivation*. This is the same critical personality state discussed in Chapter 7 as the key social-psychological explanation of why black unrest was triggered in the 1960s. The social contexts producing the sense of relative deprivation in these two instances are, of course, quite different. We saw in Chapter 7 that relative deprivation for many Negroes derived basically from not realizing their high aspirations for the future, aspirations based on their knowledge of what other American citizens enjoy. Relative deprivation for the white working-class Wallace supporters in Gary, however, derives largely from perceiving that groups regarded as lower in status and skills—especially black Americans—are unfairly gaining on their position. Yet although the contexts are different, the effects of relative deprivation are interestingly similar for the two groups.

Table 11 presents data relevant to this point. In sharp contrast with both Nixon and Humphrey supporters, Wallace supporters were far more likely to believe that the lot of "the average man is getting worse." And this psychological trend cannot be accounted for in terms of the social differences between the three types of voters that we have just been discussing. Holding constant age, education, occupation, union membership, income, religion, political party, and social-class identification (as listed in Table 7), Wallace's backers consistently tended to agree more frequently that "the average man's lot" is slipping. Table 11 gives data on this sense of relative deprivation for three of the variables—union membership, religion, and social-class identification. When the social variables are combined with this powerful social-psychological indicator, much light is thrown on the Wallace phenomenon in Gary. Thus, 63 percent of the respondents making between $7,500 and $10,000 a year who agreed with the relative-deprivation statement supported Wallace; 57 percent of the respondents who closely identified with the working class and agreed with the statement supported Wallace; and approximately half of the Protestants, the union members, and the men with a high school education who agreed with the statement supported Wallace.

The strength of these relationships suggests that we should analyze the other psychological variables while controlling for feelings of relative deprivation. When this is done, the small but consistent tendency shown in Table 8 for Wallace supporters to appear more politically alienated virtually vanishes—which indicates that relative deprivation is the more fundamental correlate. Similarly, controlling for relative deprivation to examine fear and distrust (Table 9) narrows the differences, though it does not eliminate them. Table 12 shows that prejudiced attitudes and the statement tapping relative deprivation both predict support for Wallace, though the latter once again is the stronger. At the extremes of Table 12, observe that a highly prejudiced respondent who agreed that "the lot of

Table 11   RELATIVE DEPRIVATION

	Wallace supporters	Nixon supporters	Humphrey supporters	Total
Total Sample (245)	*29.8%*	*42.0%*	*28.2%*	*100%*
"In spite of what some people say the lot of the average man is getting worse, not better." [1]				
Agree (118)	41.5	33.1	25.4	100%
Disagree (122)	18.9	49.2	32.0	100%
Union members				
Agree (76)	47.3	30.2	22.5	100%
Disagree (63)	27.0	33.3	39.7	100%
Nonmembers				
Agree (40)	27.5	40.0	32.5	100%
Disagree (59)	10.2	66.1	23.7	100%
Religion				
Protestants				
Agree (53)	50.9	34.0	15.1	100%
Disagree (45)	22.2	53.7	24.1	100%
Roman Catholics				
Agree (53)	34.0	34.0	32.1	100%
Disagree (51)	17.6	43.1	39.2	100%
Social-class Identification				
Close to the working class				
Agree (49)	57.1	18.4	24.5	100%
Disagree (36)	25.0	47.2	27.8	100%
Not close to the working class				
Agree (25)	36.0	36.0	28.0	100%
Disagree (20)	30.0	20.0	50.0	100%
Close to the middle class				
Agree (27)	25.9	44.4	29.6	100%
Disagree (40)	7.5	60.0	32.5	100%
Not close to the middle class				
Agree (15)	26.7	60.0	13.3	100%
Disagree (23)	21.7	56.5	21.7	100%

1. This item was originally introduced in: Leo Srole, "Social Interaction and Certain Corollaries: An Exploratory Study," *American Sociological Review*, 1956, Vol. 21, pp. 709–716.

Table 12   ANTI-NEGRO PREJUDICE AND RELATIVE DEPRIVATION

	Wallace supporters	Nixon supporters	Humphrey supporters	Total
Total Sample (245)	29.8%	42.0%	28.2%	100%
High anti-Negro prejudice: [1]				
Agree that "the lot of the average man is getting worse" (59)	52.5	20.3	27.1	100%
Disagree (34)	23.0	42.3	34.7	100%
Moderate anti-Negro prejudice:				
Agree that "the lot of the average man is getting worse" (38)	36.8	44.7	18.5	100%
Disagree (38)	26.3	44.7	28.9	100%
Low anti-Negro prejudice:				
Agree that "the lot of the average man is getting worse" (18)	27.7	44.6	27.7	100%
Disagree (58)	12.1	55.2	32.8	100%

1. High, moderate, and low anti-Negro prejudice are measured by a multiple item scale formed by combining all the statements except the last one of Table 10. For national results with a similar scale, the interested reader is referred to: Paul B. Sheatsley, "White Attitudes toward the Negro," in T. Parsons and K. B. Clark (eds.), *The Negro American* (Boston: Houghton Mifflin, 1966), pp. 303–324.

the average man is getting worse" was *four* times as likely to support Wallace as a tolerant respondent who did not agree (52.5 percent to 12.0 percent).

How does Wallace exploit this sense of relative deprivation among workers in the North? We have already pointed out his economic liberalism; combined with his renunciation of government policies and his anti-Negro overtones, this creates a Populist-like appeal which apparently speaks to the relative-deprivation syndrome pointedly and effectively. Significantly, the Harris Poll reported during the campaign that many more Wallace supporters in the North chose the term "radical" to describe Wallace's political outlook than chose his own preferred term, "conservative." [28]

Lipset and Raab emphasize an interesting dilemma posed for Wallace by his blend of liberalism in economics and conservatism on civil rights.[29] As has been true for similar right-wing political efforts in the past, Wallace must necessarily alienate one of his two potential constituencies: economically liberal working-class voters who are anti-Negro, or economically conservative middle-class voters who are also anti-Negro. In 1964, Goldwater antagonized the former group in his drive to attract the latter; in 1968, Wallace antagonized the latter in his drive to attract the former. Indeed, Goldwater himself attacked Wallace as not a "true conservative," on precisely these grounds.[30]

To sum up our psychological findings, then, the Wallace supporters among Gary's white men tended to be more anti-Negro and distrustful than their counterparts who did not support Wallace. But primarily, they manifest acute feelings of relative deprivation. They have typically done better than their fathers and are objectively fairly secure: but, like black Americans, they have high aspirations without a sense of making progress toward their goals. Worse, they believe that Negroes are unjustly making rapid strides forward at their expense, helped out by a too-generous Federal government, a government that has forgotten them. Spontaneous comments made it clear that more than others in their position, supporters of the American Independent Party believed that they were victims of a national effort to aid those who "refuse to work" through public welfare programs and the Office of Economic Opportunity programs by heavily taxing those who "have worked hard all their lives to get where they are now."

The bitter irony for our nation is that the same powerful social-psychological mechanism—the sense of relative deprivation—is leading to racial strife on *both* sides of the color line. As was discussed in Chapter 7, black Americans typically regard themselves as victims of injustice when they compare their low status with the higher status of other Americans. The white Wallace voters in Gary have much the same feeling. They understandably deduce from all the publicity about the progress in civil rights of the past decade that Negroes, in contrast with themselves, are in fact "making it big." Yet the hard truth is that most Negroes, as we have noted throughout this book, are not "making it"—indeed, do not as a group approach the position of the Wallace supporters who see themselves as threatened.

This ironical situation, then, is a true measure of the madness of our times. Thanks in part to an unwelcome and draining foreign war, and thanks in part to the politician's natural bent to publicize and hail progress before it has been achieved, we find ourselves as a society in the 1970s having the "worst of both worlds." On the one hand, many aspiring young members of the white working class feel as threatened and angry as they might have been expected to feel if the nation had actually fulfilled its promises to its black citizens. And on the other hand, many aspiring young Negroes are angry and frustrated because the nation did not in fact fulfill these promises for most Negroes. The Federal government, therefore, stands falsely condemned for making a lasting and significant difference for most black Americans; and truly condemned for in fact not making much difference at all. The United States finds itself thus caught in a vise of its own making, a vise which Adlai Stevenson, in the 1950s, accurately termed "the age of rising expectations."

Footnotes

1. Riley is currently a Research Associate in both the Graduate School of Education and the Department of Social Relations of Harvard University. The authors are greatly indebted to Dr. Mark Granovetter, of Johns Hopkins University, and Mr. Andrew Walker, a candidate for the Ph.D. degree in sociol-

ogy at Harvard, for their critical contributions to this chapter.

2. "Little George" is a name commonly used for Wallace in the Deep South. Beyond its reference to his modest height, the term seems to be two-edged, tempting the speculation that even some of his supporters believe he talks "mighty big and tough" for a little man. Wallace was a Golden Gloves boxer in his youth; but the "hell of a fellow" masculine type or the "good old boy" so honored in Southern folklore is supposed to be a big enough physical specimen to match his words. W. J. Cash, *The Mind of the South* (New York: Knopf, 1941).

3. Arthur C. Wolfe, "Challenge from the Right: The Basis of Voter Support for Wallace in 1968" (paper read at the meetings of the American Psychological Association in Washington, D.C., on September 1, 1969). Former President Millard Fillmore, running in 1856 under the "Know-Nothing" banner of the American Party, was a right-wing forerunner of Wallace; he received 21 percent of the popular vote. Disregarding the confused and sectional election of 1860, only two essentially "liberal" candidates have done as well as Wallace as third-party presidential nominees: Theodore Roosevelt in 1912 and Robert LaFollette in 1924.

4. *Ibid.* Extremely similar results were obtained by other survey agencies as well. See: S. M. Lipset and E. Raab, *The Politics of Unreason: Right Wing Extremism in America, 1790–1970* (New York: Harper & Row, 1970), Chapters 9 and 10.

5. The similarity between the two voting patterns in the South emerges at the precinct, county, and state levels. For instance, both men carried the "Deep South four"—Georgia, Alabama, Mississippi, and Louisiana. Wallace added Arkansas to this core; Thurmond also carried his native South Carolina, which in 1968 he managed to keep in the Republican column for Richard Nixon.

6. While Northern whites reared in the South were, according to S.R.C. data, twice as likely as other Northern whites to support Wallace (14 to 7 percent), they form too small a proportion of the Northern population to have served as the basis of Wallace's following North of the Mason-Dixon line. Also interesting as a reference-group phenomenon are the contrasting percentages for Wallace between Northern-raised (10 percent) and Southern-raised (30 percent) residents of the South. Lipset and Raab, *op. cit.*

7. Note that the only near-exception to this generalization is

central-city Richmond, the only one of the four areas where there was a significant white vote for Humphrey.

8. Lipset in particular has placed special emphasis on fundamentalism. See: S. M. Lipset, "George Wallace and the U.S. New Right," *New Society,* October, 1968, pp. 447–483.

9. Wolfe, *op. cit.* Thus, S.R.C. data indicate that Wallace voters nationwide were, when compared with Nixon and Humphrey voters, less educated and more often of below-average income, identified with the working class, and from working-class backgrounds. But aggregate analyses of Wallace's races in 1964 for the presidential nomination of the Democratic Party in the primaries of Wisconsin, Indiana, and Maryland yield conflicting results. The expected pattern—the less-prosperous areas supporting Wallace—emerge from the data for the Maryland primary; but just the opposite trend appears in the data for Indiana and Wisconsin. The discrepancy seems to stem from the relatively "open" primary systems of Indiana and Wisconsin, which make it easy for relatively affluent and arch-conservative segments of the Republican Party to switch over to cast their ballots in the Democratic Party primaries. See: M. Conway, "Wallace and the 1964 Northern Primaries: The White Backlash Re-examined" (unpublished paper of the Department of Government and Politics, the University of Maryland, College Park, Maryland); and M. Rogin, "Wallace and the Middle Class: The White Backlash," *Public Opinion Quarterly,* Spring, 1966, Vol. 30, pp. 98–108. As was mentioned in Chapter 8, Wallace amazed the nation in these three primaries by attracting from 29.8 percent of the primary vote (in Indiana) to 43 percent (in Maryland).

10. Analogies between the Nazi and neo-Nazi movements in Germany and the American Independent Party in the United States, of course, can easily be carried too far. Though the sources of lower-middle-class support are in fact similar, sharp historical and structural differences between the German and American societies create differences in the intensity and complexity of the two movements.

11. Wolfe, *op. cit.*

12. *Ibid.*

13. This interpretation is especially championed by Lipset and Raab, *op. cit.*

14. Wallace and his advisors have long recognized this fact, and they plan their campaigning for the Deep South accordingly. Along with the waving of the Confederate flag and the playing of "Dixie" (techniques he shares with other white

politicians of the area), Wallace shrewdly interjects a novel note. He openly reminds his audience of their inferiority feelings when compared with the "slick Yankees." Then he quickly points with pride to his own electoral success in the North as solid evidence not only that the South is no longer "looked down upon," but that a Southerner can now raise the old anti-Negro, anti-Federal-government refrains of the South and gain a sympathetic ear in some quarters above the Mason-Dixon line.

15. This 10 percent cutoff was adopted to ensure that our universe of precincts was overwhelmingly white in composition. It might appear, perhaps, that this is an unusually low figure; but recall that we are forced to use data for 1960. And there is good reason to suspect that many precincts in these cities which had 5 to 10 percent Negroes in 1960 had 20 to 30 percent or more by 1968. To some extent, however, we were able to update our data through use of changing voting patterns, the special 1965 census of Cleveland, and data on poverty collected for the Office of Economic Opportunity.

16. Housing data, for example, are provided by blocks; so the housing characteristics of a precinct could be derived by merely aggregating all the data of the blocks within it. But the remaining data are available only by census tracts, the boundaries of which are seldom coterminus with those of precincts. Thus, data had to be aggregated from each tract included in a precinct and weighted by the relative sizes of the populations involved.

17. The findings reported in the following two paragraphs are derived from regression analyses of the Wallace vote across white precincts using nineteen census variables: the precinct percentages of (1) "Yankees," (2) Polish Americans, (3) Czech Americans (except in Boston, where Irish and Italian Americans were substituted for Polish and Czech Americans), (4) Russian (Jewish) Americans, (5) first- plus second-generation Americans, (6) kindergarten-aged children in public school, (7) females in the labor force, (8) labor-force members who are craftsmen or foremen, and (9) families living in the same residence as in 1955, with annual incomes in 1959 (10) below $4,000, (11) between $4,000 and $9,000, and (12) over $15,000, (13) with one car, (14) paying between $100 and $150 rent, and (15) owning their own house; as well as each precinct's (16) median education of those above 24 years of age, (17) median value of houses, (18) mean rent, and (19) percentage of houses built after 1940.

Each finding reported here emerges, then, with the other eighteen variables in effect held constant. Andrew Walker was chiefly responsible for these precinct regressions in the three cities.

18. This interesting finding is amplified in the data on individuals from the survey in Gary. Wallace supporters were found to be most numerous among those with intermediate attachment to their neighborhoods. Thus, they are overrepresented among those who had lived in the area from four to ten years, who found their area only "fairly warm and friendly," and who had "some" relatives and "first-name" friends living nearby. Wallace supporters were also more likely to report that they had recently considered moving to another neighborhood. These trends remain after such critical factors as age and education are controlled. Indeed, the findings are often enhanced; among the youngest respondents (aged 20 to 35 years), for example, two-thirds of the potential "movers" but only a quarter of the "stayers" supported Wallace. Dr. Mark Granovetter uncovered these neighborhood findings in his analysis of the data of the survey in Gary.

19. Even in Gary, however, the data on individuals from the survey reveal that the ethnic supporters of Wallace were not highly identified with and enmeshed in their nationality groups. For instance, when asked how many of their friends had the same ethnic background as their own, those answering "none" or "don't know" were roughly twice as likely as other respondents to be Wallace supporters. In short, Wallace's ethnic following do not appear to regard their national background as a salient aspect of their identity.

20. This study was performed with the cooperation of the Metropolitan Applied Research Center (M.A.R.C.) of New York City, and the interviews were conducted on contract by the University of Chicago's National Opinion Research Center (N.O.R.C.). We wish to thank Professor Kenneth Clark of M.A.R.C. and Mrs. Eve Weinberg of N.O.R.C. for their invaluable assistance.

21. After carefully inspecting a number of post-election polls, Lipset and Raab (op. cit.) conclude that Wallace tended to lose, during the closing weeks of the campaign, both supporters from among working-class union members in the North and supporters from among the middle class in the South.

22. The discerning reader will note a change from the previous

chapter in the form of tables. When reviewing the data on Mrs. Hicks's support, we simply sought rough profiles of three types of voters and provided the percentages of each type having a particular characteristic. But now we are treating support for one of the three presidential candidates as a dependent variable and consequently give the percentages of a given type of voter (e.g., respondents between 21 and 34 years of age) who favor Wallace, Nixon, or Humphrey.

23. The variables listed in Table 7 all proved more important than ethnicity, about which much was made by many popular writers at the time.

24. Despite the greater favorability toward Wallace of Gary's white Protestants, respondents reared in the South made up only a small fraction of the Wallace support of our sample. The Protestant Wallace voter was typically from a small town or farm in the Midwest, a fact which is consistent with the emphasis upon fundamentalism; but observe that the findings about religion conflict with the view of the mass media that it was primarily Roman Catholic ethnics who backed Wallace in the North.

25. Wolfe, *op. cit.*

26. When education is controlled, these differences in fear and distrust remain at each educational level.

27. Richard Hofstadter, *The Paranoid Style in American Politics* (New York: Knopf, 1965), p. 4.

28. Lipset and Raab, *op. cit.*

29. *Ibid.*

30. Barry Goldwater, "Don't Waste a Vote on Wallace," *The National Review,* October 22, 1968, Vol. 20, pp. 1061–1062, 1079.

Specialization in American race relations is in many ways a strange vocation. For example, one lives in the constant hope that virtually all his predictions will prove wrong. But sometimes when the predictions are wrong, it is because matters have deteriorated even faster than was expected.

It is not surprising, then, that specialists in the field like to commiserate with each other. So it is between my friend and colleague in social psychology, Professor Kenneth Clark, and myself. I especially recall that we did this frequently in the early 1960s. Among other delightful topics, we would speculate with friends late into the night as to when the "civil rights honeymoon" would end.

It was not difficult to see that the palmy days of biracial cooperation under Dr. King's leadership would not last indefinitely. We well knew that a mood and an ideology of "black power" (by whatever name), and an understandable desire to withdraw from whites in various ways, lay just beneath the

PART FIVE

PRESENT AND FUTURE RACIAL CONTACT

ghetto's surface, as has been true throughout black American history. We realized, too, that there was a gross indignity to blacks unnecessarily built into the case often advanced for racial integration—usually implicitly, but sometimes explicitly. To prove that segregation should be abolished, integrationist spokesmen, white and black, frequently recited the cold statistics of deprivation of Negroes, of lower test scores and higher rates of crime and disease. It sounded as if getting together with whites was essential simply to better these conditions. Seldom was the other side of the argument emphasized: that whites, too, were deprived in a segregated society and could benefit enormously from integration. Nor was a case made for racial pride, for pride in diversity. Young blacks, throwing off the restraints of earlier times, could not be expected to tolerate such indignities for long.

Add these factors to the rising sense of relative deprivation among blacks (see Chapter 7) and the increasing polarization of resistant whites (see Chapters 9 and 10), and you will see how Clark and I could spend hours speculating on when and how these various forces would combine to prevent the realization of Dr. King's dream. As I remember, we guessed that they would coalesce in the early 1970s; like many others, we failed to foresee the war in Vietnam and its serious domestic consequences.

One can never prove what might have been, but I still believe that without the war we would have been essentially correct. And this could have made an enormous difference. Although a separatist reaction, white and black, may well have been inevitable, yet the consequences of such a reaction are a function of the state of race relations when it occurs. The later the reaction comes, the firmer will be the interracial bonds that have already developed; thus, the later such a reaction takes place, the milder its consequences will be. The war in Vietnam may well have cost us five to eight years of

basic progress before the "separatists era" descended—
another of the many costs of this tragic conflict. The
firmer interracial bonds and basic racial progress that
could have characterized the years 1966 to 1970 had they
been peaceful would have meant, in particular, more
interracial contact under optimal conditions on the job,
in school, and in the neighborhood.

Why is optimal contact so critical to race relations? And
how prevalent is optimal contact today? Bringing together
the threads of earlier chapters, Chapter 11 attempts to an-
swer these fundamental questions. In all truth, optimal in-
terracial contact is not the rule in the United States
today. The promises of the "civil rights honeymoon" have
not been fulfilled, and Dr. King's dream seems no closer
to becoming reality. Not surprisingly, then, a youthful move-
ment of "black separatism" has emerged, joined enthusias-
tically by white separatists. The assumptions underlying
both black and white separatism are analyzed in
detail in Chapter 12, with considerations of inter-
racial contact again the key. This final chapter poses the
thematic question of the entire book: In the future,
will we live racially separate or together?

CHAPTER ELEVEN

THE COMPLEXITY OF AMERICAN RACIAL PATTERNS

Mr. Fawks is a white American who feels he "knows" Negroes. He works in a desegregated aircraft plant in Marietta, Georgia, lives a few hundred yards from "the colored part of town," and sends his children to a school that recently received its first Negro pupil. Yet Mr. Fawks knows only three of his Negro coworkers and none of his Negro neighbors by name, and he dares not socialize with them. His professed knowledge comes, then, almost entirely from racist folklore, from which he exempts his black coworkers on the ground that they are "different."

Mr. Seemes is another white American who feels he understands the racial scene. Although he knew no Negroes as a boy and none live within miles of his suburban Connecticut town today, he has made friends with two Negroes in his New York office. They were hired a few years ago when the company became an "equal-opportunity employer" because of its many Federal contracts. Mr. Seemes genuinely likes his coworkers, though he seldom has social contacts with them after office hours. Consequently, he has decided that "the whole problem is really a matter of social class."

Mr. Brown is a black American who also has great hopes for the future of American race relations. He recently graduated from an all-Negro high school in Durham, North Carolina, and now finds himself one of the first Negroes hired in a previously all-white Southern-based insurance company. His pastor recommended him to the firm, and he started in an entirely black section of the city. But his employers urge him to develop new white business, and he selected as likely prospects liberals on the faculty of nearby Duke University.

By contrast, Mr. Davis is a black American who has given up hope that any racial change will ever improve his personal lot. He was born on a Southern farm and moved with his mother to Harlem while he was still young. And there he has remained—deep within the ghetto. Mr. Davis has had repeated contact with whites in only four roles—policemen, employers, landlords, and merchants. These formal and often financial relations with whites combine with ghetto folklore to convince him that "the man" is never going to allow significant racial alterations.

The American racial scene has always been highly complex, varied, and inconsistent, defying facile generalizations. And, as these four cases and millions like them reveal, the current period of rapid change acts to increase this complexity. It is appropriate, then, to explore this complexity and its implications for the nation's future racial patterns.

Racial Roles and Their Variations

One useful way to conceptualize American racial patterns is to describe them in terms of role theory.[1] Discriminatory encounters between whites and blacks require that both parties "play the game." The white must act out the role of the "superior"; by direct action or subtle cue, he must convey the expectation that he will be treated with deference. For his part, the black must, if traditional norms are to be obeyed, act out the role of the "inferior"; he must play the social role of "Negro." And should he refuse to play the game, he would be judged by many whites as "not knowing his place," and harsh sanctions could follow.[2]

The socially stigmatized role of "Negro" is the critical consequence of having dark skin in the United States. As far as the personality is concerned, such enforced adoption of a role divides each individual Negro both from other human beings and from himself. Of course, all social roles, necessary as they are, hinder to some extent forthright, uninhibited social interaction. An employer and employee, for example, may never begin to understand each other as complete human beings unless they break through the formality and constraints of the relationships imposed by their roles. Likewise, whites and blacks can never communicate as equals unless they break through the barriers created by their roles. As long as racial roles are maintained, both whites and blacks find it difficult to perceive the humanity behind the facade. Many whites who are by no means racists confuse the role of "Negro" with the people who must play this role. "That's just the way Negroes are," goes the phrase. Conversely, many Negroes confuse the role of "white man" with whites: "Whites are just like that; they are born thinking they should be boss."

Intimately associated with this impairment of human relatedness is an impairment of the individual's acceptance and understanding of himself. Both whites and Negroes can confuse their own roles by considering these roles as an essential part of themselves. Whites can easily flatter themselves into believing that they are in fact "superior"; after all, does not the deference of the role-playing Negro confirm this "superiority"? And Negroes in turn often accept much of the mythology; for does not the imperious behavior of the role-playing white confirm their "inferiority"?

Explanations based on role theory are supported by a

large body of social-psychological research which convincingly demonstrates the strong power of role playing to change deeply held attitudes, values, and even self-conceptions.[3] These remarkable changes have been rendered experimentally by temporary role adoptions which are, compared with the lifelong role of "Negro," exceedingly trivial in nature. Imagine, then, the depth of the effects of having to play a role which has such vast personal and social significance that it affects virtually all aspects of daily living. It is clear that racial roles have profound and direct psychological as well as behavioral effects upon those who adopt them.

Broadly speaking, these roles of "superior" white and "inferior" Negro have, historically, structured racial interaction in America. But around this basic theme there is a great range of variations, for racial patterns systematically vary according to specific situation, institution, socio-economic class, and region.

Variation by situation. Mr. Fawks, the white aircraft worker in Georgia, has never thought his interracial neighborhood was strange and accepts the desegregation of the plant in which he works, yet he objects strenuously to public school desegregation. "I never went to no school with colored people," he grumbles, "and I never thought I'd see my kids doing it." There is nothing uniquely Southern about Mr. Fawks' selective reaction to racial patterns. Mr. Seemes, the Connecticut suburbanite, approves of the interracial character of his work situation, but he entertains serious doubts about interracial neighborhoods. "I've heard Negroes' moving into an area lowers property values," he explains, "and most of my Connecticut neighbors are dead against it—so I don't think it's a good idea."

Such inconsistencies are commonplace. The reader will, for example, recall the inconsistencies, discussed in Chapter 6, in the Panama Canal Zone and the coal mines of McDowell County, West Virginia. Attitudes and behavior need not always be consistent: in spite of the attitudes they may harbor, for most people their behavior may be structured by particular situations.

Social scientists were first alerted to this by a 1934 study of "verbal" versus "actual" discrimination.[4] A Chinese couple traveled widely over the United States, stopping at 250 sleeping and eating establishments. They were refused service only once. Later, the same places received inquiries by mail as to whether or not they served "members of the Chinese race." About half did not reply; of those which did, over 90 percent stated that they did not accommodate Chinese guests. A control sample of comparable, unvisited establishments yielded similar results.

This phenomenon was also shown in eleven restaurants in a Northeastern suburban community.[5] Three women, two white and one Negro, went to the restaurants, encountered no difficulty, and in each received exemplary service. Two weeks later, requests were sent to the restaurants for reservations for a similar group. Ten of the letters went unanswered, and follow-up phone calls met great resistance. Control calls for all-white parties produced ten reservations. Obviously it is more difficult to reject another human being face to face than through impersonal letters and phone calls.

The power of specific situational norms to shape racial patterns of behavior is dramatized by the difficulties which arise when there are no such norms. One ingenious project studied facilities in New York State that were unaccustomed to black patrons.[6] Black researchers would enter a tavern, seek service, and later record their experiences, while white researchers would observe the situation and record their impressions for comparison. Typically, the first reaction of waitresses and bartenders was to turn to the owner or someone else in authority for guidance. When guidance was unavailable, the slightest behavioral cue from anyone in the situation was utilized as a gage of what was expected. And if there were no such cues, confusion often continued until somehow the threatening situation had been structured.

Variation by institution. Comparable observations have been recorded of inconsistent racial patterns in different societal institutions. For example, consider a neighborhood of white steelworkers in the Chicago area.[7] These men were all members of the same thoroughly desegregated union and worked in desegregated plants. In fact, Negroes held elected positions as shop stewards, executive board members, and vice-president of the union and shared with whites the same locker rooms, lunch rooms, showers, and toilets in both the union hall and the plants. Only 12 percent of the 151 whites who were studied evidenced "low acceptance" of Negroes in this work situation; and the deeper the involvement in union activities, the greater the acceptance of Negroes as coworkers. But neighborhood acceptance was a vastly different matter. Bolstered by a neighborhood organization which opposed desegregation, 86 percent of the white steelworkers rejected the idea of allowing Negroes to live near them, with those men most involved in the collective existence of the neighborhood evincing the most adamant opposition. The effects of harmonious interracial patterns in employment did not extend to housing. No relationship existed between acceptance of Negroes as fellow workers and acceptance of them as neighbors.

The social-psychological key to understanding this situation is the operation of the organizations in each area. Most of the steelworkers conform to what is expected of them, even when expectations contradict one another. Thus, although there appears to be inconsistency from the viewpoint of the outside observer, to the person involved such behavior is perfectly reasonable because all of it conforms to expectations. In other words, the steelworkers were living by the norms of the groups to which they referred their behavior—their *reference groups*.[8] And these reference-group norms often act in modern American society to produce apparently inconsistent racial patterns and to restrict the generalization of changes in attitude from one institution to another.

Examples abound of this distinction between attitudes and actual behavior. For example, a 1951 investigation of almost a thousand manufacturers in Texas found that their attitudes toward Negroes and their actual practices concerning the hiring of Negroes were not related.[9] And a 1953 study of thirty discriminatory fraternities at the University of Michigan found that the members were more willing to accept Jewish than Negro students as "brothers," though their attitudes were more intensely anti-Semitic than anti-Negro.[10]

Thus, in order to comprehend some of the complexity of American racial patterns, it becomes necessary to examine separately some of the major institutions of American society. In other chapters we analyzed some of these institutions. It is sufficient here to sketch the principal trends, although even these generalizations run the risk of becoming quickly outdated.

The family remains the most racially homogeneous institution in American life. Indeed, more than a dozen states still had laws against miscegenation when the Supreme Court ruled them unconstitutional in 1967. And in states where interracial marriage has been both legal and recorded—California, Hawaii, Michigan, and Nebraska— the rates of intermarriage remain very low, except for Hawaii, and appear to have increased only slightly in recent years.[11] And attitudes of white Americans toward intermarriage have shifted very little during this time of racial change. A 1963 *Newsweek* poll found that 90 percent of a representative national sample of whites objected to their "own teen-age daughter dating a Negro." [12] A more striking finding of this same poll was that among whites who had experienced previous social contact with Negroes, although they were overwhelmingly accepting of Negroes in other institutional areas, 80 percent objected to their teen-age daughter dating a Negro and 70 percent objected to a close friend or relative marrying a Negro.[13] Interracial marriages, then, are not likely to become commonplace until the special Negro stigma is eliminated.

Organized religion is also an extensively segregated institution. The vast majority of blacks who maintain religious ties are Protestant, and more than 90 percent of black Protestants belong to all-black denominations.[14] Among those relatively few Negroes who are members of predominantly white denominations, a large majority attend racially separate churches within these denominations. Moreover, church-sponsored facilities—hospitals, colleges, welfare agencies—are often more segregated than the churches—although churches are so extremely segregated that it is often impossible for these facilities to be more so.[15] Consequently, the organized church has not been a conspicuous source of interracial contact in the United States.

Racial patterns in education are now in a state of flux. In the South, public education from primary to college levels was separate until recently, but the pattern has been more varied in the North. Black ghettos in Northern cities were neither so dense nor so large before World War II as today; thus biracial education at the primary and secondary levels was quite common. This explains why many middle-aged white and Negro Northerners today recall that they knew members of the other race best during their early school days. This pattern did not, however, extend into college. Among the few Negro Northerners who managed to go on to higher education, the great majority enrolled in either all-Negro colleges in the South or similar institutions in the North—some private (for example, Lincoln University in Pennsylvania and Wilberforce University in Ohio) and some public (such as Cheyney State College in Pennsylvania).

The present educational picture is more complex. Public education in the South is no longer tightly segregated. The first two decades after the 1954 Supreme Court ruling against *de jure* segregation of public schools have witnessed slow, but fundamental, alterations. Yet, as we mentioned in Chapter 4, as *de jure* segregation of schools decreases, so-called *"de facto"* segregation is rapidly increasing. The ever-growing Negro ghettos in major cities throughout the United States combine with the neighborhood-school principle to establish an entrenched pattern of racially separate education. And to this picture must be added the bleak outlook in housing discussed in detail in Chapter 2, for increasing residential segregation obviously goes hand in hand with *de facto* school segregation. The expansion of urban ghettos and the development of *de facto* segregated education means that Negroes growing up in ghetto areas have generally had far *less* equal-status contact with whites in their formative years than Negroes of earlier generations had.

Since family, religious, educational, and housing patterns provide only limited interracial contact, encounters on the job between black and white Americans assume special importance. As was seen in Chapter 3, gains in Negro employment have hardly been impressive. Nevertheless, interracial contact in the near future depends heavily upon work patterns emerging in the 1970s.

Variation by socio-economic class. Mention of segregation reveals an interesting phenomenon having to do with socio-economic class. Higher-status whites generally give more support to racial desegregation than lower-status whites, but this tendency does not seem to hold for attitudes toward interracial housing. Thus, a 1956 national survey noted that 61 percent of college-educated whites approved of school desegregation, compared with 51 percent of the high-school-educated and 36 percent of the grammar-school-educated; and 72 percent of the college-educated approved of the desegregation of public transportation, compared with 64 percent of the high-school-educated and 46 percent of the grammar-school-educated. But virtually no difference appeared among the three groups in response to the query, "If a Negro with the same income and education as you moved into your block, would it make any difference to you?" [16]

Other research suggests that this reluctance of upper-status whites to support housing desegregation is maintained despite the fact they often realize that these beliefs are in direct conflict with their own religious and national ideals.[17] This is partly explained by the fact that housing desegregation directly affects them in a way other changes typically do not. In addition, there is a tendency for many upper-status white Americans to assume that their own values are different from those of Negroes—even when the question specifies a Negro neighbor with the same income and education.

This is not to imply that white Americans make no distinction among Negroes of different social classes. Indeed, Westie has shown that the willingness of a white to associate with a Negro is a direct function of both the social status of the respondent and that of the Negro in question.[18] That is, the higher the status of the white, the greater is his willingness to interact with Negroes and the greater is his tendency to make a differentiation between, say, a black doctor and a black machine operator. Lower-status whites are more rejecting of Negroes in general and less prepared to distinguish between Negroes of different social standing.

Westie repeated this research with blacks, measuring their social-distance attitudes toward whites, and obtained essentially the same findings.[19] Higher-status Negroes are far more willing than lower-status Negroes to interact with whites, and they make sharper distinctions among whites of various occupations. Another set of studies investigated the stereotypes of whites as a group held by Negroes of varying social classes in the North and South.[20] In general, the same overall stereotype emerged for all classes in both regions: whites tend to be seen as "ambitious, sticking together, businesslike, deceitful and tricky, feeling superior, keeping the Negro down, underestimating the Negro's ability, judging Negroes by the worst type, and not caring to be among Negroes." But higher-status Negroes, particularly those in the North, were considerably more favorable in their image of whites than other Negroes.

Variation by region. The relatively more favorable view of whites held by upper-status Negro Northerners is largely a function of their much greater opportunity for equal-status contact with whites. Though still relatively small, this group is especially significant for the future, as migration to the North and expansion of the middle class continue among Negroes. Thus, it is of interest to look at the reported interracial experiences of a representative sample of 250 middle-income Negro housewives residing in Roxbury, the Negro ghetto of Boston (see Table 13).[21]

These women typically knew whites well as children— though this is not the case for their children growing up in

Table 13 INTERRACIAL CONTACTS OF MIDDLE-INCOME NEGROES OF BOSTON

Source of contact	Percentage reporting
As a child:	
Played with white children	86.0
Lived in racially-mixed neighborhood	75.0
Attended integrated school	67.5
Today:	
Family very friendly with white people	83.1
White people visit home at least once a month	43.8
Visit white people at their home at least once a month	39.9
Husband works with white people	93.2
White work associates visit home at least once a month	37.6
Visit white work associates at their home at least once a month	34.8
Family doctor is white	56.0
Family dentist is white	40.4
Member of a church which is:	
Virtually all white	0.0
Mostly white	15.0
Roughly equal	8.4
Mostly Negro	10.3
Virtually all Negro	66.4

Source: Reanalysis of data from L. G. Watts, H. E. Freeman, H. M. Hughes, R. Morris, and T. F. Pettigrew, *The Middle-Income Negro Family Faces Urban Renewal* (Boston: Department of Commerce and Development, Commonwealth of Massachusetts, 1964). The sample consisted of 250 black housewives whose families lived in the ghetto and had a total family income of not less than $5,200 annually; the percentages exclude the few cases which did not answer the query or did not belong to a church, and so forth.

the ghetto. It appears that the husband's work is the family's principal contact with whites; mutual visiting with white work associates almost reaches the level of all such contacts with whites. An additional contact comes through professional family services—such as the family doctor and dentist. But less than one in four of the women report membership in a church attended by substantial numbers of whites.

Such interracial contacts, of course, are severely restricted for low-income Negroes in both the North and the South. They are less likely to have known whites as children; they are more likely to work in laboring and semiskilled jobs where other lower-status Negroes are their associates and whites are only supervisors and employers; they are not likely to have a family doctor or dentist, but are likely to depend upon the impersonal services of public hospitals and clinics; and they seldom belong to a church with white members.

Middle-income black Southerners are also more constrained than black Bostonians of similar status. Segregation sealed them off in ghettos with longer histories and more developed Negro infrastructures than Northern ghettos. Consequently, they, too, are less likely than their Northern counterparts to have known whites as children, to work and visit with whites, to have white physicians and dentists, and to belong to interracial church congregations. Yet here the racial patterns are rapidly changing. While the revolution of the past few years has not significantly altered the lives of most lower-status Negroes, the lives of higher-status Negro Southerners have undeniably been affected. The desegregation of public golf courses, expensive restaurants, and the Atlanta opera, and the new opportunities for skilled Negroes with Federal contractors, have not meant much yet to the poor and unskilled, but such changes have pried open the ghetto's lid for those in the middle class who want to take advantage of them. In a few years, middle-income Negroes in the urban South may report interracial patterns, especially as concerns employment, quite similar to those cited for Boston.

There are other interesting regional differences. Negroes are not strangers or interlopers on the Southern scene, as they are often perceived in the North. White and Negro Southerners are both products of the same subculture. They share a common history and a common religion; white and black Northerners frequently share neither. These advantages have tempted Southern liberals, black and white, to speculate that the South may possibly take the giant step from formal desegregation to informal integration with greater ease and alacrity than the North; the writer has at times shared this dream. But the present adoption by the urban South of strict residential segregation makes it appear that the South, too, will have to work through a difficult period of *de facto* segregation similar to that in the North today.[22]

Nevertheless, these cultural and religious bonds between Negro and white Southerners are an important element in the explanation of the present difference in moods between black communities in the South and those in the North. To risk oversimplification, this difference seems to involve hope and despair. Negroes in the South, including most lower-status Negro Southerners, still "believe," still have faith that the revolution is bringing freedom. Despite racist governors, despite police brutality and wanton murders, Negro Southerners have been rewarded in this belief by seeing *de jure* segregation crumble. In sharp contrast, Negro Northerners, particularly the lower-status residents of the ghettos, either have lost or are losing such hope for the future. A brooding despair develops when it is seen that white officials are not even budged by protests against *de facto* segregation. And when progress is stifled, despair spills over into rioting. This regional difference is made obvious by the response of a hardened Harlemite to a young black Southerner visiting New York. "Baby," he jeered, "down South you're just fighting to get where we are now—and we can tell you that once you get here it's just a solid blank wall." [23]

This dramatic regional difference in "mood" is borne out by data from national surveys. Gallup reports that between 1963 and 1965 the proportion of Negro Southerners who said that they feel they are treated "not very well" or "badly" declined from roughly 90 percent to 70 percent, while virtually no change was noted among Negro Northerners.[24] In 1966, Harris asked nine different questions of an all-Negro national sample as to whether they were better off, about the same, or worse off than they had been three years before in employment, housing, voting, pay, schooling, transportation, use of restaurants, etc. In every case, Negro Southerners were more likely to report "better off" than Negro Northerners—often by a wide margin.[25] Another important ingredient in this regional difference is the distinction between aspirations and attainment. As we discussed in Chapter 7, social motivation is more directly determined by *relative* deprivation than by absolute derivation.[26] Negro Southerners have aspired to far less than Negro Northerners, and hence have received greater reinforcement from smaller racial advances. But this situation will obviously not last much longer. As the black revolution proceeds, aspirations will tend to rise faster than actual gains. Moreover, as *de jure* segregation fuses into *de facto* segregation, gains in the South are certain to come less rapidly and less dramatically. Will the Negro Southerner continue, even then, to "believe"? The answer obviously depends largely upon the response of the urban South, a response that has not been encouraging so far.

Change in American Racial Patterns

Contact and Change

Many well-meaning Americans have expressed the opinion that if only blacks and whites could experience more contact with each other the nation's racial difficulties would solve themselves. Unfortunately, the case is not so simple. Africans and Europeans have more contact in the Republic of South Africa than anywhere else on the African continent, and black and white Americans have more contact in the South than in any other region of the nation; yet neither of these areas is conspicuous for its interracial harmony. It almost looks as if contact between two peoples exacerbates, rather than relieves, hostility; but this conclusion would be just as hasty and fallacious as the naive assumption that contact invariably lessens prejudice.

Increasing interaction, whether of groups or individuals, intensifies and magnifies processes already underway. Hence, more interracial contact can lead either to greater prejudice and rejection or to greater respect and acceptance, depending upon the situation in which it occurs. The basic issue, then, concerns the types of situations in which contact leads to distrust and those in which it leads to trust.

As was noted earlier, Gordon Allport, in his review of the relevant research, concluded that four characteristics of the "contact situation" are of utmost importance: [27] prejudice is lessened when the two groups (1) possess equal status, (2) seek common goals, (3) are cooperatively dependent upon each other, and (4) interact with the positive support of authorities, laws, or customs.

If the groups are of widely different social status, especially in the situation itself, contact between them may do little more than reinforce old and hostile stereotypes. In the typical situation of interracial contact in the South, most Negroes encountered by white Southerners are servants and other low-status service workers. Many whites eventually conclude that domestic and low-status service are the types of jobs best suited for Negroes, that somehow this is the black's "proper place." To be sure, there are Negro professionals in the South, but, as has been noted, segregation has forced them to stay deep within the Negro ghetto where whites rarely meet them. The segregationist who boasts that he "really knows Negroes" is usually referring to his casual encounters with Negroes of lower status. This is a principal reason that the plentiful black-white patterns of contact in the South have not led to more interracial understanding.

As was previously mentioned, many whites are convinced that Negroes do not share their interests and values, a belief which compounds racial prejudice with assumed value conflict. *Equal-status* contact attacks this problem in two ways. First, people of equal status are more likely than others to possess congruent outlooks and beliefs simply by virtue of their common positions in society. Second, equal-status situations provide the optimal setting in which this congruence can be perceived.

When groups work together toward *common goals,* further opportunities are presented for developing and discovering similarities of interests and values. The reduction of prejudice through contact generally requires an active, focused effort, not simply intermingling for its own sake. Athletic teams furnish a pertinent example. Interracial teams create not only an equal-status contact situation but one in which black and white team members cannot achieve their common goal of winning without the assisttance of each other. Under such conditions, race loses importance.

Not only must groups seek common goals, but the attainment of these goals must be a *mutually dependent* effort involving no competition along strictly racial lines. For instance, if the San Francisco Giants were an all-white baseball team and the Los Angeles Dodgers were all Negro, they could probably play indefinitely and not become more racially tolerant. Though equal status and common goal conditions would prevail, the lines of competition would make race relevant. Fortunately, professional athletic teams are interracial and provide a case of relatively successful desegregation. But the lesson is clear: contact situations which lead to interracial harmony must involve cooperative interdependence.

The final factor concerns the auspices of the contact. If the situation has *explicit social sanction,* interracial contact is more readily accepted and leads to more positive effects. Though the situation may be awkward at first, the support of authorities helps make it seem "right." Failure of local authorities, laws, and customs to bolster even minimal desegregation in much of the South is a chief reason for the failure of many white Southerners to respect Federal court orders.

Research literature abounds with examples of these contact principles in operation. One study found that white members of the Merchant Marine tended to hold racial attitudes in direct relation to how many voyages they had taken with equal-status blacks—the more desegregated voyages, the more positive their attitudes.[28] Another investigation noted that white policemen in Philadelphia who had personally worked with Negro colleagues were far more favorable toward the desegregation of their force than other white policemen.[29] A study of white government workers, veterans, and students found that those who had known Negro professionals were far less prejudiced toward Negroes than those who had known only unskilled Negroes.[30]

Evidence appears even in times of crisis. While black and white mobs raged during the Detroit race riot of 1943, integrated coworkers, university students, and neighbors of long standing peacefully carried on their lives side by side.[31] Research into neighborhood integration introduces the most solid evidence available. Repeated studies have found that integrated living in public housing developments which meet all four of Allport's criteria for contact sharply reduces racial prejudice among both black and white neighbors.[32] And these same studies demonstrate that living in segregated, but otherwise identical, housing developments affects interracial contact in such a way that, if anything, racial bitterness is enhanced. Additional data derive from the desegregation of the Armed Forces.[33] Once again, conditions involving equal status, cooperative striving toward common goals, and support by authority led directly to the reduction of racial prejudice among both black and white servicemen. As a black officer in Korea candidly phrased it: "After a while you start thinking of whites as people."

But it will be remembered from Chapter 6 that one important qualification must be made: at least in the initial stages, change in attitude is often limited to the specific situation which produced it. This limitation is a result of the extent to which segregation has snarled the vital fabric of American life. Untying any one tangle is not a solution; but as desegregation proceeds there should be increasing generalization from one situation to another.

The Law and Change

From this perspective, a reappraisal can be made of the old saw "Laws cannot change the hearts and minds of men." A case in point is the 1945 anti-discrimination employment legislation enacted by New York State. This law led to the first hiring of Negroes as sales clerks in New York City department stores. Two investigators conducted separate tests of the effects of this law-induced desegregation. One study of white sales personnel revealed that those who had experienced the new equal-status job contact with Negroes held more favorable attitudes toward interracial interaction in the work situation.[34] Once again, however, the initial effects of this contact did not extend beyond the immediate situation; equal-status clerks were not more accepting of Negroes in eating and residential situations. The other investigation questioned customers.[35] Their responses showed widespread acceptance of this change. They were concerned largely with shopping conveniently and efficiently; many hesitated to challenge the *fait accompli* established by the law; and for many the new pattern was consistent with their belief in the American creed of equal opportunity for all.[36]

Contrary to the old adage, then, laws *can* change the

hearts and minds of men. They do so through a vital inter-mediate step. Laws first act to modify behavior, and this modified behavior in turn changes the participants' atti-tudes. Notice that precisely the opposite sequence is com-monly believed to be the most effective method of social change: when people are convinced to be less prejudiced through informational and goodwill campaigns, conven-tional reasoning asserts, then they will discriminate less. To be sure, this sequence is sometimes effective, but the preponderance of social-psychological evidence attests to the greater efficacy of the opposite approach. Behaving differently more often precedes thinking differently.

The celebrated rituals of Brotherhood Week, brother-hood dinners, and brotherhood awards illustrate the point. While they remind participants of their religious and na-tional ideals and strengthen the already convinced, these events are apparently of limited value in convincing the unconvinced. The basic problem with such observances is that they do not require participants to change their be-havior. The interracial contact is brief and artificial, and the emphasis is placed on exhortation and influencing atti-tudes directly. A vast body of psychological data indicates that prejudiced individuals in such situations will avoid the message altogether, deny its relevance for themselves, or find ways of twisting its meaning.[37] In addition, ritualistic exhortations for brotherhood may often serve an unantici-pated negative function. By attending the annual dinner and paying the tax-deductible $50 or $100 per plate, many individuals of considerable influence regularly relieve their guilt. Having gone through the motions of supporting "equality for all," participants are psychologically re-leased to go on discriminating as before.

Anti-discrimination laws can also be tuned out by the prejudiced and used as salves by the guilty. Frequently, the laws remain unenforced except on a case-by-case basis, failing to attack the structure that supports discrimi-nation. But such legislation offers a potential means of achieving behavioral change, a means not offered by exhortation. Several reasons for this are apparent. There is, of course, the threat of punishment and unfavorable publicity for recalcitrants. But more important is the "off-the-hook" function such laws provide. Thus, the department stores in New York City may each have been afraid to hire Negro sales personnel as long as there were no assurances that their competitors would follow suit. But the anti-discrimination law, applied to all stores, furnished this needed assurance. And the legally established *fait accompli,* unlike exhortations for tolerance, generates its own acceptance.[38] The improvement it achieves is a year-round process, a constant, institutionalized reminder that racial harmony is the sanctioned norm. Finally, the new behavior required by the law psychologically commits the individual, for when a person has behaved publicly in a new manner and has been rewarded for doing so, he is likely to become personally committed to the behavior.[39]

A Microcosmic Case

The fundamental principles underlying change in racial attitudes are dramatically highlighted by an ingenious field study conducted in Oklahoma.[40] Twenty young boys, of homogeneous backgrounds but previously unacquainted with one another, attended an experimental summer camp. From the start, the boys were divided into two groups— "The Rattlers" and "The Eagles." The first stage of the experiment was designed to develop high *esprit de corps* within each of the groups. Separated from each other, the Rattlers and Eagles engaged in a variety of satisfying experiences, and each group soon evidenced the pride and sense of "we-ness" characteristic of strong ingroup solidarity.

The second stage brought the groups face-to-face in a series of grimly competitive tasks—tugs-of-war, baseball and football games, and tent pitching. In all of these contact situations, only one group could win and the other had to lose. The inevitable intergroup animosity soon appeared. Derogatory songs and slogans were composed;

destructive raids on "the enemy's" cabin began; negative stereotypes developed; and preferences for group segregation were voiced. Competitive contact had wreaked its usual havoc.

The third stage tried to mend the damage. The "brotherhood dinner" was the first approach. The boys met in such noncompetitive situations as eating good food in the same room, shooting off fireworks, and attending a movie together—all of them involving passive conduct without common goals or interdependence. Understandably, friction between the groups did not abate; in fact, the boys employed these unfocused events as opportunities for further vilification of their rivals. Next, the investigators introduced carefully contrived problems whose solutions required the cooperation of both groups. Fixing the damaged water tank that supplied the whole camp, raising funds to show a favorite movie, and other functionally dependent behavior achieved a striking decrement in intergroup hostility. At the close of the competitive second stage over half of the characteristics assigned by the boys to the rival group were sharply unfavorable; but at the close of the interdependent third stage over two-thirds of such judgments were favorable. Moreover, the percentage of friendships across group lines multiplied fourfold.

One final result of this intriguing investigation replicates the limited nature of the attitude change initially induced even under optimal contact conditions. The first interdependent encounters of the two groups by no means removed all of the bad feeling between them. But as these socially sanctioned encounters continued, they took on more power to reduce prejudice. This suggests that, as the desegregation process proceeds, it may well receive increasingly greater support and have increasingly greater effects upon the participants, both black and white.

Contrasting Strategies for Change

The Rattlers and the Eagles demonstrate a basic principle involved in changing racial patterns in the United States:

effective efforts must attack the patterns directly. It is not enough to be concerned with reducing anti-Negro prejudice. Indeed, the very changes that eliminate social barriers to progress by Negroes structure new situations which in turn alter individual attitudes to the greatest possible extent. Allport's four situational criteria for lessening prejudice are virtually impossible to achieve without first eliminating racial discrimination.

At the broadest level, eliminating discrimination requires the development of institutional protections for minorities, as was mentioned in Chapter 8. Such protections have been emphasized throughout this book; suffice it to add that these protections often appear in forms not ostensibly related to minorities and come in a variety of ways. For example, changes in municipal property-tax laws are desperately needed by many Negroes and whites, because property-tax structures tend to foster and perpetuate slum housing in many cities, in that slum landlords are encouraged to allow property to deteriorate in the ghetto by tax incentives and lack of enforcement of building and sanitation codes.

The United States government is not the only sponsor of institutional protections, but it has become by far the chief agent of planned change in race relations. And frequently a conflict confronts government officials in this and other areas: "success strategy" versus "test strategy."

Consider an official with a reasonably tight budget, a limited staff, and a broad legislative mandate for immediate action. He could be an official of the Office of Education charged with enforcing Title VI of the 1964 Civil Rights Act and preparing to withhold Federal funds from a variety of school districts which refuse to comply with the nondiscriminatory provisions of the Act. Or he could be an official administering the Manpower Retraining Act or similar programs and preparing to select the blacks and whites for the program out of the vast pool of people who need and want such training. In each of these situations the organizers must decide where to focus the limited resources. Should the principal effort be directed at those cases which are most likely to change easily and thus will demonstrate that the program is a success—the so-called "skimming-off-the-cream" approach? Or should it be directed at those cases which are least likely to change easily and thus will provide a rigorous test of the program? Or should it be directed primarily at cases of medium difficulty, or at some combination of these possibilities?

Frequently, specialists in civil rights have criticized Federal programs for following the path of least resistance and tackling only the easy cases. Yet a reasonable argument can be made for this approach: why not change those who obviously can be changed? Indeed, this policy yields more conspicuous gain per dollar spent than any other strategy—a not irrelevant consideration. Consequently, it appeals to those with political purposes and to administrators with their own future careers in mind. In addition, early success safeguards the program's continuance, making it theoretically possible to attack the core of the problem later on from a stronger posture, and can enhance the program's image as one that is making progress.

But maximizing early success has its obvious drawbacks as a strategy for planned change. If the Office of Education followed this approach, it would reward the most belligerent and recalcitrant school districts practicing racial discrimination by exempting them from the initial stages of the enforcement of Title VI. In job training programs, this process would differentially operate against the enrollment of Negroes because the floor of deprivation among Negroes is qualitatively and quantitatively below that of disadvantaged whites. Fundamentally, then, the dangers of the "early success" approach are that it may squander a major chance for basic and needed change and ease consciences while only scratching the surface of the problem.

These weaknesses point up the advantages of the counterstrategy—the need to put programs to the test by concentrating upon the most difficult cases. In enforcing Title VI, this test strategy would require the use of virtually all resources for school districts in Alabama, Mississippi, Louisiana, northern Florida, and southwest Georgia; in the Manpower Retraining and Job Corps programs, it would necessitate accepting only the hard-core unemployed, with the consequence that the most debilitated segments of the black ghetto would be far more likely to be included in significant numbers. In addition to affording a real test of the program, such a strategy provides a genuine attempt at initiating the basic institutional alterations that are needed before much wider solutions are possible.

Basic institutional alterations, however, are generally politically dangerous; and there is a greater chance of short-run failure with the "test" strategy. Moreover, greater expenditures of public funds for less conspicuous success will generally be involved, for the cost per person effectively prepared for the labor market in, say, the Manpower Retraining program would necessarily be greater if the hard-core unemployed were the principal clientele. Thus, the test strategy may seriously jeopardize the continuation of the whole program.

The complementary nature of the advantages and disadvantages of these rival strategies suggests that a third possibility may be useful. A dual strategy might involve a judicious mixture of the success and test strategies, employed simultaneously, taking as many of the easiest and hardest cases as resources allow while omitting the middle range. The political need for early success can be met largely with the easier cases; the more difficult cases allow head-on grappling with the most recalcitrant and early experience with the fundamental issues of the problem at its worst.

The most effective methods for the easy cases will almost undoubtedly not be the same as those for the difficult cases. Modern social science has no bag of tricks or even of well-tested techniques for tasks like training the most seriously disadvantaged young people, such as were enrolled in the Job Corps. A successful attack on the effects of racism and poverty must have an evolving strategy; it must learn as it unfolds, and it probably cannot do so if it does not have, on the one hand, easy instances for reasons of publicity, politics, and its own future and, on the other hand, difficult instances from which its administrators can learn how to shape the program in the future.

Future American Racial Patterns

At first glance, the plight of blacks trapped in urban ghettos recalls the immigrant ghettos of previous generations. Both Negroes and immigrants moved from near-peasant status to form the lower classes of large metropolitan centers. But beyond that, the analogy breaks down. As Talcott Parsons ably demonstrates, the black American poses a sharply different problem than immigrant Americans as concerns inclusion into America's "societal community." [41] The analogy is, therefore, exceedingly misleading. It provokes the often-heard query: "What's so special about Negroes? We Irish (or Italians or Jews) made it on our own—why all this fuss over the Negro's problems?" In addition to its debatable accuracy concerning how immigrants were absorbed into American society, such a question overlooks all that is unique about the case of Negroes from slavery to the present. In particular, the analogy obscures the principal social-psychological problem of race relations in the United States—the persistent fact that there is in American society a special and debilitating *stigma* placed upon the Negro.

The concept of "stigma" is here used in its social-psychological sense: that is, "stigma" signifies a handicap which disqualifies an entire class of persons from full social acceptance.[42] It need *not* be a permanent handicap, and the concept should not be confused with certain popular usages of the term as a lasting physical mark of blemish. The Negro stigma revolves largely around the assumption of primitive inferiority.[43] Manifestations of the stigma include the attitudes of whites toward interracial marriage, cited earlier, and the expected subservient role of "Negro." The special stigma becomes apparent when the Negro's position in society is compared with that of other deprived groups. Negro Texans, for example, have a median of two years' more education than Texans of Mexican descent, yet their median family income falls well below even that of the Mexican—and this despite the fact that the Mexican Americans face special language and cultural barriers. Nor is this stigma a matter of mere color and visibility: compare the black American's place in American society with that of Japanese and Chinese Americans.

Stigmata placed on outgroups, as we noted in Chapter 8, often takes one or two contrasting forms: superego images and id images. The id stigma placed upon the Negro American is only now beginning to recede. A study of Princeton University undergraduates in 1950, following up a study made in the early 1930s, found that the Negro stereotype, like other stereotypes, had lost some of its salience. The percentage of students regarding the Negro American as "superstitious" had declined from 84 to 41 percent, as "lazy" from 75 to 31 percent, as "happy-go-lucky" from 38 to 17 percent, and as "ignorant" from 38 to 24 percent.[44] Evidence of a similar trend for the entire adult population comes from repeated surveys of the National Opinion Research Center asking a question concerning intelligence of Negroes (see Chapter 8).

For striking evidence of how this shift is reflected in the mass media, one need only compare contemporary material with, say, the early issues of *Life Magazine*.[45] While occasionally portraying blacks neutrally or as "credits to their race," *Life* in the late 1930s overwhelmingly presented them either as musical, primitive, amusing, or religious, or as violent and criminal; occupationally, they were pictured as either servants, athletes, or entertainers, or as unemployed. Pictures included a Negro choir at a graveside funeral, an all-Negro chain gang, and Negro W. P. A. workers beating a drum "in tribal fashion" at a W. P. A. circus. Dialect was common: to the question of who was Father Divine's father, "Mrs. Mayfield cackled, 'Lawd, chile, that been so long ago, I done fergit.' " Descriptions of Negroes dancing included such terms as "barbaric," "jungle," and "native gusto." Today the mass media would not consider such material.

This is not to imply that the id stigma of blacks has faded completely from view. A 1966 national survey of white Americans revealed that 56 percent still believe that blacks "laugh a lot," 52 percent that they "smell different," 50 percent that they "have looser morals," and 43 percent that they "want to live off the handout." [46] Nevertheless, the id stigma is slowly receding, as a result of the upgrading of the Negro labor force and the improvement of the racial content of the mass media combined with the assertive resourcefulness of the black revolution. The pace at which it recedes will be directly related to how dysfunctional it becomes for American society, but the process will undoubtedly require a number of generations before the most entrenched aspects of the stigma are eradicated.

Erasure of the Negro stigma will in large part be a function of changing interracial patterns. The current black revolution makes it certain that there will be changes in these patterns; but it is equally certain that these changes will come unevenly.

Racial patterns in 1984, to select a fateful year, will differ most from those of today in the area of employment and least in the areas of housing and family. Employment contact—much of it meeting Allport's criteria for reducing intergroup animosity—will expand rapidly in the future, so that by the 1980s only pockets of the economic sector (for example, automobile executives) will lack at least token Negro representation. Nevertheless, these occupational gains will be limited by the capacity of public education and effective intervention programs of the Federal government to upgrade skills among Negroes. This educational factor may well prove to be a severe limitation. Here the importance of *de facto* segregation of schools looms large, for Negroes cannot be expected to work in interracial situations at high standards if they have overwhelmingly been trained in uniracial schools with low standards. The racial balancing of schools, however, may be a slow process at best in the future unless designs such as metropolitan parks are relied upon (see Chapter 4). And it will probably require initiatives created by state and Federal legislatures, as opposed to judicial action against *de jure* school segregation. At any rate, public education will provide steadily increasing opportunities in higher education for interracial contact that meets Allport's criteria; but these opportunities will not increase so rapidly as employment and may deter the racial integration of the American labor force.

The whole issue of *de facto* segregation in schools, churches, and other neighborhood-based institutions revolves around residential segregation. Interracial housing trends of recent years portend a future generation resembling the one just past—that is, a period of rapid racial change in other realms with housing integration lagging far behind. Some of the barriers to interracial housing are structural. Further progress, as we have seen, is inseparably intertwined with such larger issues as the total supply of low-cost housing, property-tax laws, and land-use planning. These are not issues for which picketing, sit-ins, and other protest techniques are ideally suited. Some of the barriers are less subtle and are erected by fierce resistance from whites. Racial discrimination in housing is usually blatant and entrenched, and it is pervasive throughout the nation and the class structure. It feeds on bigotry and on fears about status and finances; in addition, it is encouraged by much of the real-estate industry.

In addition to resistance from whites, recall from Chapter 2 that the lack of insistence by blacks is a critical barrier to the alteration of housing patterns. Segregation has produced large and concentrated Negro ghettos in a great majority of America's cities; and each of these ghettos has developed institutions and a community life in many ways distinct from and independent of the wider community. These deep-rooted black communities present formidable barriers to an eventual integrated society. As Franklin Frazier often pointed out, separate community life causes many Negroes to develop a vested interest in segregation.[47] Thus, Negro professionals and businessmen enjoy a captive market within the walls of a tight ghetto, but they must meet extensive competition in a desegregated society. Likewise, the all-black church and other all-black institutions naturally thrive best in a racially segregated society. Consequently, there is every reason to expect that even when residential discrimination essentially ends and Negroes as a group are prosperous enough to afford a wide range of housing, there will be binding ties in the ghetto that restrain many Negroes from moving to interracial areas.

Yet some change, even in housing patterns, can be expected during the next generation. Such change will definitely be selective, however, unless massive Federal intervention in housing occurs along lines far different from the efforts of the past, which have usually acted to tighten the ghetto. There may well be more Federally sponsored interracial contact in low-cost housing. But in general only the prospering middle-class Negroes in the urban North will be able to purchase or rent the type of housing that will be available in interracial areas on the private market.

The selective nature of this housing trend will give many white Americans living in the "better" residential districts the strong impression that considerable change is underway. After all, their suburban neighborhoods are likely to shift from having no Negro residents whatsoever to one Negro family or even an "invasion" of two or three Negro families. This will mean that token integration in suburban churches and schools is likely to become the rule, while the ghettos of the central cities grow ever larger.[48] Such a prospect is greeted with enthusiasm these days by black and white separatists; and it is the assumptions of these separatists to which we turn in the final chapter.

Footnotes

1. An extended application of role theory to race relations in the United States is provided in: T. F. Pettigrew, *A Profile of the Negro American* (Princeton: Van Nostrand, 1964).

2. The terror such a subordinate role can have for a white person, inexperienced in its subtleties, is described in: John Griffin, *Black Like Me* (New York: Signet Books, 1961).

3. Pettigrew, *op. cit.*

4. R. T. LaPiere, "Attitudes versus Actions," *Social Forces,* 1934, Vol. 13, pp. 230–237.

5. B. Kutner, C. Wilkins, and P. R. Yarrow, "Verbal Attitudes and Overt Behavior Involving Racial Prejudice," *Journal of Abnormal and Social Psychology,* 1952, Vol. 47, pp. 649–652.

6. M. L. Kohn and R. M. Williams, Jr., "Situational Patterning in Intergroup Relations," *American Sociological Review,* 1956, Vol. 21, pp. 164–174.

7. J. D. Lohman and D. C. Reitzes, "Note on Race Relations in Mass Society," *American Journal of Sociology,* 1952, Vol. 58, pp. 240–246; J. D. Lohman and D. C. Reitzes, "Deliberately Organized Groups and Racial Behavior," *American Sociological Review,* 1954, Vol. 19, pp. 342–344; and D. C. Reitzes, "The Role of Organizational Structures: Union versus Neighborhood in a Tension Situation," *Journal of Social Issues,* 1953, Vol. 9, No. 1, pp. 37–44.

8. Note that a "reference group" is not the same as a "membership group." People may or may not be members of their reference groups. What is critical is that the reference group supplies standards which an individual may use to guide his own behavior and with which he may compare his own position in life. See H. H. Hyman, "The Psychology of Status," *Archives of Psychology,* 1942, Vol. 38, No. 269, pp. 5–94; H. H. Kelley, "Two Functions of Reference Groups," in G. E. Swanson, T. M. Newcomb, and E. L. Hartley (eds.), *Readings in Social Psychology* (New York: Holt, Rinehart, and Winston, 1952), pp. 410–414; and R. K. Merton and A. S. Kitt, "Contributions to a Theory of Reference Group Behavior," in R. K. Merton and P. F. Lazarsfeld (eds.), *Studies in the*

Scope and Method of "The American Soldier" (Glencoe, Ill.: Free Press, 1950). All these important works and others, can be found in: H. H. Hyman and E. Singer, *Readings in Reference Group Theory and Research* (New York: Free Press, 1968).

9. H. A. Bullock, "Racial Attitudes and the Employment of Negroes," *American Journal of Sociology*, 1951, Vol. 56, pp. 448–457.

10. A. Kapos, "Some Individual and Group Determinants of Fraternity Attitudes Toward the Admission of Members of Certain Minority Groups" (unpublished doctoral dissertation, University of Michigan, 1953).

11. D. M. Heer, "Negro-White Marriage in the United States," *New Society*, August 26, 1965, Vol. 6, No. 152, pp. 7–9.

12. W. Brink and L. Harris, *The Negro Revolution in America* (New York: Simon & Schuster, 1964), p. 148. The comparable percentages for white Southerners are 97 and 91 objecting.

13. *Ibid.*

14. G. E. Simpson and J. M. Yinger, *Racial and Cultural Minorities,* 3d ed. (New York: Harper & Row, 1965), p. 401.

15. T. F. Pettigrew, "Our Caste-Ridden Protestant Campuses," *Christianity and Crisis,* 1961, Vol. 21, pp. 88–91; and T. F. Pettigrew, "Wherein the Church Has Failed in Race," *Religious Education,* 1964, Vol. 59, pp. 64–73.

16. H. H. Hyman and P. B. Sheatsley, "Attitudes Toward Desegregation," *Scientific American,* 1956, Vol. 195, pp. 35–39.

17. R. W. Friedrichs, "Christians and Residential Exclusion: An Empirical Study of a Northern Dilemma," *Journal of Social Issues,* 1959, Vol. 15, No. 4, pp. 14–23.

18. F. R. Westie, "Negro-White Status Differentials and Social Distance," *American Sociological Review,* 1952, Vol. 17, pp. 550–558.

19. F. R. Westie and D. H. Howard, "Social Status Differentials and the Race Attitudes of Negroes," *American Sociological Review,* 1954, Vol. 19, pp. 584–591.

20. T. C. Cothran, "Negro Conceptions of White People," *American Journal of Sociology,* March, 1951, Vol. 56, pp. 458–467; and P. A. McDaniel and N. Babchuk, "Negro Conceptions of White People in a Northeastern City," *Phylon,* Spring 1960, Vol. 21, pp. 7–19.

21. L. G. Watts, H. E. Freeman, H. M. Hughes, R. Morris, and T. F. Pettigrew, *The Middle-Income Negro Family Faces Urban Renewal* (Boston: Department of Commerce and Development, Commonwealth of Massachusetts, 1964).

22. T. F. Pettigrew, "De Facto Segregation, Southern Style," *In-*

tegrated Education, October—November, 1963, Vol. 1, No. 5, pp. 15—18; and T. F. Pettigrew, "Continuing Barriers to Desegregated Education in the South," _Sociology of Education,_ Winter 1965, Vol. 38, pp. 99—111.

23. N. Hentoff, personal communication. For a vivid and penetrating analysis of this mood in Northern ghettos, see: K. B. Clark, _Dark Ghetto_ (New York: Harper & Row, 1965).

24. G. Gallup, "Negroes, Whites Disagree on Treatment of Former" (American Institute of Public Opinion, May 4, 1965).

25. W. Brink and L. Harris, _Black and White_ (New York: Simon and Schuster, 1967), pp. 222—231.

26. Pettigrew, _Profile of the Negro American, op cit.,_ Chap. 8.

27. G. W. Allport, _The Nature of Prejudice_ (Cambridge, Mass.: Addison-Wesley Publishing Co., 1954), Chap. 16.

28. I. N. Brophy, "The Luxury of Anti-Negro Prejudice," _Public Opinion Quarterly,_ Winter 1945—46, Vol. 9, pp. 456—466. One possible explanation for the results of this study and others cited below is that the people who were the least prejudiced to begin with sought out interracial contact. Most of these studies, however, rule out the operation of this self-selection factor.

29. W. M. Kephart, _Racial Factors and Urban Law Enforcement_ (Philadelphia: University of Pennsylvania Press, 1957), pp. 188—189.

30. B. MacKenzie, "The Importance of Contact in Determining Attitudes Toward Negroes," _Journal of Abnormal and Social Psychology,_ October, 1948, Vol. 43, pp. 417—441.

31. A. M. Lee and N. D. Humphrey, _Race Riot_ (New York: Dryden, 1943), pp. 97, 130, 140.

32. M. Deutsch and M. Collins, _Interracial Housing: A Psychological Evaluation of a Social Experiment_ (Minneapolis: University of Minnesota Press, 1951); M. Jahoda and P. West, "Race Relations in Public Housing," _Journal of Social Issues,_ 1951, Vol. 7, Nos. 1 and 2, pp. 132—139; D. M. Wilner, R. Walkley, and S. W. Cook, _Human Relations in Interracial Housing: A Study of the Contact Hypothesis_ (Minneapolis: University of Minnesota Press, 1955); and E. Works, "The Prejudice-Interaction Hypothesis from the Point of View of the Negro Minority Group," _American Journal of Sociology,_ July, 1961, Vol. 67, pp. 47—52.

33. S. A. Stouffer, E. A. Suchman, L. C. DeVinney, S. A. Star, and R. M. Williams, Jr., _Studies in Social Psychology in World War II,_ Vol. 1, _The American Soldier; Adjustment During Army Life_ (Princeton, N. J.: Princeton University Press, 1949), Chap. 10.

34. J. Harding and R. Hogrefe, "Attitudes of White Department Store Employees Toward Negro Co-Workers," *Journal of Social Issues*, 1952, Vol. 8, No. 1, pp. 18–28.

35. G. Saenger and E. Gilbert, "Customer Reactions to the Integration of Negro Sales Personnel," *International Journal of Opinion and Attitude Research*, Spring 1950, Vol. 4, pp. 57–76.

36. Prohibition provides an interesting contrast. It apparently failed largely because it was not rigorously enforced and, despite its moral overtones for some Protestants, it did fit in with national traditions or ease the consciences of many Americans.

37. E. Cooper and M. Jahoda, "The Evasion of Propaganda: How Prejudiced People Respond to Anti-Prejudice Propaganda," *Journal of Psychology*, January, 1947, Vol. 23, pp. 15–25; and H. H. Hyman and P. B. Sheatsley, "Some Reasons Why Information Campaigns Fail," *Public Opinion Quarterly*, Fall 1947, Vol. 11, pp. 413–423.

38. For an interesting political example of this phenomenon, see: H. Cantril (ed.), *Gauging Public Opinion* (Princeton, N. J. Princeton University Press, 1944), pp. 226–230.

39. W. A. Scott, "Attitude Change Through Reward of Verbal Behavior," *Journal of Abnormal and Social Psychology*, July, 1957, Vol. 55, pp. 72–75; and W. A. Scott, "Attitude Change by Response Reinforcement: Replication and Extension," *Sociometry*, December, 1959, Vol. 22, pp. 328–335.

40. M. Sherif, D. J. Harvey, B. J. White, W. R. Hood, and C. Sherif, *Intergroup Conflict and Cooperation: The Robbers Cave Experiment* (Norman, Okla.: University of Oklahoma, 1961).

41. T. Parsons, "Full Citizenship for the Negro American? A Sociological Problem," in Parsons and Clark (eds.), *The Negro American* (Boston: Houghton Mifflin, 1966), pp. 709–754.

42. E. Goffman, *Stigma: Notes on the Management of Spoiled Identity* (Englewood Cliffs, N. J.: Prentice-Hall, 1963).

43. B. Bettelheim and M. Janowitz, *Social Change and Prejudice* (New York: Free Press of Glencoe, 1964); and T. W. Adorno, E. Frenkel-Brunswik, D. J. Levinson, and R. N. Sanford, *The Authoritarian Personality* (New York: Harper and Row, 1950).

44. D. Katz and K. W. Braly, "Racial Stereotypes of 100 College Students," *Journal of Abnormal and Social Psychology*, October–November, 1933, Vol. 28, pp. 280–290; and G. M. Gilbert, "Stereotype Persistence and Change Among College Students," *Journal of Abnormal and Social Psychology*, April, 1951, Vol. 46, pp. 245–254.

45. I am indebted to Dr. Patricia Pajonas, for her analysis of all

racial material appearing in thirty-four issues of *Life* sampled from November, 1936, to March, 1938.

46. Brink and Harris, *op. cit.,* p. 136.

47. E. F. Frazier, "The Negro Middle Class and Desegregation," *Social Problems,* April, 1957, Vol. 4, pp. 291–301.

48. This pattern of tokenism in the suburbs and segregation in the central city suggests one important and largely untapped source of future interracial contact. This would entail programs where the suburbs cooperate with the central city by accepting in their schools a specified number of black children from the inner city, by accepting low-cost public housing, and so forth. Better still, of course, are large-scale cooperative ventures like the metropolitan educational parks described in Chapter 4.

CHAPTER TWELVE

RACIALLY SEPARATE OR TOGETHER? [1]

The United States has had an almost perpetual racial crisis for a generation. But the last third of the twentieth century has begun on a new note, a change of rhetoric and a confusion over goals. Widespread rioting is just one expression of this. The nation hesitates: it seems to have lost its confidence that the problem can be solved; it seems unsure as to even the direction in which a solution lies. In too simple terms, yet in the style of the fashionable rhetoric, the question has become: Shall Americans of the future live racially separate or together?

This new mood is best understood when viewed as part of the eventful sweep of recent years. Ever since World War I, when war orders combined with the curtailment of immigration to encourage massive migration to industrial centers, Negro Americans have been undergoing rapid change as a people. The latest products of this dramatic transformation from Southern peasant to Northern urbanite are the second and third generations of young people born in the North. The most significant fact about this "newest new Negro" is that he is relatively released from the principal social controls recognized by his parents and grandparents, from the restraints of an extended kinship system, a conservative religion, and an acceptance of the inevitability of white supremacy.

Consider the experience of the 20-year-old Negro in 1971. He was born in 1951; he was only 3 years old when the Supreme Court ruled against *de jure* public school segregation; he was only 6 years old at the time of the disorders over desegregation in Little Rock, Arkansas; he was 9 years old when the student-organized sit-ins began at segregated lunch counters throughout the South; he was 12 when the dramatic march on Washington took place and 15 when the climactic Selma march occurred. He has witnessed during his short life the initial dismantling of the formal structure of white supremacy. Conventional wisdom holds that such an experience should lead to a highly satisfied generation of young black Americans; but newspaper headlines and social-psychological theory tell us that precisely the opposite is closer to the truth, as we discussed in Chapter 7.

The young black surveys the current scene and observes correctly that the benefits of recent racial advances have disproportionately accrued to the expanding middle class, leaving the urban lower class ever further behind. While the middle-class segment of Negro America has expanded from roughly 5 to 25 percent of the Negroes since 1940,[2] the vast majority of blacks remain poor. The young Negro has been raised on the proposition that racial integration is the basic solution to racial injustice, but his doubts grow as opportunities open for the skilled while the daily lives of the unskilled go largely unaffected. Accustomed to a rapid pace of events, many Negro young people wonder if integration will ever be possible in an America where the depth of white resistance to racial change becomes painfully more evident: in 1964, the equivocation of the Democratic Party Convention when faced with the challenge of the Mississippi Freedom Democratic Party; in 1965, the brutality at the bridge in Selma; in 1966, the summary rejection by Congress of anti-discrimination legislation for housing; in 1968, the wanton assassinations within ten weeks of two leading symbols of the integration movement; and, finally, the retrogression in Federal action for civil rights under the Nixon administration. These events create understandable doubts as to whether Dr. Martin Luther King's dream of equality can ever be achieved.

It is tempting to project this process further, as many analyses in the mass media unhesitantly have done, and suggest that all of black America has undergone this vast disillusionment, that blacks now overwhelmingly reject racial integration and are instead turning to separatist goals. As we shall note shortly when reviewing evidence from surveys, this is not the case. Strictly separatist solutions for the black ghettos of urban America have been most elaborately and enthusiastically advanced not by Negro writers but by such popular white writers as the newspaper columnist Joseph Alsop and William H. Ferry, formerly of the Center for the Study of Democratic Institutions.[3] These white analysts, like many white spokesmen for three centuries before them, are prepared to abandon the American dream of equality as it should apply to blacks, in the name of "hard realities" and under a conveniently mistaken notion that separatism is what blacks want anyway.

Yet the militant stance and rhetoric have shifted in recent years. In a real sense, integration has not failed in America, for it still remains to be tried as a national policy. Many Negroes of all ages sense this; they feel that the nation has failed integration rather than that integration has failed the nation. Influential black opinion turned in the late 1960s from integration as the primary goal to other goals—group power, culture, identity, integrity, and pride. Only a relatively small segment of blacks see these new goals as conflicting with integration; but this segment and their assumptions are one focus of this chapter, for they play a disproportionately critical role for the two chief concerns of this volume—racial integration and white racism. The principal contention throughout this book has been that *integration is a necessary condition for the eradication of white racism at both the individual and institutional levels.* But no treatment of this thesis in America of the 1970s would be complete unless it included a brief discussion of this new black mood and its apparently separatist fringe.

Even much of this fringe of young ideological blacks should be described as "apparently" separatist, for the labels that make sense for white Americans necessarily must shift meaning when applied to black Americans. Given the national events that have occurred in their short lives, it is not surprising that this fringe regard racial integration less as an evil than as irrelevant to their preoccupations. They often call for *selective* separatism of one or more aspects of their lives while also demanding their rights of entry into the society's principal institutions. It is no accident that the most outspoken members of this faction are college students in prestigious and predominantly white universities.

Through the eyes of some whites, this behavior seems highly inconsistent; it looks as though they talk separation and act integration. But actually the inconsistency is often, though not always, more apparent than real. Consistent with the new emphasis upon power and pride, these young blacks are attempting to define their situation for themselves with particular attention to group autonomy. They are generally as opposed to forced separatism as were Negroes of past generations, and they reject other imposed doctrines as well. And for many of them, integration appears to be imposed by white liberals. "Why is it that you white liberals only insist on *racial* integration," they often ask, "when separation by class and ethnicity is a widespread fact of American life? Why is it no one gets upset by Italian separatism or Jewish separatism, only black separatism?" That the imposed separation of Negroes in America is qualitatively different and more vast than that practiced against or by any other sizable American minority, that integration as a doctrine was a creation not of white liberals but of their own fathers and grandfathers—these answers to the young blacks' insistent question are intellectually sound. But such responses do not relate to the feelings underlying the question, for they ignore the positive functions of the new emphasis which excite many young black Americans today.

The positive functions of the new militancy and ideology are exciting precisely because they go to the heart of many young blacks' personal feelings. If the new ideology's analysis of power at the societal level is incomplete, its analysis of racial self-hate at the individual level is right on the mark. Its attention to positive identity and "black is beautiful" is needed and important. Indeed, the abrupt shift from "Negro" to "black" is an integral part of this movement. Many members of older generations would have taken offense at being called "black"; it was considered a slur. But in facing the issue squarely, young blacks want to be called by the previously forbidden term in order to externalize the matter and convert it into a positive label. The fact that the historical justification sometimes cited for the shift is thin at best is not the point.[4] The important consideration is psychological, and on this ground there is every reason to believe that the change is healthy.

But the point often overlooked about this new movement is that its cultural and psychological aspects do not require racial separatism. At the close of this chapter, we shall review evidence indicating that this fact is clearly perceived by the great majority of black Americans, who want racial pride and integrity together with integration. Not only is there no necessary contradiction between these two goals, but, once established, group pride is developed best in heterogeneous settings which allow for both individual and group autonomy.

Racial integration has shifted, then, in much black thought from the status of a principal goal to that of one among other mechanisms for achieving "liberation." "Liberation," in its broadest meaning for American race relations, means the total elimination of racial oppression. Similar to the older usage of "freedom," "liberation" means the eradication of the burden of racism that black Americans have borne individually and collectively since 1621. From this particular black perspective, "racially separate or together" is not the issue so much as what mix of strategies and efforts can actually achieve liberation. This view predominated in the August, 1970, issue of *Ebony,* which was completely devoted to the topic: "Which Way Black America? Separation? Integration? Liberation?" *Ebony*'s Senior Editor, Lerone Bennett, Jr., puts it forth bluntly:

. . . The fundamental issue is not separation or integration but liberation. The either/or question of integration or separation does not speak to that proposition; for if our goal is liberation it may be necessary to do both or neither.[5]

We shall return to this point shortly; and we will note that when the much-abused term "integration" is adequately defined, the position advocated throughout this volume resembles Bennett's in all but rhetoric.

There are, then, positive functions internal to black communities and individuals which this new stance and line of thought appear to have. Much of the present writing in race relations is devoted to these positive functions. But what do these trends spell for the possibility of effectively combating white racism? While accepting the conclusion of the Kerner Commission that this is the basic problem, some recent black thought takes the position that wholly *black* concerns must take such precedence that the fight against white racism is, if not irrelevant, at least of secondary importance. Worse, some elements of the separatist fringe actively contribute to the growth and legitimacy of white racism. Hence, when Roy Innis, the national chairman of the Congress of Racial Equality (CORE), goes on a publicized tour to meet governors of the Deep South in order to advocate his program of separate-but-equal public schools, it hardly helps the effort to eliminate white racism.

This truly separatist fringe, then, is neither necessary to nor typical of the new black thrust. It gains its importance from, and becomes potentially dangerous because of, the way it nourishes white racism at both the individual and institutional levels. And it is for this reason that we need to compare it with white segregationist thought. Obviously, the two groups of separatists have sharply different sources of motivation: the blacks to withdraw, the whites to maintain racial supremacy. Nor are their assumptions on a par for destructive potential. But the danger is that black and white separatism could congeal as movements in the 1970s and help perpetuate a racially separate and racist nation. Because of this danger, it is well to examine the basic assumptions of both groups.

Separatist Assumptions

White segregationists, both in the North and in the South, base their position upon three bedrock assumptions. *Assumption 1* is that separation benefits both races because each feels awkward and uncomfortable with the other: *Whites and Negroes are happiest and most relaxed when in the company of "their own kind."* [6]

Assumption 2 is blatantly racist: *Negroes are inherently inferior to whites, and this is the underlying reality of all racial problems.* The findings of both social and biological science place in serious jeopardy every argument put forward for this assumption, and a decreasing minority of white Americans subscribe to it.[7] Yet it remains the essential substratum of the thinking of white segregationists; racial contact must be avoided, according to this reasoning, if standards of whites are not to be lowered. Thus, attendance at a desegregated school may benefit black children, but it is deemed by segregationists to be inevitably harmful to white children.[8]

Assumption 3 is derived from this assumption of white superiority: *Since contact can never be mutually beneficial, it will inevitably lead to racial conflict.* The White Citizens' Councils in the Deep South, for example, insist that they are opposed to violence and favor racial separation as the primary means of maintaining racial harmony. As long as Negroes "know their place," as long as white supremacy remains unchallenged, strife will be at a minimum.

Black separatists base their position upon three somewhat parallel assumptions. They agree with Assumption 1, that both whites and Negroes are more at ease when separated from each other. It is a harsh fact that blacks have borne the heavier burden of desegregation and have entered previously all-white institutions where open hostility is sometimes practiced by segregationist whites in order to discourage the process, and this is a partial explanation of agreement among blacks with Assumption 1. Yet some of this agreement stems from more subtle situations: the demands by some black student organizations on interracial campuses for all-black facilities have been predicated on this same assumption.

A second assumption of black separatists focuses directly upon white racism. Supported by the chief conclusion of the National Advisory Commission on Civil Disorders, black separatists consider that white racism is the central problem, and that "white liberals" should confine their energies to eradicating it.[9] Let us call this *Assumption 4: White liberals must eradicate white racism.* This assumption underlies two further contentions: namely, that "white liberals" should stay out of the ghetto except as their money and expertise are explicitly requested, and that it is no longer the job of black militants to confront and absorb the abuse of white racists.

The third assumption of black separatists is the most basic of all, and is in tacit agreement with the segregationist notion that interracial contact as it now occurs makes only for conflict. Interaction between black and white Americans, it is held, can never be truly equal and mutually beneficial until blacks first gain personal and group autonomy, self-respect, and power. This makes *Assumption 5: Autonomy is necessary before contact.* It often underlies a two-step theory of how to achieve meaningful integration: the first step requires separation so that Negroes can regroup, unify, and gain a positive self-image and identity; only when this is achieved can the second step, real integration, take place. Ron Karenga, a black leader in Los Angeles, states the idea forcefully: "We're not for isolation, but interdependence. But we can't become interdependent unless we have something to offer. We can live with whites interdependently once we have black power." [10]

Each of these ideological assumptions deserves examination in the light of social-psychological theory and findings.

Social-Psychological Considerations of Separatist Assumptions

Assumption 1: Whites and Negroes Are More Comfortable Apart than Together

There can be no denying that many black and white Americans initially feel uncomfortable and ill at ease when they encounter each other in new situations. This reality is so vivid and so generally recognized that both black and white separatists use it widely in their thinking, though they do not analyze the nature and origins of the situation.

The literature of social science is replete with examples of the phenomenon. Irwin Katz has described the initial awkwardness in biracial task groups in the laboratory: white partners usually assumed an aggressive, imperious role, black partners a passive role. Similarly, Yarrow found initial tension and keen sensitivity among many Negro children in an interracial summer camp, much of which centered on fears that they would be rejected by white campers.[11] But, more important, such tension does not continue to pervade a truly integrated situation. Katz noted that once blacks were cast in assertive roles, behavior in his small groups became more equalitarian and this improvement generalized to new situations. Yarrow, too, observed a sharp decline in anxiety and sensitivity among the black children after two weeks of successful integration at the summer camp. As was discussed previously, similar increments in cross-racial acceptance and reductions in tension have been noted in new interracial situations in department stores,[12] the Merchant Marine,[13] the armed forces,[14] and public housing,[15] and even among the Philadelphia police.[16]

This is not to say that new interracial situations invariably lead to acceptance. As we have seen, the *conditions* of the interracial contact are crucial; and even under optimal conditions, the cross-racial acceptance generated by contact is typically limited to the particular situation which created it. A segregated society restricts the generalization effects of even truly integrated situations; and at times like the present, when race assumes such overwhelming salience, the racial tension of the larger society may even poison previously successful interracial settings.

Acquaintance and similarity theory helps to clarify the underlying process. Newcomb states the fundamental tenet as follows:

Insofar as persons have similar attitudes toward things of importance to both or all of them, and discover that this is so, they have shared attitudes; under most conditions the experience of sharing such attitudes is rewarding, and thus provides a basis for mutual attraction.[17]

Rokeach has applied these notions to race relations in the United States with some surprising results. He maintains that rejection of black Americans by white Americans is motivated less by racism than by assumed differences in beliefs and values. In other words, whites generally perceive Negroes as holding beliefs contrasting with their own, and it is this perception—not race *per se*—that leads to rejection. Indeed, a variety of subjects have supported Rokeach's ideas by typically accepting in a social situation a Negro with beliefs similar to their own over a white with different beliefs.[18]

Additional work has specified the phenomenon more precisely. Triandis and Davis have shown that the relative importance of belief and race in attraction is a joint function of personality and the interpersonal realm in question. Similarity of beliefs is most critical in more formal matters of general personal evaluation and social acceptance, where racial norms are ambiguously defined. Race is most critical in intimate matters of marriage and neighborhood, where racial norms are explicitly defined. For interpersonal realms of an intermediate degree of intimacy, such as friendship, both beliefs and race appear important. There are wide individual differences in the application of these concerns, however, especially in areas where the degree of intimacy is intermediate.[19]

Seen in the light of this work, racial isolation has two negative effects, both of which operate to make optimal interracial contact difficult to achieve and initially tense. First, isolation prevents each group from learning of the beliefs and values they do in fact share. Consequently, Negroes and whites kept apart come to view each other as very different; this belief, combined with racial considerations, causes each race to reject contact with the other. Second, isolation leads in time to the evolution of genuine differences in beliefs and values, making interracial contact in the future even less likely.[20]

A number of findings of social-psychological research support this extrapolation of interpersonal-attraction theory. Stein et al. noted that relatively racially isolated white ninth-graders in California assumed an undescribed Negro teen-ager to be similar to a Negro teen-ager who was described as being quite different from themselves.[21] Smith et al. found that similarity of beliefs was more critical than racial similarity in desegregated settings, less critical in segregated settings.[22] And the U. S. Commission on Civil Rights, in its study of *Racial Isolation in the Public Schools,* found that both black and white adults who as children had attended interracial schools were more likely as adults to live in an interracial neighborhood and hold more positive racial attitudes than comparable adults who had known only segregated schools.[23] Or, to put it negatively, Americans of both races who experienced only segregated education are more likely to reflect separatist behavior and attitudes as adults.

Racial separatism, then, is a cumulative process. It feeds upon itself and leads its victims to prefer continued separation. In an open-choice situation in Louisville, Kentucky, black children were far more likely to select predominantly white high schools if they were currently attending predominantly white junior high schools.[24] From these data, the U. S. Commission on Civil Rights concluded: "The inference is strong that Negro high school students prefer biracial education only if they have experienced it before. If a Negro student has not received his formative education in biracial schools, the chances are he will not choose to enter one in his more mature school years."[25] Similarly, Negroes who attended segregated schools, the Civil Rights Commission finds, are more likely to believe as adults that interracial schools "create hardships for Negro children" and are less likely to send their children to desegregated schools than are Negroes who attended biracial schools.[26] Note that those who most fear discomfort in biracial settings are precisely those who have experienced such situations *least*. If desegregation actually resulted in perpetual and debilitating tension, as separatists are so quick to assume, it seems unlikely that children already in the situation would willingly opt for more, or that adults who have had considerable interracial contact as children would willingly submit themselves to biracial neighborhoods and their children to biracial schools.

Moreover, in dealing with the fact that some tension does exist, a social-cost analysis is needed. The question becomes: What price comfort? Racially homogeneous settings are often more comfortable for members of both races, though, as we have just noted, this seems to be most true at the start of the contact and does not seem to be so debilitating that those in the situation typically wish to return to segregated living. But those who remain in racial isolation, both black and white, find themselves increasingly less equipped to compete in an interracial world. Lobotomized patients are more comfortable, too, but they are impaired for life.

Moreover, there is nothing inevitable about the tension that characterizes many initial interracial encounters in the United States. Rather, tension is the direct result of the racial separation that has traditionally characterized our society. In short, separation is the cause of awkwardness in interracial contacts, not the remedy for it.

Assumption 2: Negroes Are Inferior; and Assumption 4: White Liberals Must Eradicate White Racism.

These two assumptions, though of vastly different significance, raise related issues; and both also are classic cases of self-fulfilling prophecies. Treat a people as inferior, force them to play subservient roles,[27] keep them essentially separate, and eventually the people produced by this must come to support the initial racist notions. Likewise, assume that whites are unalterably racist, curtail efforts by Negroes to confront racism directly, separate Negroes from whites even further, and the result will surely be a continuation, if not a heightening, of racism.

The core of racist attitudes, the assumption of innate racial inferiority, has been under sharp attack from social science for over three decades.[28] Partly because of this work, attitudes of white Americans have undergone massive change over these years. Yet a sizable minority of white Americans, perhaps still as large as a fifth of the adult population, persist in harboring racist attitudes in their most vulgar and naive form. This is an important fact in a time of polarization, such as the present, for this minority becomes the vocal right anchor in the nation's process of social judgment. Racist assumptions not only are nourished by separatism but in turn rationalize separatism. Equal-status contact is avoided because of the racist stigma placed on black Americans by three centuries of slavery and segregation. But changes are evident both here and in social-distance attitudes. Recall from Chapter 8 that between 1942 and 1963 the percentage of white Americans who favored racially desegregated schools rose from 30 to 63; the percentage of those with no objections to a Negro neighbor rose from 35 to 63.[29] And recall, too, that this trend did not abate during the mid-1960s of increasing white polarization mistakenly labeled "white backlash." This trend slowed, however, at the very close of the 1960s and in the early 1970s— possibly as a result of less insistence for integration.

The slow but steady erosion of racist and separatist attitudes among white Americans occurred during years of confrontation and change, although the process has been too slow to keep pace with the Negro's rising aspirations for full justice and complete eradication of racism. In a period of confrontation, dramatic events can stimulate surprisingly sharp changes in a short period of time.[30] Consider the attitudes of white Texans before and after the assassination of Martin Luther King, Jr., the riots that followed his murder, and the issuance of the forthright Report of the National Advisory Commission on Civil Disorders.[31] Table 14 shows the data collected before the assassination (in November, 1967, and February, 1968) and after the assassination (in May, 1968, and August, 1968). Observe that there were especially large changes in the four areas of relatively formal contact—desegregation in buses, jobs, restaurants and hotels. In areas of relatively informal contact—desegregation of schools and churches —there was moderate change. And in areas of intimate contact—desegregation of social gatherings, housing, swimming pools, house parties, and college dormitories— there was no significant change. Despite the ceiling ef-

Table 14 PERCENT OF WHITE TEXANS WHO APPROVE *

Area of Desegregation	Nov. 1967	Feb. 1968	May 1968	Aug. 1968	$\dfrac{May + Aug.}{2} - \dfrac{Nov. + Feb.}{2}$ Raw change
Formal contact					
Same buses	62.9	64.5	74.3	69.7	+8.3
Same jobs	66.8	69.1	76.1	76.4	+8.2
Same restaurants	57.9	59.9	66.8	66.4	+7.7
Same hotels	53.0	53.8	60.2	59.6	+6.5
Informal contact					
Same schools	53.7	57.6	61.4	61.7	+5.8
Same churches	57.4	60.0	62.5	65.4	+5.2
Teach your child	49.4	51.2	54.3	55.6	+4.7
Intimate contact					
Same social gatherings	39.3	38.9	41.8	44.2	+3.9
Live next door	29.5	32.1	32.0	36.6	+3.5
Same swimming pools	30.9	27.1	29.5	34.6	+3.1
Same house party	26.2	26.2	26.5	29.0	+1.5
College roommate of your child	17.4	17.8	17.1	18.0	0.0

* These results are taken from R. T. Riley and T. F. Pettigrew, "Dramatic Events and Racial Attitude Change" (unpublished paper, Harvard University, August, 1970). The data are from probability samples of white Texans drawn and interviewed by Belden Associates of Dallas, Texas.

fect,[32] approval increased most for those items already most approved. One is reminded of Triandis and Davis's breakdown of racial realms by degree of intimacy.[33] The changes in attitudes also varied among different types of white Texans; the young and the middle class shifted positively the most, again despite ceiling effects.[34] The tentative generalization growing out of these data is that in times of confrontation, dramatic events can achieve positive attitude changes among those whites and in those areas least subject to separatist norms.

The most solid social-psychological evidence about changes in racial attitudes comes from the studies of contact reviewed in Chapter 11. Repeated research in a variety of newly desegregated situations showed that the attitudes of whites and blacks toward each other markedly improved: in department stores, public housing,[35] the armed services,[36] and the Merchant Marine,[37] and among government workers,[38] the police,[39] students,[40] and general small-town populations.[41] Some of these findings can be interpreted not as results of contact, but as an indication that more tolerant white Americans seek contact with Negro Americans. A number of the investigations, however, restrict this self-selection factor, making the effects of the new contact itself the only explanation of the significant alterations in attitudes and behavior.

Surveys bear out these findings on a national scale. Hyman and Sheatsley found that among whites the most extensive changes in racial attitudes have occurred where extensive desegregation of public facilities had already taken place.[42] Recall, too, that data from the Coleman Report indicate that white students who attend public schools with blacks are the least likely to prefer all-white classrooms and all-white "close friends"; and this effect is strongest among those who began their interracial schooling in the early grades.[43] This fits neatly with the findings of the U. S. Commission on Civil Rights for both black and white adults who had attended biracial schools as children.[44]

Not all intergroup contact, of course, leads to increased acceptance; sometimes it only makes matters worse. Keep in mind Allport's criteria: prejudice is lessened when the two groups (1) possess equal status in the situation, (2) seek common goals, (3) are cooperatively dependent upon each other, and (4) interact with the positive support of authorities, laws, or customs.[45] These criteria are actually an application of the broader theory of interpersonal attraction. All four conditions maximize the likelihood that shared values and beliefs will be evinced and mutually perceived. Rokeach's belief-similarity factor is, then, apparently important in the effects of optimal contact. Following Triandis and Davis's findings,[46] we would anticipate that alterations in attitudes achieved by intergroup contact, at least initially, will be greatest in formal areas and least in intimate areas—as was true of the changes in attitudes of white Texans, brought about by dramatic events in the early spring of 1968.

From this social-psychological perspective, the assumption of black separatists that "white liberals" should eliminate white racism seems to be an impossible and quixotic hope. One can readily appreciate the militants' desire to avoid further abuse from white racists; but their model for change is woefully inadequate. White liberals can attack racist attitudes publicly, conduct research on racist assertions, set the stage for confrontation. But with all the will in the world they cannot accomplish by themselves the needed push, the dramatic events, the actual interracial contact which have gnawed away at racist beliefs for a generation. A century ago the fiery and perceptive Frederick Douglass phrased the issue pointedly:

I have found in my experience that the way to break down an unreasonable custom is to contradict it in practice. To be sure in pursuing this course I have had to contend not merely with the white race but with the black. The one has condemned me for my presumption in daring to associate with it and the other for pushing myself where it takes it for granted I am not wanted.[47]

Racially Separate or Together?

Assumption 3: Contact Must Lead to Conflict; and
Assumption 5: Autonomy Is Needed before Contact

History reveals that white separatists are correct when they contend that racial change creates conflict, that if only the traditions of white supremacy were to go unchallenged racial harmony might be restored. One of the quietest periods in American racial history, 1895–1915, witnessed the construction of the massive system of institutional racism as it is known today—the "nadir of Negro American history," as Rayford Logan calls it.[48] The price of those two decades of relative peace is still being paid by the nation. Even if it were possible now to gain racial calm by inaction, the United States could not afford the enormous cost.

But if inaction is clearly impossible, the types of action necessary are not so clear. Black separatists believe that efforts to further interracial contact should be abandoned or at least delayed until greater personal and group autonomy is achieved by Negroes. This view and the attitudes of white separatists just mentioned are two sides of the same coin. Both leave the struggle against racism in attitudes completely in the hands of "white liberals." And the two assumptions run a similar danger. Racism is reflected not only in attitudes but, more importantly, in institutionalized arrangements that operate to restrict the choices open to blacks. Both forms of racism are fostered by segregation, and both have to be confronted directly by Negroes. To withdraw into the ghetto, psychologically tempting as this may be for many, is essentially to give up the fight to alter the racially discriminatory operations of the nation's chief institutions. The Rev. Jesse L. Jackson, the Chicago black leader of Operation Breadbasket, makes the same point in forceful terms:

Let's use this analogy. Assuming that racism is a hot fire. If we're gonna take over things and run them and destroy racism;

we got to get to the core of the fire. You can't destroy it by running away from it. The fact is, at this point in American history, racism is in trouble in terms of the government, economy, political order and even the psychological order.[49]

The issues involved are shown schematically in Figure 13. By varying contact–separation and an ideologically vague concept of "autonomy," four cells may be set up that represent the various possibilities under discussion. Cell A, true integration, refers to institutionalized biracial situations where there is cross-racial friendship, racial interdependence, and a strong measure of personal and group autonomy. Such situations do exist in America today, but they are rare islands in a sea of conflict. Cell B represents the autonomous ghetto postulated by advocates of black separatism, relatively independent of the larger society and far more viable than is commonly the case now. This is an ideologically derived hypothetical situation, for no such urban ghettos exist today. Cell C stands for merely desegregated situations. These are often mistakenly called "integrated." They are institutionalized biracial settings

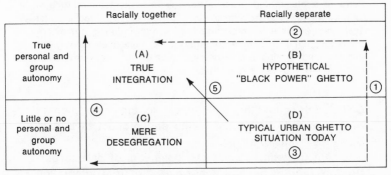

Figure 13. Schematic diagram of autonomy and contact–separation. Dotted lines denote hypothetical paths; solid lines, actual paths. The author is indebted to Professor Karl Deutsch of Harvard University for several stimulating conversations out of which came this diagram.

Racially Separate or Together?

313

which involve little cross-racial acceptance and, often, patronizing legacies of white supremacy. Cell D represents today's typical highly separate urban ghetto with little or no personal or group autonomy.

Definitional confusions may obscure the meaning of Figure 13, especially the definition of "integration." This term became almost a hallowed symbol of the civil rights movement of previous decades, and its present disparagement in newer black thought may be traced in part to this fact. But most disparagement of "integration" is due to definitional confusion between it and "assimilation" and between it and desegregation as diagramed in Figure 13. As Lerone Bennett rightly points out, these confusions among both whites and blacks stem from employing exclusively a white standard of reference:

> . . . One of the greatest enemies of integration in America today is the word integration. Contrary to the hopes of some and the fears of others, integration does not mean black elimination. Integration may or may not lead to assimilation, but assimilation does not necessarily mean the disappearance of a minority. . . . [D]ifferences can be eliminated in favor of a creative minority. Both "integrationists" and "separatists" forget that there is a blackening process as well as a whitening process. Liberationists, who recognize this dialectic, say blacks must assimilate and not be assimilated. . . . Integration is not disappearance; nor is it simple contiguity . . . since men have given the word integration a bad name, we shall use the word *transformation* to refer to the real thing.[50]

Cell A refers to "the real thing," to the integration of *whites* as well as blacks, to the end product of Lerone Bennett's "transformation."

Except for white separatists, observers of diverse persuasions agree that the achievement of true integration (cell A) should be the ultimate goal. But there are, crudely speaking, three contrasting ways of getting there from the typical current situation (cell D). The black separatist assumes that only one route is possible: from the depressed ghetto of today to the hypothetical ghetto of tomorrow and then, perhaps, on to true integration (lines 1 and 2 in Figure 13). The desegregationist assumes precisely the opposite route: from the present-day ghetto to mere desegregation and then, hopefully, on to true integration (lines 3 and 4 in Figure 13). But there is a third, more direct route, right across from the current ghetto to true integration (line 5 in Figure 13). Experience to date combines with a number of social-psychological considerations to favor the last of these possibilities with some important qualifications.

The route favored by black separatists has a surprising appeal for an untested theory; besides those whites who welcome any alternative to integration, it seems to appeal to militant black leaders searching for a new direction into which to channel the ghetto's rage, and to blacks who just wish to withdraw as far away from whites as possible. Yet, on reflection, it can be seen that the argument involves the perverse notion that the way to bring two groups together is to separate them further. One is reminded of the detrimental consequences of isolation in economics, through "closed markets," and in genetics, through "genetic drift." In social psychology, isolation between two contiguous groups generally leads to: (1) the development of diverse values, (2) reduced intergroup communication, (3) uncorrected perceptual distortions of each other, and (4) the growth of vested interests within both groups for continued separation. Race relations in the United States already suffer from each of these conditions; and the proposal for further separation, even if a gilded ghetto were possible, can only exacerbate them.

In fairness, it should be emphasized again that the criticisms here are directed against the concept of the insulated ghetto, not the shrewder and more subtle notions of power and regrouping combined with challenges to the restriction of choice imposed by the nation's leading institutions. As was mentioned at the beginning of this chapter, a much larger segment of militant blacks, judging from their actions, adheres to the latter program. The fascinations of the more romantic notions of a totally self-sufficient black community and even occasional expressions of black chauvinism are apparently diminished by many of the unromantic facts of the situation.

We will not pursue the many economic and political difficulties inherent in the concept of the insulated ghetto, but it should be mentioned that the resources immediately available in the ghetto for the task are meager. Recognizing this limitation, black separatists call for massive Federal aid with no strings attached. But this requires a national consensus. Some separatists consider that the direct path to integration (line 5 in Figure 13) is idealistic dreaming, then turn and assume that the same racist society that resists integration will unhesitatingly pour a significant portion of its treasure into the ghetto. "Local control" without access to the necessary tax base is not control. This raises the question of the political limitations of this route. Irish-Americans entered the mainstream through the political system, and this method is often cited as appropriate to black separatism—but is it really? Faster than any other immigrant group except Jewish Americans, the Irish have assimilated on the direct route of Figure 13. Forced to remain in ghettos at first, the Irish did not settle for "local control" but strove to win city hall itself. Boston's legendary James Michael Curley won "Irish power" not by becoming mayor of the South Boston ghetto, but by becoming mayor of the entire city. Analogies between immigrants and blacks contain serious inaccuracies, however, since immigrants never suffered from slavery and legalized segregation. But to the extent an analogy is appropriate, Mayor Carl Stokes of Cleveland, Mayor Richard Hatcher of Gary, and Mayor Kenneth Gibson of Newark are far closer to the Irish-American model than are black separatists.

A critical part of the thinking of black separatists centers on the psychological concept of "fate control" —more familiar to psychologists as Rotter's internal control of reinforcement variable.[51] "Until we control our own destinies, our own schools and areas," goes the argument, "blacks cannot possibly achieve the vital sense of fate control." Data from the Coleman Report are cited to show that fate control is a critical correlate of achievement in school for black children.[52] But no mention is made of the additional fact that levels of fate control among black children were found by Coleman to be significantly higher in interracial schools than in all-Negro schools. Black separatists brush this important finding aside because all-Negro schools today are not what they envision for the future. Yet the fact remains that interracial schools appear to be facilitating the growth of fate control among Negro students now; the ideological contention that fate control can be developed as well or better in uniracial schools remains an untested and hypothetical assertion.

Despite the problems, black separatists feel that their route (lines 1 and 2 in Figure 13) is the only way to true integration, in part because they regard the indirect route of desegregation (lines 3 and 4) as an affront to their dignity. Anyone familiar with the blatantly hostile and subtly rejecting acts that typify some interracial situations will understand this repudiation of nonautonomous desegregation (cell C).[53] The U.S. Commission on Civil Rights, in reanalyzing Coleman's data, found that this provided the tool for distinguishing empirically between effective and ineffective biracial schools where whites form the majority. Achievement, college aspirations, and the sense of fate control by Negro students proved to be highest in truly integrated schools when these schools are independently defined as biracial institutions characterized by no racial tension and widespread cross-racial friendship.

Merely desegregated schools, defined as biracial institutions typified by racial tension and little cross-racial friendship, have scant benefits over segregated schools.[54]

This finding reflects Allport's conditions for optimal contact. Truly integrated institutions afford the type of contact that maximizes cross-racial acceptance and the similarity of beliefs described by Rokeach.[55] They apparently also maximize the positive and minimize the negative factors which Katz has isolated as important for performance of Negroes in biracial task groups.[56] And they also seem to increase the opportunity for beneficial cross-racial evaluations, which may well be critical mediators of the effects of biracial schools.[57] Experimental research following up these leads is now called for to detail the precise social-psychological processes operating in the truly integrated situation.[58]

The desegregation route (lines 3 and 4 in Figure 13) has been successfully navigated, though the contention of black separatists that Negroes bear the principal burden for this effort is undoubtedly true. Southern institutions that have attained integration, for example, have typically traveled this indirect path. This route, then, is not as hypothetical as the route advocated by black separatists, but it is hardly to be preferred over the route of direct integration (line 5).

Why not the direct route, then? The standard answer is that it is impossible, that demographic trends and resistance from whites make it out of the question in our time. One is reminded of the defenders of slavery in the 1850s, who attacked the Abolitionists as unrealistic dreamers and insisted that slavery was so deeply entrenched that efforts should be limited to making it into a benign institution. If the nation acts on such speculations, of course, they will probably be proven correct. What better way is there to prevent racial change than to act on the assumption that it is impossible?

The belief that integration is impossible, however, is based on some harsh facts of urban racial demography.

Between 1950 and 1960, the average annual increment of Negro population in the central cities of the United States was 320,000; from 1960 to 1966 the estimated annual growth climbed to 400,000, though reduced in-migration from the rural South has lowered this annual growth rate considerably since 1966.[59] In the suburbs, however, the average annual growth of the Negro population declined from 60,000 between 1950 and 1960 to an estimated 33,000 between 1960 and 1966, though it has sharply increased since 1966.[60] In other words, it would require several times the present trend in growth of Negro populations in the suburbs just to maintain the sprawling central-city ghettos at their present size. In the nation's largest metropolitan areas, then, the trend is still pushing in the direction of ever increasing separatism.

But these bleak data are not the whole picture. In the first place, they refer especially to the very largest of the metropolitan areas—to New York City, Chicago, Los Angeles, Philadelphia, Detroit, Washington, D.C., and Baltimore. Most Negro Americans do not live in these places, but rather in areas where racial integration is in fact possible in the short run if attempts in good faith are made. There are more Berkeleys—small enough for school integration to be effectively achieved—than there are New York Cities. In the second place, the presumed impossibility of reversing racial trends in the central city are based on anti-metropolitan assumptions. We noted repeatedly throughout Part One of this volume that without metropolitan cooperation central cities—and many suburbs, too—will find their racial and other basic problems continuing. Do we need to assume such cooperation impossible? We previously proposed effective state and Federal incentives to further this cooperation. Moreover, some large black ghettos are already extending into the suburbs (e.g., east of Pittsburgh and west of Chicago); the first tentative metropolitan schemes to aid racial integration are emerging in a variety of cities (e.g., Boston, Hartford, Rochester, and Portland, Oregon); and several major metropolitan areas have even consolidated (e.g., Miami-Dade County and Nashville-Davidson County). Once the issue is looked at in metropolitan terms, its dimensions become more manageable. Black Americans are found in America's metropolitan areas in almost the same ratio as white Americans: about two-thirds of each group reside in these 212 regions. On a metropolitan basis, therefore, Negroes are not disproportionately metropolitan.

Yet it must be admitted that many young blacks, separatist and otherwise, are simply not convinced by such arguments. Such large-scale proposals as metropolitan educational parks (Chapter 4) strike them as faraway pipe dreams of no significance to their immediate problems. Contact theory holds little appeal. They rightfully argue that Allport's four conditions do not typify the American national scene. How often, they ask, do blacks actually possess equal status in situations with whites? And in struggles for racial power, as they view it, can there be a cooperative seeking of common goals? And as for the possibility that true integration of cell A will be sanctioned by those in authority, they say ruefully, consider the public images on racial matters of Nixon, Mitchell, Agnew, Carswell. Maybe the demographic arguments against the possibility of integration are overdrawn, they concede, but can one realistically expect Allport's conditions of positive contact to become the rule in the foreseeable future of the United States?

Underlying this criticism is less a theoretical and ideological difference than a sharply contrasting assessment of the probabilities and possibilities of America's race relations. These black spokesmen may well be right. The United States may indeed be so racist both as to individuals and structure that the type of institutional changes advocated throughout this volume will never be achieved. No footnoting of references or social-psychological theory can refute this possibility, but I hope it is wrong. The entire analysis of this book is predicated on the more optimistic view that somehow American society will muddle through. To assume otherwise, once again, is to risk contributing to the problem by engaging in a self-fulfilling prophecy.

Moreover, the attack on contact theory is based in part on a misreading of it. *Situations* meeting Allport's four conditions do exist in the United States, and we have seen that they are becoming more numerous in such realms as employment. True, as noted, these truly integrated situations are still isolated islands and together do not constitute a critical mass nationally. Yet the status of Negroes is rising in the United States. Indeed, the personal lives of the black critics themselves typically attest to this social mobility, for roughly 90 percent of middle-class blacks today derive from families which were lower class in 1940. But we noted in Chapter 7 how these very gains create rapidly rising expectations and a keen sense of relative deprivation, some of which gets channeled among some blacks into the separatist ideology under discussion.

Nor are power struggles as completely racial and competitive as critics claim. For one thing, power conflicts almost invariably involve class as well as racial interests, and to the extent that class is involved there are at least potential white allies. White Americans, after all, are an even more diverse assortment than black Americans. Thus, Mayor Carl Stokes received 22 percent of the white vote in Cleveland in November of 1969, Thomas Bradley 40 percent in the Los Angeles mayoralty run-off in June of 1969, Mayor Kenneth Gibson 16 percent in Newark in June of 1970. The percentages are low because of racism, but they do occur and rise over time (Stokes received in general elections only 11 percent in 1965, and 19 percent in 1967). But actually the theory requires only that blacks and some whites share common goals to the point where coalitions become important to both; one of these coalitions is called the Democratic Party, which since Franklin Roosevelt has consisted of a precarious combination of minorities which together total a registration far larger than that of the rival party.

Finally, concerning Allport's fourth condition on the sanction of laws and authorities, there is solid evidence in civil rights legislation and other institutional changes that moving toward the sanctioning of true integration. By and large, of course, America's institutions still do not play this role; they are racist, in the Kerner Commission's plain language, in that their normal operations still act typically to restrict choice for blacks. But positive change is evident from the appearance of Negroes on television to their participation in former bastions of white privilege. True, as far as race is concerned the Nixon Administration is a throwback to the naivete of early twentieth-century administrations; it offers no "authority sanction," nor does it promise to in its remaining years. Yet there are other political alternatives which would willingly offer the racial leadership the nation so desperately needs. To opt out of the opposition, to assume that the Mitchells and Agnews are inevitable and typical products of the American political system, is to ensure that such men will in fact remain in power.

To argue for route 5 in Figure 13 is not to assume that it will be easy to achieve, or that Allport's optimal conditions for intergroup contact apply generally throughout America at present. The direct path does stress that *simultaneous* attention must be given to both integration and individual and collective autonomy, for today's cell D has neither and tomorrow's cell A must have both. And neither the desegregation (paths 3 and 4 of Figure 13) nor the separatist (paths 1 and 2) route gives this simultaneous attention. Once again, Bennett phrases the argument cogently:

It is impossible, Simon de Beauvoir said, to draw a straight line in a curved space. Both "integrationists" and "separatists" are trying to create right angles in a situation which only permits curves. The only option is Transformation of a situation which does not permit a clear-cut choice in either direction. This means that we must face the fact that it is impossible to move 30 million African-Americans anywhere.[61]

Implications for Policy

Much of the confusion over policy seems to derive from the assumption that since *complete* integration in the biggest cities will not be possible in the near future, present efforts toward opening opportunities for integration for both Negro and white Americans are premature. This thinking obscures two fundamental issues. First, the democratic objective is not total racial integration and the elimination of black neighborhoods; the idea is simply to provide an honest choice between separation and integration. Today only separation is available; integration is closed to blacks who would choose it. The long-term goal is not a complete obliteration of cultural pluralism, of distinctive Negro areas, but rather the transformation of these ghettos from racial prisons to ethnic areas freely chosen or not chosen. Life within ghettos can never be fully satisfactory as long as there are Negroes who reside within them only because discrimination requires them to.

Second, the integrationist alternative will not become a reality as long as we disparage it or abandon it to future generations. *Exclusive* attention to programs for enriching life in the ghetto is almost certain, to use Kenneth Clark's pointed word, to "embalm" the ghetto, to seal it in even further from the rest of the nation (making line 2 in Figure 13 even less likely). This danger explains the recent interest of conservative whites in enrichment programs for the ghetto. The bribe is straightforward: "Stop rioting and stop demanding integration, and we'll minimally support separatist programs within the ghetto." Even black separatists are understandably ambivalent about such offers, as they come from sources long identified with opposition to all racial change. Should the bargain be struck, however, race relations in the United States will be dealt still another serious blow.

Yet a policy concentrating *exclusively* on integration, like one concentrating exclusively on enrichment, runs its own danger of worsening the situation. As many black spokesmen correctly point out, a single-minded pursuit of integration is likely to blind us to the urgent requirements of today's black ghettos. Either policy followed mechanically and exclusively, then, has serious limitations which the rival strategy is designed to correct. This fact strongly suggests that a national transformation from a racist society to an open society will require a judicious mix of both the strategies.

The outlines of the situation, then, are these: (1) Widespread integration is possible everywhere in the United States except in the largest central cities. (2) It will not come unless present trends are reversed and considerable resources are provided for the process. (3) Big central cities will continue to have significant concentrations of Negroes even with successful metropolitan dispersal. (4) Large Negro ghettos are presently in need of intensive enrichment. (5) Some enrichment programs for the ghetto run the clear and present danger of embalming the ghetto further.

Given this situation and the social-psychological considerations we have been discussing throughout this book, the overall strategy needed must contain the following elements:

1 A major effort toward racial integration must be mounted in order to provide genuine choice to all Negro Americans in all realms of life. This effort should envisage complete attainment of the goal in smaller communities and cities by the late 1970s and a halting of separatist trends in major central cities, with a movement toward metropolitan cooperation.

2 A simultaneous effort is required to enrich the vast central-city ghettos of the nation, to change them structurally, and to improve life in them. In order to avoid "embalming" them, however, strict criteria must be applied to proposed enrichment programs to insure that they will not hinder later dispersal and integration. Restructuring the economics of the ghetto, especially by developing urban cooperatives, is a classic example of productive enrichment. Effective job training programs offer another example of productive enrichment. The building of enormous public housing developments within the ghetto presents a good illustration of counterproductive enrichment. Some programs, such as the decentralization of huge public school systems or the encouragement of business ownership by Negroes, can be either productive or counterproductive depending upon how they are focused. A decentralization plan of many small homogeneous school districts for New York City is clearly counterproductive for later integration; a plan involving a relatively small number of heterogeneous school districts for New York City could well be productive. Likewise, black entrepreneurs who are encouraged to open small shops and are expected to prosper with an all-black clientele are not only part of a counterproductive plan, but are probably commiting economic suicide. Negro businessmen who are encouraged to pool their resources to establish somewhat larger operations and to appeal to white as well as black customers on major traffic arteries in and out of the ghetto could be an important part of a productive plan.

In short, a mixed strategy is called for—both integration and enrichment—and it must contain safeguards that the two aspects will not impede each other. Results of recent surveys strongly suggest that such a mixed strategy would meet with widespread approval among black Americans. On the basis of their extensive survey of black residents in fifteen major cities in 1968, Campbell and Schuman conclude:

Separatism appeals to from five to eighteen per cent of the Negro sample, depending on the question, with the largest appeal involving black ownership of stores and black administration of schools in Negro neighborhoods, and the smallest appeal the rejection of whites as friends or in other informal contacts. Even on questions having the largest appeal, however, more than three-quarters of the Negro sample indicate a clear preference for integration. Moreover, the reasons given by respondents for their choices suggest that the desire for integration is not simply a practical wish for better material facilities, but represents a commitment to principles of nondiscrimination and racial harmony.[62]

Young men prove to be the most forthright separatists, but even here the percentages of men aged 16 to 19 who were separatists ranged only from 11 to 28. An interesting interaction between type of separatism and educational level of the respondent appears in Campbell and Schuman's data. Among the 20- to 39-year-olds, college graduates tended to be more separatist in those realms where their training gives them a vested interest in positions free of competition—black-owned stores for black neighborhoods, black teachers in mostly black schools. The poorly educated were most likely to believe that whites should be discouraged from taking part in civil rights organizations and to agree that "Negroes should have nothing to do with whites if they can help it" and that "there should be a separate black nation here." [63]

But if separatism draws little favorable response even in the most politicized ghettos, positive aspects of cultural pluralism attract wide interest. For example, 42 percent endorse the statement that "Negro schoolchildren should study an African language." And this interest seems rather general across age, sex, and education categories. Campbell and Schuman regard this as evidence of a broadly supported attempt ". . . to emphasize black consciousness *without* rejection of whites. . . . A substantial number of Negroes want *both* integration and black identity." [64] Or, in the terms of this chapter, they prefer cell A in Figure 13—"true integration."

When viewed historically, this preferred combination of black consciousness without separation is not a new position for black Americans. It was, for example, their dominant response to the large-scale movement of Marcus Garvey in the 1920s. Garvey, a West Indian, stressed pride in Africa and black beauty and successfully mounted a mass movement throughout the urban ghettos of the day, but his famous "back to Africa" separatist appeals were largely ignored as irrelevant.

Campbell and Schuman's data indicate little if any change from the prointegration results of earlier surveys.[65] And they are consistent with the results of surveys in Detroit, Miami, New York City, and other cities.[66] Data from Bedford-Stuyvesant in Brooklyn are especially significant, for here separatist ideology and a full-scale enrichment program are in full view. Yet when asked if they would prefer to live on a block with people only of the same race or people of every race, 80 percent of the Negro respondents chose an interracial block. Interestingly, the largest Negro segment choosing integration—88 percent—consisted of residents of public housing where a modest amount of interracial tenancy still prevails.[67]

A final study from Watts links these surveys to the analysis of this chapter. Ransford found that willingness of Negroes to use violence was closely and positively related to a sense of powerlessness, feelings of racial dissatisfaction, and limited contact with whites. Respondents who indicated that they had no social contact with white people, "like going to the movies together or visiting each other's homes," were significantly more likely to feel powerless and express racial dissatisfaction as well as to report greater willingness to use violence.[68] The personal, group, and national costs of racial separatism are clearly great.

A Final Word

Racially separate or together? Our social-psychological examination of separatist assumptions leads to the assertion of one imperative: the attainment of a viable, democratic nation, free from personal and institutional racism, requires extensive racial integration in all realms of life as well as vast programs of ghetto enrichment. To prescribe more separation because of discomfort, racism, conflict, or the need for autonomy is like getting drunk again to cure a hangover. The nation's binge of *apartheid* must not be exacerbated but alleviated.

Footnotes

1. An earlier draft of this paper was the author's presidential address to the Society for the Psychological Study of Social Issues, delivered at the annual convention of the American Psychological Association in San Francisco, California, on September 1, 1968.

2. These figures derive from three gross estimates of "middle class" status: annual family income of $6,000 or more, high school graduation, or white-collar occupation. Thus, in 1961 roughly one-fifth of Negro families received in excess of $6,000 (a percentage that now must approach one-fourth, even in constant dollars); in 1960, 22 percent of Negroes over 24 years of age had completed high school; and in 1966, 21 percent of employed Negroes held white-collar occupations.

3. J. Alsop, "No More Nonsense About Ghetto Education!" *New Republic,* July 22, 1967, Vol. 157, pp. 18–23; and "Ghetto Schools," *New Republic,* Nov. 18, 1967, Vol. 157, pp. 18–23. (For answers to these articles, see: R. Schwartz, T. Pettigrew, and M. Smith, "Fake Panaceas for Ghetto Education," *New Republic,* Sept. 23, 1967, Vol. 157, pp. 16–19; and "Is Desegregation Impractical?" *New Republic,* Jan. 6, 1968, Vol. 157, pp. 27–29.) W. H. Ferry, "Black Colonies: A Modest Proposal," *The Center Magazine,* January 1968, Vol. 1, pp. 74–76. Ferry even proposes that "black colonies" be formally established in American central cities, complete with treaties enacted with the Federal government. The position of black militants is in sharp contrast to this; they complain of having a colonial status now and do not consider it a desirable state of affairs.

4. It is sometimes held that "Negro" was the term for slaves; but actually both "Negro" and "black" were frequently used in documents concerning slaves. Some critics argue that the true skin color of Negro Americans is basically brown, not black, and that the term "black" is therefore inappropriate. But of course "white" Americans are seldom

white either; besides, "Negro" is simply the Spanish word for "black." The importance of the term "black" is in fact basically psychological. I have used both terms interchangeably because surveys indicate each is preferred by different segments of the Negro community.

5. Lerone Bennett, Jr., "Liberation," *Ebony,* August 1970, Vol. 25, 1970, Vol. 25, pp. 36–43.

6. C. P. Armstrong and A. J. Gregor, "Integrated Schools and Negro Character Development: Some Considerations of the Possible Effects," *Psychiatry,* 1964, Vol. 27, pp. 69–72.

7. T. F. Pettigrew, *A Profile of the Negro American* (Princeton, N.J.: Van Nostrand, 1964).

8. Analysis specifically directed on this point shows that this contention is not true for predominantly white classrooms as contrasted with comparable all-white classrooms. [United States Commission on Civil Rights, *Racial Isolation in the Public Schools* (Washington, D.C.: U.S. Government Printing Office, 1967), Vol. 1, p. 160.]

9. National Advisory Commission on Civil Disorders, *U.S. Riot Commission Report* (Washington, D.C.: Government Printing Office, 1968).

10. B. E. Calame, "A West Coast Militant Talks Tough But Helps Avert Racial Trouble," *The Wall Street Journal,* July 26, 1968, Vol. 172, No. 1, p. 15. Karenga's contention that blacks presently have nothing "to offer" a racially interdependent America strangely echoes similar contentions of white racists.

11. I. Katz, "Review of Evidence Relating to Effects of Desegregation on the Performance of Negroes," *American Psychologist,* 1964, Vol. 19, pp. 381–399; and M. R. Yarrow (ed.), "Interpersonal Dynamics in a Desegregation Process," *Journal of Social Issues,* 1958, Vol. 14, No. 1, pp. 3–63.

12. J. Harding and R. Hogrefe, "Attitudes of White Department Store Employees Toward Negro Co-workers," *Journal of Social Issues,* 1952, Vol. 8, pp. 18–28; and G. Saenger and E. Gilbert, "Customer Reactions to the Integration of Negro Sales Personnel," *International Journal of Opinion and Attitude Research,* 1950, Vol. 4, pp. 57–76.

13. I. N. Brophy, "The Luxury of Anti-Negro Prejudice," *Public Opinion Quarterly,* 1946, Vol. 9, pp. 456–466.

14. S. A. Stouffer, E. A. Suchman, L. C. DeVinney, S. A. Star, and R. M. Williams, Jr., *Studies in Social Psychology in World War II,* Vol. 1, *The American Soldier: Adjustment During Army Life* (Princeton: Princeton University Press, 1949).

15. M. Deutsch and M. Collins, *Interracial Housing: A Psycho-*

logical Evaluation of a Social Experiment (Minneapolis: University of Minnesota Press, 1951); M. Jahoda and P. West, "Race Relations in Public Housing," *Journal of Social Issues,* 1951, Vol. 7, pp. 132–139; D. M. Wilner, R. Walkley, and S. W. Cook, *Human Relations in Interracial Housing: A Study of the Contact Hypothesis* (Minneapolis: University of Minnesota Press, 1955); and E. Works, "The Prejudice-Interaction Hypothesis from the Point of View of the Negro Minority Group," *American Journal of Sociology,* 1961, Vol. 67, pp. 47–52.

16. W. M. Kephart, *Racial Factors and Urban Law Enforcement* (Philadelphia: University of Pennsylvania Press, 1957).

17. T. M. Newcomb, R. H. Turner, and P. E. Converse, *Social Psychology: The Study of Human Interaction* (New York: Holt, Rinehart and Winston, 1965).

18. M. Rokeach, P. Smith and R. Evans, "Two Kinds of Prejudice or One?" in M. Rokeach (ed.), *The Open and Closed Mind* (New York: Basic Books, 1960); M. Rokeach and L. Mezei, "Race and Shared Belief as Factors in Social Choice," *Science,* 1966, Vol. 151, pp. 167–172; C. R. Smith, L. Williams, and R. H. Willis, "Race, Sex and Belief as Determinants of Friendship Acceptance," *Journal of Personality and Social Psychology,* 1967, Vol. 5, pp. 127–137; D. D. Stein, "The Influence of Belief Systems on Interpersonal Preference," *Psychological Monographs,* 1966, Vol. 80, No. 616; and D. D. Stein, J. A. Hardyck, and M. B. Smith, "Race and Belief: An Open and Shut Case," *Journal of Personality and Social Psychology,* 1965, Vol. 1, pp. 281–290.

19. H. C. Triandis and E. E. Davis, "Race and Belief as Determinants of Behavioral Intentions," *Journal of Personality and Social Psychology,* 1965, Vol. 2, pp. 715–725. This resolution of the earlier controversy between Triandis and Rokeach takes on added weight when the data from studies favorable to Rokeach's position are examined carefully. (H. C. Triandis, "A Note on Rokeach's Theory of Prejudice," *Journal of Abnormal and Social Psychology,* 1961, Vol. 62, pp. 184–186; and M. Rokeach, "Belief versus Race as Determinants of Social Distance: Comment on Triandis' Paper," *Journal of Abnormal and Social Psychology,* 1961, Vol. 62, pp. 187–188). That interpersonal realms lead to varying belief-race weightings is borne out by Table 4 in Stein *et al., op. cit.;* that intensely prejudiced subjects, particularly in environments where racist norms even extend into less intimate realms, will act on race primarily is shown by one sample of whites in the Deep South in Smith *et al., op. cit.*

20. Both black and white observers tend to exaggerate racial differences in basic values. Rokeach and Parker note from data from national surveys that, while there appear to be real value differences between the rich and the poor, once socioeconomic factors are controlled there are no sharp value differences between black and white Americans. M. Rokeach and S. Parker, "Values as Social Indicators of Poverty and Race Relations in America," *Annals of the American Academy of Political and Social Science,* 1970, Vol. 388, pp. 97–111.

21. Stein *et al., op. cit.*

22. Smith *et al., op. cit.*

23. United States Commission on Civil Rights, *op. cit.*

24. For twelve junior highs, the Spearman-Brown rank-order correlation between the white junior high percentage and the percentage of Negroes choosing predominantly white high schools is +.82 (corrected for ties)—significant at better than the 1 percent level of confidence.

25. United States Commission on Civil Rights, *Civil Rights USA: Public Schools, Southern States, 1962* (Washington, D.C.: U.S. Government Printing Office, 1963).

26. United States Commission on Civil Rights, *Racial Isolation in the Public Schools, op. cit.*

27. For a role-analysis interpretation of racial interactions in the United States, see Pettigrew, *A Profile of the Negro American, op. cit.*

28. One of the first significant efforts in this direction was the classic intelligence study by O. Klineberg, *Negro Intelligence and Selective Migration* (New York: Columbia University Press, 1935). For a summary of current scientific work relevant to racist claims regarding health, intelligence and crime, see Pettigrew, *A Profile of the Negro American, op. cit.*

29. H. H. Hyman and P. B. Sheatsley, "Attitudes Toward Desegregation," *Scientific American,* July, 1964, Vol. 211, pp. 16–23; and P. B. Sheatsley, "White Attitudes Toward the Negro," in T. Parsons and K. B. Clark (eds.), *The Negro American* (Boston: Houghton Mifflin, 1966).

30. R. T. Riley and T. F. Pettigrew, "Dramatic Events and Racial Attitude Change" (unpublished paper, Harvard University, August, 1970).

31. National Advisory Commission on Civil Disorders, *op. cit.*

32. "The ceiling effect" occurs when initial approval is already so high, so near its "ceiling" of 100 percent, that further

gains in approval would not generally be as large as when there is less initial approval.

33. Triandis and Davis, *op. cit.*

34. Similar to these results was an overall shift of approximately 5 percent toward favoring the racial desegregation of public schools noted among white Texans between two surveys taken immediately before and after the 1957 school crisis in Little Rock. And once again, the most positive shifts were noted among the young and the middle class. (R. T. Riley and T. F. Pettigrew, *op. cit.*)

35. Deutsch and Collins, *op. cit.*; Jahoda and West, *op. cit.*; Wilner *et al.*, *op. cit.*; and Works, *op. cit.*

36. Stouffer *et al.*, *op. cit.*; and B. MacKenzie, "The Importance of Contact in Determining Attitudes Toward Negroes," *Journal of Abnormal and Social Psychology*, 1948, Vol. 43, pp. 417–441.

37. Brophy, *op. cit.*

38. MacKenzie, *op. cit.*

39. Kephart, *op. cit.*

40. MacKenzie, *op. cit.*

41. R. M. Williams, Jr., *Strangers Next Door: Ethnic Relations in American Communities* (Englewood Cliffs, N.J.: Prentice-Hall, 1964).

42. Hyman and Sheatsley, *op. cit.* This is, of course, a two-way causal relationship. Not only does desegregation erode racist attitudes, but desegregation tends to come first to areas where white attitudes are least racist to begin with. Hyman and Sheatsley's finding, however, specifically highlights the former phenomenon: "In those parts of the South where some measure of school integration has taken place official action has *preceded* public sentiment, and public sentiment has then attempted to accommodate itself to the new situation."

43. J. S. Coleman, E. Q. Campbell, C. J. Hobson, M. McPartland, A. M. Mood, F. D. Weinfield, and R. L. York, *Equality of Educational Opportunity* (Washington, D.C.: U.S. Government Printing Office, 1966).

44. U.S. Commission on Civil Rights, *Racial Isolation in the Public Schools, op. cit.*

45. G. W. Allport, *The Nature of Prejudice* (Cambridge, Mass.: Addison-Wesley, 1954).

46. Triandis and Davis, *op. cit.*

47. F. Douglass, *Life and Times of Frederick Douglass: The Complete Autobiography* (New York: Collier Books, 1962), pp. 366–367 (original edition in 1892).

48. R. W. Logan, *The Negro in the United States: A Brief History* (Princeton, N.J.: Van Nostrand, 1957).

49. J. L. Jackson and A. F. Poussaint, "A Dialogue on Separatism," *Ebony,* August, 1970, Vol. 25, pp. 62–68.

50. Bennett, *op. cit.,* pp. 37–38.

51. J. B. Rotter, "Internal versus External Control of Reinforcement," *Psychological Monographs,* 1966, Vol. 80, No. 609.

52. Coleman *et al., op. cit.*

53. For extreme examples of this phenomenon in public schools in the Deep South, see: M. Chessler, *In Their Own Words* (Atlanta: Southern Regional Council, 1967).

54. U. S. Commission on Civil Rights, *Racial Isolation in the Public Schools, op. cit.* More recent evidence for this distinction is provided in: S. Koslin, B. Koslin, R. Pargament, and H. Waxman, "Classroom Racial Balance and Students' Interracial Attitudes," (unpublished paper, Riverside Research Institute, New York City, 1970).

55. Another white observer enthusiastic about black separatism even denies that the conclusions of the contact studies are applicable to the classroom and other institutions which do not produce "continual and extensive equal-status contact under more or less enforced conditions of intimacy." Stember selectively cites the investigations of contact in public housing and the armed forces to support his point (C. H. Stember, "Evaluating Effects of the Integrated Classroom," *The Urban Review,* June, 1968, Vol. 2 [3–4], pp. 30–31); but he has to omit the many studies from less intimate realms which reached the same conclusions—such as those conducted in schools (T. F. Pettigrew, "Race and Equal Educational Opportunity," *Harvard Educational Review,* 1968, Vol. 38, pp. 66–76) and employment situations (Harding and Hogrefe, *op. cit.;* Kephart, *op. cit.;* MacKenzie, *op. cit.;* and Williams, *op. cit.*), and even one involving brief contact between clerks and customers (G. Saenger and E. Gilbert, "Customer Reactions to the Integration of Negro Sales Personnel," *International Journal of Opinion and Attitude Research,* 1950, Vol. 4, pp. 57–76).

56. I. Katz, *op. cit.;* and I. Katz, "The Socialization of Competence Motivation in Minority Group Children," in D. Levine (ed.), *Nebraska Symposium on Motivation, 1967* (Lincoln: University of Nebraska Press, 1967).

57. T. F. Pettigrew, "Social Evaluation Theory: Convergences and Applications," in D. Levine, *op. cit.*

58. Pettigrew, "Race and Equal Educational Opportunity," *op. cit.*

59. U. S. Depts. of Labor and Commerce, *The Social and Economic Status of Negroes in the United States, 1969* (Washington, D.C.: U.S. Government Printing Office, 1970), pp. 5–7.

60. *Ibid.*

61. Bennett, *op. cit.*, p. 38.

62. A. Campbell and H. Schuman, "Racial Attitudes in Fifteen American Cities," in The National Advisory Commission on Civil Disorders, *Supplemental Studies* (Washington, D.C.: U.S. Government Printing Office, 1968), p. 5.

63. *Ibid.*, p. 19.

64. *Ibid.*, p. 6.

65. W. Brink and L. Harris, *The Negro Revolution in America* (New York: Simon and Schuster, 1964); and W. Brink and L. Harris, *Black and White: A Study of U.S. Racial Attitudes Today* (New York: Simon and Schuster, 1967).

66. P. Meyer, *A Survey of Attitudes of Detroit Negroes after the Riot of 1967* (Detroit, Mich.: Detroit Urban League, 1968); P. Meyer, "Miami Negroes: A Study in Depth," *The Miami Herald,* 1968; and Center for Urban Education, "Survey of the Residents of Bedford-Stuyvesant." Unpublished paper, 1968.

67. *Ibid.*

68. H. E. Ransford, "Isolation, Powerlessness, and Violence: A Study of Attitudes and Participation in the Watts Riot," *American Journal of Sociology,* 1968, Vol. 73, pp. 581–591.

INDEXES

NAME INDEX

Braly, K. W., 293n.
Brimmer, A. F., 47n.
Brink, W., 126n., 151, 152,
   162n., 201n., 209n., 291n.,
   292n., 294n., 334n.
Brinton, C., 155, 163n.
Brophy, I. N., 292n., 329n., 332n.
Brown, R. W., 121n.
Bruner, J. S., 133, 141n.
Buckley, W. M., 221
Bullock, H. A., 291n.

Cabot, H., 201n.
Calame, B. E., 329n.
Campbell, A., 325–327, 334n.
Campbell, D. T., 122n.
Campbell, E. Q., 125n., 126n.,
   332n.
Cancian, F., 124n.
Cantril, H., 150, 154, 162n., 173,
   199n., 293n.
Carey, J. W., 200n.
Carswell, G. Harold, 320
Cash, W. J., 252n.
Cayton, H., 90
Chessler, M., 333n.
Churchill, Sir Winston, 90
Clark, K. B., 31n., 34n., 47n.,
   48n., 99, 140n., 209n., 229n.,
   249n., 255n., 258, 292n.,
   293n., 323, 331n.
Clemence, T., 30n., 31n.
Cleveland, S., 82n.
Coleman, A. L., 99, 124n.
Coleman, J. S., 52–55, 58, 60–
   69, 81n., 82n., 86, 87, 152,
   162n.

Collins, M., 31n., 292n., 329n.,
   332n.
Connelly, G. M., 200n.
Converse, P. E., 330n.
Conway, M., 253n.
Cook, S. W., 31n., 106, 125n.,
   292n., 330n.
Cooley, C. H., 91, 98
Cooper, E., 293n.
Coser, L. A., 97, 98, 124n.
Cothran, T. C., 291n.
Coughlin, Father, 245
Craig, T., 15n.
Cramer, M. R., 103n., 114,
   124n., 125n., 126n., 203n.
Crawford, T., 211, 229n.
Crutchfield, R. S., 137, 142n.
Curley, Mayor James Michael,
   316

Dabney, V., 89, 121n.
Davies, J. C., 147, 156, 162n.,
   163n.
Davis, A., 142n., 163n.
Davis, E. E., 305, 310, 311,
   330n., 332n.
Davis, F. J., 32n.
Davis, J. A. S., 95, 123n.
Davis, J. P., 31n., 32n., 47n.,
   203n.
de Beauvoir, Simone, 322
Descartes, Rene, 91
Deutsch, K., 313
Deutsch, M., 31n., 292n., 329n.,
   332n.
DeVinney, L. C., 141n., 292n.,
   329n.

Divine, Father, 287
Dodson, D., 83n., 104
Dollard, J., 113, 142n.
Douglass, Frederick, 311, 332n.
Douglass, J. H., 32n., 33n.
Drake, St. C., 90
Duncan, B., 33n.
Duncan, O. D., 48n.

Eisenstadt, S. M., 124n.
Elkins, S. M., 201n.
Erskine, H. G., 124n., 198n.,
    200n., 209n.
Essien-Udom, E. U., 124n.
Evans, R., 330n.

Fein, R., 36, 46n., 48n.
Fenton, J. M., 209n.
Ferry, W. H., 297, 328n.
Festinger, L., 137, 142n.
Field, H. H., 200n.
Fillmore, President Millard,
    252n.
Frazier, E. F., 90, 121n., 153,
    163n., 201n., 289, 294n.
Freeman, H. E., 33n., 271n.,
    291n.
Frenkel-Brunswick, E., 127n.,
    142n., 201n., 293n.
Freud, S., 189
Frieden, B., 6n., 26, 33n., 34n.
Friedrichs, R. W., 291n.

Gallup, G., 274, 292n.
Gardner, B., 142n., 163n.

Gardner, M., 142n., 163n.
Garvey, Marcus, 326
George, W. C., 89, 121n.
Geschwender, J. A., 162n.
Gibson, Mayor Kenneth, 316,
    321
Gilbert, E., 293n., 329n., 333n.
Gilbert, G. M., 191, 203n., 293n.
Ginzberg, E., 47n., 48n.
Glass, B., 201n.
Glenn, N., 81n.
Gockel, G., 31n.
Goffman, E., 91, 121n., 122n.,
    293n.
Goffman, I. W., 123
Goldwater, Senator Barry, 166,
    175, 183, 200n., 220–222,
    229n., 250, 256n.
Gore, P. M., 123n., 156, 163n.
Gouldner, A. W., 109, 112, 126n.
Granovetter, M., 251n., 255n.
Gregor, A. J., 329n.
Grier, E., 20, 21, 30, 31n., 32n.,
    33n., 34n.
Grier, G., 20, 21, 30, 31n., 32n.,
    33n., 34n.
Griffin, J., 290n.
Grigg, C., 124n., 125n., 126n.
Grimshaw, A. D., 8, 15n.
Guetzkow, H., 142n.

Halpern, B., 178, 201n.
Hamilton, C. H., 4, 6n.
Harding, J., 141n., 293n., 329n.,
    333n.
Hardyck, J. A., 330n.
Hargis, Rev. B. J., 166

Triandis, H. C., 305, 310, 311, 330*n*., 332*n*.
Truman, President Harry S., 87
Tumin, M. M., 126*n*.
Turner, R. H., 154, 162*n*., 163*n*., 330*n*.

Ulman, N., 34*n*.

Vander Zanden, J. W., 124*n*., 126*n*.
Viereck, P., 166

Walker, A., 251*n*., 255*n*.
Walkley, R., 31*n*., 292*n*., 330*n*.
Wallace, Governor George C., 57, 172, 173, 175, 207, 208, 209*n*., 231–251, 252*n*., 253*n*., 254*n*., 255*n*., 256*n*.
Wallace, Vice-President Henry, 245
Watts, L. G., 33*n*., 34*n*., 271*n*., 291*n*.
Waxman, H., 333*n*.
Weinberg, Eve, 255*n*.
Weinberg, M., 125*n*.
Weinfield, F. D., 332*n*.
Welch, R., 166, 198*n*.
West, P., 31*n*., 292*n*., 330*n*., 332*n*.
Westie, F. R., 163*n*., 270, 291*n*.
Westin, A., 166, 196
White, B. J., 293*n*.

White, J. G., 163*n*., 164*n*.
White, Mayor Kevin, 214
White, R. W., 133, 141*n*.
Wilkins, C., 290*n*.
Williams, J. A., 123*n*.
Williams, L., 330*n*.
Williams, R. M., 100, 126*n*., 141*n*., 202*n*., 203*n*., 290*n*., 292*n*., 329*n*., 332*n*., 333*n*.
Willis, R. H., 330*n*.
Wilner, D. M., 31*n*., 292*n*., 330*n*., 332*n*.
Wilson, A. B., 58–60, 62, 81*n*.
Wilson, J. Q., 9, 11, 12, 16*n*.
Wilson, M. O., 142*n*.
Wirth, L., 90
Wolfe, A. C., 231, 235, 241, 252*n*., 253*n*., 256*n*.
Wolfgang, M., 7, 15*n*.
Works, E., 32*n*., 124*n*., 292*n*., 330*n*., 332*n*.
Wright, Frank Lloyd, 1
Wurster, C. B., 17, 30*n*.

Yancey, W., 48*n*.
Yankauer, M. P., 33*n*.
Yarrow, M. R., 122*n*., 303, 304, 329*n*.
Yarrow, P. R., 290*n*.
Yinger, J. M., 291*n*.
York, R. L., 332*n*.

Zelditch, M., 123*n*.
Zinn, H., 141*n*.

SUBJECT INDEX

Anti-Negro prejudice:
  salience of, 184–185, 197,
    202n.
  and social class, 182, 202n.,
    269–270, 291n.
  stereotype of black Ameri-
    cans, 178–182, 201n.
  survey of social distance,
    184, 202n.
  and voting: for Louise Hicks,
    216–219
    for George Wallace in
      1968, 241–244
  of white Americans, 205–
    207, 208n.–209n.
  (See also Racism, white)
Anti-Semitic prejudice:
  ability of opinion surveys to
    measure, 169–171
  and anti-Negro prejudice,·
    136, 146, 165–203
  and attitudes toward Joe
    McCarthy, 183, 202n.
  decreases in, 167–169
  discriminatory practices
    continue, 171, 199n.
  and fraternity discrimina-
    tion, 267, 269n.
  less extensive in the South
    and Far West, 135, 185–
    188, 197, 202n.–203n.
  Nazi need for, 195, 203n.
  rumors during World War II,
    136, 186, 202n.
  salience of, 184–185, 202n.
  and social class, 182, 202n.
  stereotype of Jews, 178–182,
    201n.

Anti-Semitic prejudice:
  survey of social distance,
    184, 202n.
Apartheid, 328
Arkansas, 3, 252
  (See also Little Rock,
    Arkansas)
Assimilation:
  of black Americans, xvii
  of immigrant Americans,
    316–317
Atlanta, Georgia, 4
  elementary school segrega-
    tion in, 57
  overcrowded housing of
    blacks in, 22
Attitude(s):
  toward black Americans: in
    Boston, 215–218
    and voting for Louise
      Hicks, 216–219
  of blacks toward whites by
    social class, 270, 291n.
  concept of, 133–135
  toward desegregated
    schools, 176–177, 200n.,
    216–218, 269, 291n.
  toward desegregation of
    public transportation,
    269, 291n.
  dramatic events and racial,
    308–311, 331n.–332n.
  future in U. S. of anti-minor-
    ity prejudiced, 192–196,
    203n.
  toward housing desegrega-
    tion: and social class,
    269–270, 291n.

Black American(s):

assimilation of, xvii, 181–182

attitudes in Boston toward, 215–218

attitudes toward, and voting for Louise Hicks, 216–219

attitudes toward intelligence of, 185, 202*n*., 215, 229*n*., 286, 307–308, 331*n*.

attitudes toward intermarriage with, 181, 201*n*.–202*n*., 267, 291*n*.

attitudes toward whites and social class, 270, 291*n*.

birth rates, 5

broadening of comparative reference groups among, 153–156

Caucasian genes among, 180, 201*n*.

changing moods of, 258–259, 274, 292*n*.

children and friendships with whites, 67–68

and the city, 1–83

community ties, 26, 288–289, 294*n*.

compared to Chinese and Japanese Americans, 37, 286

compared to Mexican Americans in Texas, 286

consequences of unemployment among, 38–40

contacts with whites of

Black American(s):

Boston middle-income, 271–273, 291*n*.

decreasing discrimination against, 171

differences from Jewish Americans, 179–182, 201*n*., 285

discrimination against: in administration of justice, 7

in housing, 21–24

economic polarization among, 37, 47*n*.

and education, 51–83, 268–269, 287–288

and employment, 35–50, 287–288

exclusion from fraternities of, 267, 291*n*.

gains in housing of, 23

and housing, 17–34, 288–290

housing choices of middle-income, 26

and the immigrant analogy, 285, 293*n*.

increase in home ownership among, 23

increased status inconsistency among, 152–153

low expectation of Nixon Administration by, 160

mental illness among, 182, 202*n*.

middle-class percentage of, 62, 296, 328*n*.

Black American(s):

migration of, 2–6, 318–320, 334*n*.

1960 employment gains of, 35, 287–288

1968 Presidential voting of, 234

versus "non-whites" as concept, 32*n*., 37

optimism for the future among, 149–152, 274, 292*n*.

overcrowded housing of, 22

and the police, 7–16

police employment of, 10, 12–14

population changes of, 2–6, 318–320, 334*n*.

protest leadership by middle-class, 155, 156, 158

relative deprivation among, 94–95, 250–251

results of integrated education on adult, 64–65

sentiment for integration and separatism among, 297–301, 325–327, 334*n*.

separatism versus Italian and Jewish American separatism, 298–299

shift from "Negro" to "black" as label, 299, 328*n*.–329*n*.

social mobility of middle-class, 321

soldiers in World War II, 93

unemployment of, 36

unrest, 147–164

Black American(s):

values held by, 180–181, 201*n*., 331*n*.

youth, 296–300

[*See also* Racial role(s); Stereotype(s); Stigma]

Black Belt areas of the South, structural analysis of, 95–97

Black experience, xix

Black Muslims, 98, 124*n*., 153, 163*n*.

Black Panthers, 98, 161

Black Power, ideology of, 258

Black separatism, 259

Boston, Massachusetts, 319

attitudes toward blacks in, 215–218

and black policemen, 10

desegregation results of school redistricting in, 70

Louise Hicks supporters in, 211–229

inferior housing of blacks in, 22

interracial contacts of blacks in, 271–273, 291*n*.

"Irish power" in, 316

mayor of, 214

middle-income black housing choices in, 26

school districts in metropolitan, 56

study of bigotry in, 211–229

voting for George Wallace in, 236–238, 254*n*., 255*n*.

Boston, Massachusetts:
"white backlash" and school
committee elections in,
174–175, 211–213, 218–
220
white private school attendance in, 57
Boston Pilot, 212
Brookline, Massachusetts,
innovative educational
leadership in, 71
Brotherhood Week, dinners
and awards, 279, 281–282,
293*n*.
Buffalo, New York, housing
segregation in, 18
Bundy Report on School Decentralization in New York
City, 80

California:
Advisory Committee to the
United States Commis-
sion on Civil Rights, 8,
15*n*., 16*n*.
rates of interracial marriage
in, 267, 291*n*.
referendum on anti-discrimination housing statute,
21–22, 213
Center for the Study of Democratic Institutions, 297,
328*n*.
Change:
in American racial patterns,
274–285

Change:
and contact, 274–281
contrasting strategies for,
281–285
(*See also* Remedies)
Charleston, South Carolina,
129
Charlotte, North Carolina, bad
desegregation publicity
about, 102
Chattanooga, Tennessee, 129
Cheyney State College, 268
Chicago, 3, 70, 104, 319
black population growth in
suburbs of, 19, 32*n*.
de facto school segregation
by design in, 57
elementary school segregation in, 57
neighborhood and union desegregation in metro-
politan, 266, 290*n*.
Operation Breadbasket in,
312
prejudice study of veterans
in, 184, 202*n*.
race riot in, 8
rent discrimination in, 22–23
South Side, 69
Chinese:
acceptance in U.S. public
accomodations of, 265,
290*n*.
Americans, 37, 286
merchants of Malaysia and
Indonesia stereotype,
179

Demographic trends:
  black, 2–6, 318–320, 334*n.*
  school segregation and, 56
Desegregation, xvii
  attitudes toward neighborhood and union, 266, 290*n.*
  attitudes toward school, 176–177, 200*n.*, 216–218
  and autonomy, 313–315
  defined in terms of self-definition, 91–92
  ecological prediction of school, 101–103
  housing definition of, 30*n.*
  ignorance of techniques for achieving school, 217–218
  versus integration, 63–64, 313–314, 317–318, 333*n.*
  and interracial contact effects, 277–278, 310, 332*n.*
  and models of social change, 97–98, 124*n.*
  pattern of violence over, 130
  as a response to strains in the social system, 95–97
  social class and attitudes toward housing, 269–270, 291*n.*
  social psychology and research on, 129–143
  sociology and, 89–127

Desegregation:
  and Title VI of 1964 Civil Rights Act, 34*n.*
  (*See also* Contact; *De facto* segregation; *De jure* segregation; Integration; Segregation)
Despair, mood of, xxii
Detroit, Michigan, 3, 4, 319
  black American attitudes in, 327, 334*n.*
  and black policemen, 10
  1943 race riot in, 8, 156, 277
  1967 race riot in, 8
  referendum on anti-discrimination housing statute, 21–22, 213
  school districts in metropolitan, 56
  sociologist as City Councilman in, 105, 125*n.*
Discrimination (*see* Racial discrimination)
"Drafts riots" of 1863, 156
Dramatic events and racial attitude change, 308–311, 331*n.*–332*n.*
Duke University, 262
Durham, North Carolina, 262

Easttown Township, Pennsylvania, court decision against zoning requirements of, 34*n.*

Ecological fallacy, 238
  definition of, 199*n.*
  example of, 173
Economic(s):
  analogy to "closed markets" in, 315
  factors in housing segregation, 19
  polarization among black Americans, 37, 47*n.*
  progress of blacks and general economic growth, 48*n.*
Education:
  anti-metropolitan organization of public schools, 56
  causes of segregated, 56–57
  consequences of integrated, 57–69
  desegregated verşus integrated, 57–69
  extent of segregated, 51–56
  and race, 51–83
  racial segregation in elementary schools, 54–56
  rising enrollments in public, 78
  school social class level and consequences in, 58–63
Elementary and Secondary Educational Act (1965), "river and harbors bill" principle in, 72, 73
Elmira, New York, prejudiced attitudes in, 184, 202*n.*

Employment:
  critical importance of black, 269
  labor force changes in, 40–41
  1960 gains in black, 35
  public service, 41–42
  and race, 35–50
England, toleration of political nonconformists in, 192–193, 196, 203*n.*
Equal Employment Opportunity Commission (EEOC), 43–44
Equality of Educational Opportunity (Coleman Report), 310, 322*n.*
  on "academic self-concept," 65–66
  criticism of, 62
  data on extent of segregated education in, 51–56, 81*n.*
  on "fate control," 65–66, 152, 162*n.*, 317, 333*n.*
  key conclusion of, 58, 60–61
  as a political case study, 86–87
  racial significance of, 62–69
  on "social evaluation" in interracial classroom, 65–68
  summary evaluation of, 68–69

Fair Housing Act of 1968, 24, 28–29
Family Allowance Plan, 49*n.*

Family disorganization:
   and unemployment, 39–40
   and welfare programs, 45
Farmers, views concerning the
   rights of labor, 123n.–
   124n.
"Fate control," 65–66, 152,
   162n., 317, 333n.
   and black participation in
   protest, 123n.
Federal government:
   as employer of blacks, 43
   funding, 5
   1964 Civil Rights Act of, 27
   1968 Fair Housing Act of,
   24, 28–29
   reluctance to support desegregation research
   by, 105–107
   Rent Supplement Program
   of, 29
Federal Housing Administration, racial discrimination
   in housing of, 20
Florida, 101, 103, 284
   desegregation brief to Supreme Court of, 110
Florida State University, 110
Fort Lauderdale, Florida:
   housing segregation in, 18
   Nova educational complex
   near, 76
Foundation for Cooperative
   Housing, 34n.
Foundations, private, reluctance to support desegregation research of,
   105–107, 125n.

Free-Masons, 242
Frustration-aggression theory
   of prejudice, 134

Galveston, Texas, lunch-counter sit-in protest in, 104,
   125n.
Garvey Movement, 326–327
Gary, Indiana, 316
   elementary school segregation in, 57
   voting for George Wallace
   in 1968 in, 236–251
Genetic drift, 315
Georgia, 6n., 133, 252n., 264,
   284
Germany, 179
Ghetto, black: and autonomy,
   313–322, 333n.–334n.
   hypothetical "black power" and autonomy,
   313–322, 333n.–334n.
   small versus big, 69–70
Gross National Product (GNP):
   black employment gains and
   increase in, 38
   increase between 1970 and
   1980 predicted in, 40
Guilt of white Americans, xxii
Gypsies, stereotype of, 179

Harlem, 69, 262, 273
   1943 race riot in, 156
   (See also New York City)
Hartford, Connecticut, 319
Harvard University, 229n.,
   251n.–252n.

Hawaii, rates of interracial marriage in, 267, 291*n*.

Hicks, Representative Louise Day:

analysis of elections of, 211–230, 256*n*.

school board elections of, 174–175

supporters of, 208, 211–230

and themes of Barry Goldwater and Spiro T. Agnew, 220–222

(*See also* Boston, Massachusetts; Voting)

Homicide, racial discrimination in trials for, 7

Housing:

causes of segregation in, 19–26

improvement in black, 23

1969 Congressional rejection of anti-discrimination legislation for, 296–297

and race, 17–34

remedies for segregation in, 26–30

segregation in, 17–19, 113–114, 269

shortage of, 24–25

social class and attitudes toward desegregation of, 269–270, 291*n*.

suburban zoning barriers in, 25–26

ties within black community as cause of segregation in, 26

(*See also* Segregation)

Housing Development Corp., 34*n*.

Indiana:

1968 Presidential primary vote for Eugene McCarthy, 245

the George Wallace phenomenon in Gary, 236–251

(*See also* Gary, Indiana)

Institutional protections for minorities, 193–198

activities of radical right against, 195–196

contrasting strategies for establishing, 281–285

(*See also* Law)

Integration:

and autonomy, 313–314

consequences of school, 57–69

defined in terms of self-definition, 91–92

definition of, xvii

versus desegregation, 63–64, 313–314, 317–318, 333*n*.

failure to try as national policy, 297

and ghetto enrichment as overall strategy, 322–327, 334*n*.

housing definition of, 30*n*.

indignity of some arguments for, 258

"Kafka problem" of school impersonalization, 78–79
Kentucky, 3
Kerner Commission Report (*see* National Advisory Commission on Civil Disorders)
Know-Nothings, 242, 252*n.*
Ku Klux Klan, 98, 113, 124*n.*, 126*n.*, 198*n.*

Labor force:
  employment changes within, 40–41
  expansion in, 40
  predictive value of percent of white women in, 101, 125*n.*
Labor market, racial necessity of a tight, 42–43
"Latent liberals," 139–140, 205–206, 208*n.*–209*n.*
Law, the, and contact and change, 278–280, 293*n.*
  (*See also* Institutional protections for minorities)
Liberation, 299–300, 314, 329*n.* 333*n.*
Life magazine, 286–287, 293*n.*– 294*n.*
Lincoln University (Pennsylvania), 268
Little Rock, Arkansas:
  actions in racial crisis of, 113
  bad desegregation publicity about, 102

Little Rock, Arkansas:
  desegregation violence in, 130, 296
  elementary school segregation in, 57
  school desegregation conflict in, 227
  White Citizens' Council in, 165
  white liberal clergy in, 109
Los Angeles, California, 3, 7, 70, 319
  elections of right-wing mayors in, 221
  1943 race riot, 156
  overcrowded housing of blacks in, 22
  race riot in Watts, 8–9
  white vote for Thomas Bradley in, 321
Los Angeles Dodgers, 276
Los Angeles Times, 86
Louisiana, 6*n.*, 204, 252*n.*
Louisville, Kentucky, school preferences of black children in, 64, 306, 331*n.*
Lynchburg, Virginia, 110

McCarthy, Senator Eugene J., 1968 Indiana Presidential primary vote for, 245
McCarthy, Senator Joseph R.:
  prejudice and attitudes toward, 183, 202*n.*
  supporters of, 242

McDowell County, West Virginia, study of racial contact in, 131–132, 141*n.*, 264

Manpower Report of the President (1967), 40

Manpower Retraining Act, 44–45, 282, 284

Marietta, Georgia, desegregated aircraft plant in, 261

Marshall Field Foundation, 125*n.*

Maryland, 95

Massachusetts:
backed-up demand for public housing in, 24–25
Secretary of State of, 214
statute against racially imbalanced schools, 227
(*See also* Boston, Massachusetts)

Memphis, Tennessee, 4
elementary school segregation in, 57

Metropolitan Applied Research Center (MARC), 255*n.*

Metropolitan Cooperation, 1–2
in education, 72
educational lack of, 56
in housing, 27–28, 30

Metropolitan Educational Parks, 69–80, 83*n.*, 218, 229

Metropolitan Educational Parks:
advantages of, 74–77

Metropolitan Educational Parks:
and community control, 80
disadvantages of, 77–80
incentive for, 72–73
and school decentralization, 80

Metropolitan Job Councils, 41

Mexican Americans compared to black Americans in Texas, 286

Miami, Florida:
black American attitudes in, 327, 334*n.*
housing segregation in, 18
metropolitan consolidation of, 320

Michigan, rates of interracial marriage in, 267, 291*n.*

Migration of black Americans, 2–6

Milpitas, California, racial discrimination in housing by zoning barrier, 25

Milwaukee, Wisconsin, 3

Minneapolis, Minnesota, elections of right-wing mayors in, 221

Mississippi, 3, 6*n.*, 252*n.*, 284

Mississippi Freedom Democratic Party, 296

"Moderate," 139

Moynihan Report and the Politics of Controversy, The, 48*n.*

Muslim Indian merchants of East and South Africa stereotype, 179

Nashville, Tennessee:
differential acceptance of school and lunch-counter integration in, 132
metropolitan consolidation of, 320
National Advisory [Kerner] Commission on Civil Disorders, report of, xviii, xxii–xxiii, 6n., 31n., 33n., 308, 331n.
basic conclusion of, 300, 302
and black policemen, 10
on improving police and community relations, 14, 15n., 16n.
on nation's racist institutions, 322
on race riots, 9
National Association for the Advancement of Colored People (NAACP), 98, 104
National Housing Corp., proposal for, 28, 34n.
National Humanities Foundation, 87
National Opinion Research Center (NORC), 168, 170, 208n.–209n., 286
interracial housing study by, 18–19, 31n.
survey in Boston, 213
survey of Gary by, 255n.
survey on Joe McCarthy, 183, 202n.

National Opinion Research Center (NORC):
survey on "white backlash" by, 175, 199n.
National Police Cadet Training Corps, proposal for, 14, 16n.
National Science Foundation, 87
National Social Science Foundation, proposal for, 87
Nazi(s):
analogies with George Wallace phenomenon, 253n.
need for anti-Semitism, 195, 203n.
popularity among authoritarian men, 234
Nebraska, rates of interracial marriage in, 267, 291n.
Negative Income Tax, 45–46
Negro American [see Black American(s)]
Neighborhood involvement:
and 1968 voting for George Wallace in Gary, 255n.
and voting for Louise Hicks, 222–226
Newark, New Jersey, 4, 317
white vote for Mayor Gibson in, 321
New Jersey, pluralistic ignorance about housing desegregation in suburban, 104–105
(See also Newark, New Jersey)

Ohio, 268

Oklahoma, intergroup contact study in, 280–281, 293n.

Oklahoma City, Oklahoma, elementary school segregation in, 57

Omaha, Nebraska, elementary school segregation in, 57

Orlando, Florida, housing segregation in, 18

Other-directed individuals, 132

"Other Negro America," 37–39

Panama Canal Zone, study of racial contact in, 131–132, 141n., 264

Parents and Taxpayers Association, 213, 221

Pennsylvania, 268

Personality and attitudes, 133–135

Philadelphia, Pennsylvania, 3, 4, 7, 70, 319

police and racial bigotry, 11, 304, 310, 330n., 332n.

racial trends in housing of metropolitan, 31n.

Urban League proposal for nonmetropolitan educational parks, 83n.

white private school attendance in, 57

Pittsburgh, Pennsylvania, 319

Action Housing, Inc., in, 34n.

Frank Lloyd Wright's comment on, 1

Pluralistic ignorance about housing desegregation in suburban New Jersey, 104–105

Police:

alienation in Chicago, 9

and all-white review boards, 8, 13

behavior styles of, 11, 16n.

and black charges of brutality, 8–9, 14

and favorable interracial contact, 277, 292n.

and hiring of blacks, 10, 12–14

murders of blacks by, 160

and race, 7–16

and race riots, 8–9, 159

racial bigotry of, 11

and U.S. Supreme Court, 9

Population, black American changes of, 2–6

Populism:

supporters of, 242

and George Wallace phenomenon, 235–236, 249–250, 253n.

Portland, Oregon, 319

Potomac Institute, 104, 125n.

Prejudice, psychological theories of, 134–135

Princeton Plan of School Desegregation, 69

Princeton University, studies of stereotypes in, 191, 203n., 286, 293n.

Prohibition, 194

Project One Hundred Thousand, 45

Psychoanalytic theory of prejudice, 134

Public Housing Programs, 20–21

accounts for one percent of nation's housing, 33n.

backed-up demand in Massachusetts for, 24–25

as latter-day version of poor house, 29

Race:

as applied to Jews, 180, 182

of interviewer effects, 122n.

as a measure of social distinction, 91

as a social concept, 121n.

Race riot(s), 7–8

in Detroit in 1943, 8

explanations for, 157–160

in Los Angeles in 1965, 8–9

and police, 8–9, 159

versus rebellion, 159

size of ghetto and, 163n.–164n.

Racial attitudes, trends in since World War II, 145–203

Racial change and social science, 85–143

Racial discrimination:

in Chicago rents, 22–23

in employment, 37–40

in homicide trials, 7

in housing, 21–24

in Schenectady, New York, 33n.

in pay of "nonwhites" within occupational categories, 47

vicious circle in, 44

in zoning barrier: in Deerfield, Illinois, 25

in Milpitas, California, 25

Racial integration (see Integration)

Racial patterns:

change in American, 274–285

complexity of American, 261–294

future of American, 285–290

Racial role(s), 262–274, 290n.

impairments of, 263–264

"Negro," 263–264

white, 262–264

Racial segregation (see Segregation)

Racism, white: assumption that white liberals alone must eradicate, 302, 307–311

at the ballot box, 205–256

basic assumption of, 301–302, 307–311

versus belief similarity, 304–305, 330n.–331n.

Racism, white: construction of
institutional, 312, 333*n.*
individual, xviii, 312
institutional, xviii, 312
integration as a neces-
sary condition for
the eradication of,
xvii, 297–298
and myth of backlash, 102
not in psychological vac-
uum, 207–208
(*See also* Anti-Negro prejudice)
Raleigh, North Carolina, lack
of desegregation violence
in, 130
Randolph-Macon Women's
College, 110
Reference group(s), 266,
290*n.*–291*n.*
broadening of, among black
Americans, 153–156
Relative deprivation:
in "age of rising expectations," 208, 251
among black Americans,
94–95, 250–251
"egoist" versus "fraternalist," 154–155
as explanation for popular
uprisings, 147–160,
162*n.*–163*n.*
four processes underlying,
147–156
regional differences in, 274,
292*n.*

Relative deprivation:
and George Wallace vote in
1968, 241, 246–251
Remedies, xviii–xix, xxi
for educational segregation,
69–80
financial pressure in general racial, 227–229
general strategy for racial,
322–327, 334*n.*
for housing segregation,
26–30
for facial economic prob-
lems, 40–46
for police and racial problems, 12–15
(*See also* Change)
Rent Supplement Program, 29
Republican Party, xxii
preference of youth for, 59
and radical right, 195
and George Wallace phe-
nomenon, 234–235,
239–240, 253*n.*
Residential segregation (*see*
Housing; Segregation)
Richmond, Virginia:
elementary school segregation in, 57
George Wallace vote in
metropolitan, 232–233,
252*n.*–253*n.*
Richmond Times Dispatch, 89,
121*n.*
Rochester, New York, 319
housing segregation in, 18

Roman Catholic(s):

  parochial school cooperation with public schools, 76–77

  parochial school effects on public school segregation, 57

  parochial school student selection, 83n.

  percent of black Americans who are, 57

St. Louis, Missouri, 3

  white private school attendance in, 57

St. Paul, Minnesota, highway displacement of blacks in, 32n.

San Antonio, Texas, lunch-counter sit-in protest in, 104, 125n.

San Francisco, 3, 8

  college aspirations of high school youth in metropolitan, 58–59

San Francisco Giants, 276

San Jose, California, housing segregation in, 18

San Mateo County, California, police complaint procedure of, 13

Savannah, Georgia, prejudiced attitudes in, 184, 202n.

Schenectady, New York, blatant racial discrimination in housing in, 33n.

Seattle, Washington, referendum on anti-discrimination housing statute, 21–22, 213

Segregation:

  basic assumptions of white and black, 301–322, 329n.–334n.

  causes of educational, 56–57

  consequences of school, 57–69

  in elementary schools, 54–56

  of the family, 267, 291n.

  in higher education, 268

  in housing, 17–30, 113–114, 226, 269

  housing definition of, 30n.

  versus integration, 295–334

  Massachusetts statute against school, 227

  negative effects of, 305–307, 315, 331n.

  of organized religion, 267–268, 291n.

  as racially comfortable, 301, 303–317

  voting for Louise Hicks: and attitudes toward housing, 223–226

  and attitudes toward school, 216–218

  (See also *De facto* segregation; *De jure* segregation; Desegregation; Integration)

Sociology:
  its use and disuse in the
    desegregation process,
    89–128
  why potential of not fulfilled,
    105–119
South, the:
  changes in, 2, 187–188
  migration of blacks from,
    2–6
  reduced anti-Semitism in,
    135, 185–188, 197,
    202*n.*–203*n.*
  voting for Wallace in 1968
    in, 231–235
South Africa, Republic of:
  anti-African attitudes in,
    142*n.*
  interracial contact in, 275
South Carolina, 6*n.*, 232, 252*n.*
Southern Regional Council,
  104, 125*n.*
Springfield, Massachusetts, 8
Stamford, Connecticut, Foundation for Cooperative
  Housing in, 34*n.*
Status inconsistency:
  as concept in sociology,
    94–95, 122*n.*–123*n.*
  increases among black
    Americans in, 152–153
  and mental illness among
    blacks, 162*n.*–163*n.*
Stereotype(s):
  of black Americans, 168,
    178–181, 184–187,
    198*n.*, 200*n.*–203*n.*,
    286–287, 293*n.*–294*n.*

Stereotype(s):
  of Chinese merchants of
    Malaysia and Indone-
    sia, 179
  of gypsies, 179
  id versus superego, 178–
    179, 196–197, 201*n.*,
    286
  of Jewish Americans, 178–
    189
  of Muslim Indian merchants
    of East and South
    Africa, 179
  Princeton University studies
    of, 191, 203*n.*, 286, 293*n.*
  reinforcement of hostile,
    275
  of southern Italians, 179,
    201*n.*
Steubenville, Ohio, prejudiced
  attitudes in, 184, 202*n.*
Stigma:
  as applied to role of
    "Negro," 263–264
  concept of, as applied to
    race, 91–92, 121*n.*–
    122*n.*, 179–182, 285–
    287, 293*n.*
Stockton, California, damag-
  ing effects of urban renewal project in, 32*n.*
Survey Research Center (SRC)
  of the University of Michigan, 231, 232, 235, 236,
  252*n.*, 253*n.*

Taconic Foundation, 125*n.*

Tennessee, 101, 103
Texas, 95
    attitudes toward hiring
        blacks of manufactur-
        ers in, 266–267, 291n.
    black and Mexican Ameri-
        cans in, 286
Theory (see Social psychol-
    ogy; Sociology)
Toledo, Ohio, growth of black
    home owners in, 33n.
Transformation, 314, 322,
    333n., 334n.
"Transtolerance," 166, 183,
    196

"Uncle Tom," 139
Unemployment:
    of black Americans, 36
    and black family disorgani-
        zation, 39–40
    consequences of black, 38–
        40
United Party:
    Presidential race in 1936,
        245
    supporters of, 242
United States Army:
    effects of desegregation in,
        277–278, 292n., 304,
        329n.
    Project One Hundred Thou-
        sand of, 45
United States Commission on
    Civil Rights:
    California Advisory Commit-
        tee to, 8, 15n., 16n.

United States Commission on
    Civil Rights:
    Racial Isolation in the Pub-
        lic Schools by, 51, 58,
        62–64, 66, 81n., 306–307,
        317–318, 331n., 333n.
    study of black student pref-
        erences for integration,
        64, 306, 331n.
    survey of urban adults in
        North and West by, 64–
        65, 306–307, 310, 331n.,
        332n.
United States Department of
    Labor, 41
United States Job Corps, 284–
    285
United States Merchant Ma-
    rine, 277, 292n., 304, 310,
    329n., 332n.
United States Office of Eco-
    nomic Opportunity, 250,
    254n.
United States Office of Educa-
    tion, 58, 282–283
United States Supreme Court,
    106, 110, 145
    attitudes toward, 183, 202n.
    and the police, 9
    rules anti-miscegenation
        laws illegal, 267
    and school desegregation,
        17, 149, 268, 296
    segregationist attack upon,
        89
    social science footnote in
        desegregation opinion
        of, 90

Watts, Los Angeles:
overcrowded housing of blacks in, 22
travel time of black workers in, 45
Wayne State University, 105
Welfare programs:
incentives for dependence and unemployment in, 45
"reform" proposals of Nixon Administration, 49n.
"White backlash," xx, 169
as activation phenomenon, 177
myth of, 102, 171–178, 196, 238, 308
and voting for Louise Hicks, 211, 218–220
White Citizens' Council, 98
in Little Rock, 165
White House Conference "To Fulfill These Rights":
on black gains and gross national product increases, 48n.

White House Conference "To Fulfill These Rights":
on housing segregation, 21, 32n.
on housing shortage, 24–25, 33n.
on improving police and community relations, 14, 15n., 16n.
on remedies for racial problems in housing, 27–28, 30, 34n.
on suburban zoning barriers, 25, 38n.
on youth unemployment, 46n.
White racism (see Racism, white)
White Sulphur Springs, West Virginia, student strike over desegregation in, 104
Wilberforce, 268
Winston-Salem, North Carolina, lack of desegregation violence in, 130